APPALACHIAN ODYSSEY

A 28-YEAR HIKE ON AMERICA'S TRAIL

Written and photographed by Jeff Ryan

Enjoy the journey!

DownEastBooks
CAMDEN, MAINE

Down East Books

Published by Down East Books
An imprint of Globe Pequot
Trade division of The Rowman & Littlefield Publishing Group, Inc.
4501 Forbes Boulevard, Suite 200, Lanham, Maryland 20706
www.rowman.com

Unit A, Whitacre Mews, 26-34 Stannary Street, London SE11 4AB, United Kingdom

Distributed by NATIONAL BOOK NETWORK

Designed by Hillary Steinau, Camden Design

Maps by Rachel Carter and Puelle Design.

Copyright © 2016 by Jeffrey H. Ryan

British Library Cataloguing in Publication Information Available

Library of Congress Cataloging-in-Publication Data Available

ISBN 978-1-60893-578-9 (paperback : alk. paper)
ISBN 978-1-60893-579-6 (electronic)

♾️™ The paper used in this publication meets the minimum requirements of American National Standard for Information Sciences—Permanence of Paper for Printed Library Materials, ANSI/NISO Z39.48-1992.

Printed in the United States of America

Dedication

This book is dedicated to everyone that encouraged and contributed to my love of the outdoors, starting with Don and Dody Ryan, who knew they had a climber on their hands from the beginning and encouraged me to keep on exploring.

Contents

A message to readers who are thinking about hiking the AT

This book isn't a trail guide. The profile maps created for this book are meant to portray general elevation loss and gain and to indicate the places we camped. They are not designed for, nor should be used for navigation. If you are planning a hike on the AT, I recommend purchasing and carrying a trail map and guide (preferably one published by the Appalachian Trail Conservancy).

The guidebooks to each trail section (generally one guide per state) contain detailed trail descriptions, profile maps and topographic maps. These three pieces of information are not only critical to navigating the trail, finding water sources, etc., they can also provide a much needed perspective on how to get to help should you encounter a medical emergency (either yours or that of another hiker).

Carrying a guide book and maps is more than common sense. The proceeds from the guides also support the efforts of the chapter clubs that work tirelessly to maintain the AT and surrounding trails for everyone's enjoyment. Please consider supporting their work by making an additional donation or becoming a volunteer or member.

Preface

This book, like anything worthwhile, didn't happen overnight. It was a vision that formed slowly, solidified, then was continually shaped by the forces of nature, time and circumstance—much like the immense granite boulders on Katahdin's summit plateau.

Like those boulders, visions can stay up in the clouds, seen and pondered from afar, yet never fully examined. That was never the case for me and this 2,000 mile walk. Even though I didn't know that I was "doing the AT" when I started (and perhaps because of it) I began this journey simply by following my passion. And when the vision became something I was fully participating in, I was able to accept the way it unfolded, even when changing plans was inevitable.

After almost three decades of walking, I discovered that the secret the trail repeatedly held for me was this:

If we head in the direction of our dreams and accept the winds and rains that will test our resolve, we can experience the deep satisfaction of looking back upon the path of a life well lived.

Here's to everyone who finds and follows their own path.

Portland, Maine
March, 2016

About the Appalachian Trail

The idea to create the Appalachian Trail (AT) is widely credited to Benton MacKaye, a regional planner who envisioned a network of work, study and farming camps stretching from Mt. Washington in New Hampshire to Mt. Mitchell in North Carolina.

The vision for the trail was first publicized in October of 1921. By 1925, the first Appalachian Trail Conference was convened to get the project off the ground. Like most large scale projects, the creation of the Appalachian Trail happened in fits and starts. While the trail was completed as a continuous footpath in 1937, it wasn't until 1968 that it was designated as a national scenic trail and afforded federal protection (along with The Pacific Crest Trail).

The Appalachian Trail Conservancy provides a detailed history of the trail on their website.

The Appalachian Trail is a mountain trail. It is mentally and physically demanding. While it has been portrayed as "a walk in the woods", there are precious few sections that allow one to stroll. The fact that many underestimate the terrain and what it takes to complete a through-hike is illustrated by a single statistic: 75% of people who begin the hike don't finish.

AT Mileage by State*

Maine: 281.4 miles

New Hampshire: 160.9 miles

Vermont: 149.8 miles

Massachusetts: 90.2 miles

Connecticut: 51.6 miles

New York: 88.4 miles

New Jersey: 72.2 miles

Pennsylvania: 229.6 miles

Maryland: 40.9 miles

West Virginia: 4 miles

Virginia: 550.3 miles

Tennessee: 287.9 miles

North Carolina: 95.5 miles

Georgia: 76.4 miles

*Based on 2006-2011 data compiled by the Appalachian Trail Conservancy

APPALACHIAN TRAIL STATS

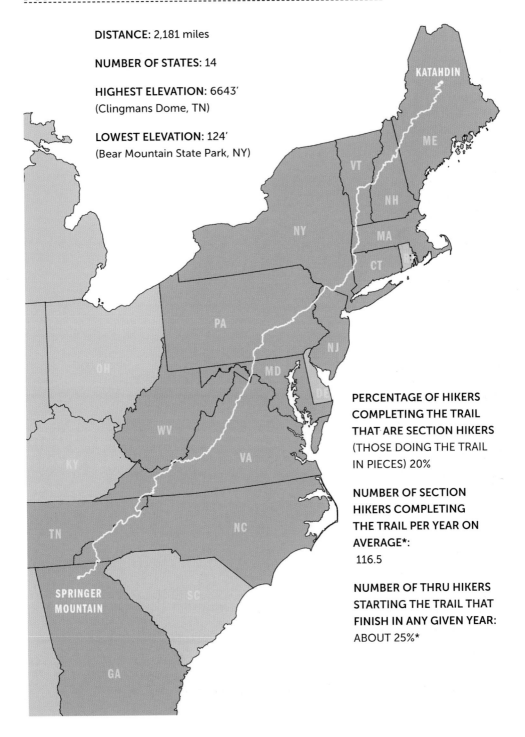

DISTANCE: 2,181 miles

NUMBER OF STATES: 14

HIGHEST ELEVATION: 6643'
(Clingmans Dome, TN)

LOWEST ELEVATION: 124'
(Bear Mountain State Park, NY)

PERCENTAGE OF HIKERS
COMPLETING THE TRAIL
THAT ARE SECTION HIKERS
(THOSE DOING THE TRAIL
IN PIECES) 20%

NUMBER OF SECTION
HIKERS COMPLETING
THE TRAIL PER YEAR ON
AVERAGE*:
116.5

NUMBER OF THRU HIKERS
STARTING THE TRAIL THAT
FINISH IN ANY GIVEN YEAR:
ABOUT 25%*

CHAPTER 1

Katahdin

What began as a day hike to the summit of Maine's fabled mountain became a 28-year adventure to places and events I could not have imagined.

Katahdin summit via the Hunt Trail (AT)

TRIP STATS
September 7, 1985
10.4 miles round trip
5.2 AT miles

By the time I met up with eight friends to climb Katahdin at age 28 in September of 1985, I had already covered quite a bit of ground.

Two years before, I spent six months on the Pacific Crest Trail (PCT) walking from Mexico to Canada. The highlights included crossing the Mojave Desert and walking the length of the Cascades through Oregon and Washington. Every day of that trip was an adventure—a test of stamina and mental health set against a stunning backdrop whose scenes I can still render in my mind's eye.

When I returned to Maine from the PCT, I gave a slide show to my cohorts at work. Afterwards, a guy I knew vaguely as "Ed" ambled over and asked if I would be interested in doing a hike with him.

"Absolutely," I said.

As it turned out, "a hike" was a gross understatement. Between April 1985 and March 1986, Ed and I climbed the 50 highest mountains in Maine in one year (it took us 47 weekends to top them all).

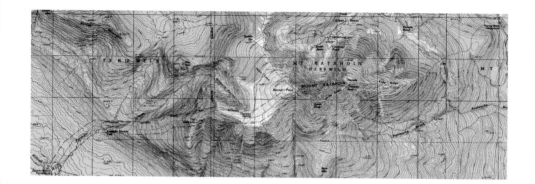

In the midst of the chase for Maine's top 50, I took a three-day hiatus to climb Katahdin with another new hiking buddy, Wayne Cyr, and some of his friends from Connecticut.

I had also met Wayne in the aftermath of my Pacific Crest Trail adventure. He attended the University of Maine in Orono, where he was a roommate of one of my childhood friends.

One day Wayne mentioned hiking, and his roommate steered him my way. Not long after that, we went on our first hike together in western Maine. We weren't even back to the car yet before we planned an autumn trip to Katahdin.

Katahdin is an amazing mountain. It is also powerful symbol of enduring wilderness. The mountain rises so dramatically from the landscape that it demands your reverence. From many angles, it looks more like a mesa than the other mountains along the Appalachian chain (even those right next door, like Coe, Barren and Doubletop). From above, Katahdin looks like an octopus, with tentacles extending out in all directions.

The mountain is a hiker's dream, with numerous approaches through the basins, up and over huge blocks of granite and onto the tableland toward the summit.

At the time of this hike, I had already climbed Katahdin over 30 times (including earlier in the year with Ed). Yet I yearned to see again what one of my favorite places on earth held for me.

Even though it was a four-hour drive to get there, I had come to know the area well enough to know some great (free) places to camp outside of the park. (Inside the park, camping reservations were required and hard to get, especially on short notice.)

I took Friday off from work. It was a nearly cloudless fall day and I was primed to climb. The only slight concern I had was the size of our hiking party. There were nine of us. It's easy to be nimble when there are two or three of you on the trip. The more people you add, the more unwieldy it can get. If the "herding cats" scenario took root, there was no way we'd get to the summit and back. I was quite willing to bail on climbing Katahdin and go for a shorter hike if needed. I figured if we were not on the Hunt Trail by 8:00 a.m., we should go with "Plan B."

The Hunt Trail

The Hunt Trail and the Appalachian Trail are one and the same, although the idea for the AT was hatched decades after Irving O. Hunt (who owned and operated a nearby

Why Katahdin?

- Until 1933, it was thought that the northern terminus of the AT should (and would) be New Hampshire's Mount Washington. The feeling was that extending the trail into the wilds of Maine would create vast stretches that would be difficult to reach and therefore maintain.

- Maine native (and Chairman of the Appalachian Trail Conference from 1931-1952) Myron Avery thought differently. He advocated for (and with the help of a dedicated handful of others) mapped and blazed the route of the AT in Maine between 1933 and 1939.

- Without Avery's vision, the AT would have been at least 10% shorter and would have resulted in a significantly diminished wilderness experience.

sporting camp) blazed this path from Katahdin Stream Campground to the summit of the mountain between 1904 and 1908. He could not have known that he was also blazing a path to what would become the northern terminus of a 2,100-plus mile trail (much like I did not know that 77 years after Hunt created the trail that bore his name, I would be standing on the edge of an adventure all my own).

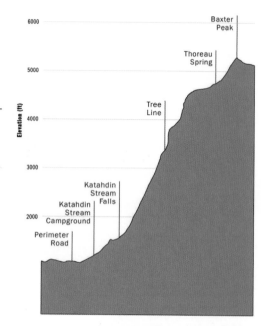

The primary access to Baxter State Park, and most of its trails, is the often narrow, winding way known to one and all as the Perimeter Road. It is unpaved because of the vision of Governor Percival Baxter. In the 1930s, Baxter began purchasing plots of land, starting with Katahdin itself, with the idea of establishing a state park. In subsequent years, he kept buying adjacent parcels (27 more, totaling over 200,000 acres), which he also turned over to the state of Maine to increase the size of the park.

There were few a conditions attached. One of the most important ones was that the park would "remain forever wild."

The spirit of Baxter's generosity is captured in his famous quote, "Man is born to die, his work short lived, buildings crumble, monuments decay, wealth vanishes, but Katahdin, in all its glory, shall forever remain the mountain of the people of Maine. Throughout the ages it will stand as an inspiration to the men and women of the state."

To help make sure it stayed that way, upon his death at age 87 in 1969, Baxter left $7 million to maintain the park that bears his name.

I am reasonably certain that Irving O. Hunt was a young man when he blazed his trail. I say that because it is much less a trail in places than a rock climbing route, particularly the steep, one-mile ascent of huge boulders, where a giant metal staple and a few metal hand and footholds are there to assist you. God help the person who tries to negotiate through this stretch with a full pack on!

Fortunately, most hikers opt for the 10.4 mile round trip with day packs, as we did on this early September day.

After a late night of rehydrating and swapping stories around the campfire, I was doubting the troops would rally for an early wake up call. I was pleasantly wrong. We passed the trailhead sign and started up the trail at 7:47 a.m.

Whenever I step on the trail, I am hit with a giant wave of relief. This is my home. I can't wait to turn my feet over and connect with my surroundings. Some friends who have observed this phenomenon have likened my behavior as being like an Irish Setter who has been let out of the car after a long ride. I can't wait to be in the woods and, ideally, to climb up for a view. With so many people on this trip, I had to temper my rush of enthusiasm a bit. I could dash ahead, but I'd have to wait to make sure everyone

was making progress. The rule of thumb is that the group should roughly keep the pace of the slowest hiker. Fortunately, we were young. That makes up for a lot of other sins, such as eating from the junk food pyramid and staying up late partying—both of which happened just a few hours before.

The trail begins with a short, gentle warm up along the appropriately granite-boulder-filled Katahdin Stream, where crystal clear mountain water alternatively surges and pools. The number of little side trails cut down to the stream's edge tell the story of the thousands of hikers who have come before us.

The trail climbs gently up the ridge, never quite leaving the refreshing sound of Katahdin Stream. Just over a mile from the campground, the trail crosses the stream one final time via a manmade wooden bridge, then begins climbing in earnest. Over the next four miles, it climbs over 3700' to the summit.

I knew from experience that the bridge was the place to stop and wait for the rest of the gang. It was a splendid scene. Mosses and ferns everywhere. Small spruce trees thrived, protected from the harsh winds that can blow across the tableland above.

I was sweating like crazy. I set my day pack down and found a nice piece of granite to sit on while I waited. There were a few bugs and, true to form, they found me. Generally, if there is a black fly within 10,000 miles, it will find its way to my ear canal (most always after taking a bite out of the back of my neck). Like the black flies, I was determined to reach my goal. When everyone was assembled and hydrated, I urged forward progress. We had a big climb ahead of us.

Just after the falls, the trail climbs steeply via huge rock steps installed to battle erosion. These works are an impressive and nearly indestructible ode to a man named Lester Kenway.

Lester was the trail steward in Baxter State Park for many years. It is here that he honed his incredible skill at designing improvements that at once protect the footpath, fit the landscape and defy gravity.

One of the greatest challenges to a trail is erosion. An inherent problem is that once a section of trail gets muddy, hikers will start cutting paths around the mud. These paths in turn start getting muddy and hikers carve increasingly wider routes. Soon there is one giant manmade bog.

Another challenge is water management. If rain isn't diverted from the trail, it will eventually get either washed out or converted into a new flowing stream.

All along the AT, a dedicated network of volunteers does their best to help hikers stay

Lester Kenway designed and, with the help of his trail crew, installed steps on the steep slopes of Katahdin to prevent erosion and provide stable footing for generations.

true to the path. They build bog bridges, replace bridges over streams, build rock steps and in some cases, reroute the trail to make the hike more pleasant and protect the surroundings.

The hallmark of Lester Kenway's work is enormous undertakings. If you are on the AT (particularly in Maine) and encounter a section of trail that makes you wonder out loud, "How the hell did they get these boulders in place and how did they do such an incredible job (including factoring in how they would otherwise want to shift downslope)?", it was probably the vision of Lester and the hard work of one of his crews.

Lester Kenway's use of slings, tripods, rock cutters and other tools of the trade have made him a legend well beyond Maine and the AT community, so much so, that he started a trail building consultancy company. His work now appears on trails throughout North America, due to his ongoing design work and his in-the-field workshops that teach trail building techniques to other trail groups.

The relentless climb up the shoulder of Katahdin is spectacular. It leads you around and over an astoundingly huge jumble of boulders that begins below tree line, then suddenly thrusts you into a world of stellar views of The Owl, Barren, Doubletop and surrounding peaks.

On a blue-sky day, the experience will leave you breathless. But exposed ridges can also hold significant and unexpected dangers.

In 1846, Henry David Thoreau climbed to Katahdin's tablelands by way of a route approximating the one that Hunt would formally establish almost 60 years later.

When storm clouds rolled in to obscure the summit above, he decided to turn back and rejoin the rest of his party, who had stopped to harvest the wild cranberries that proliferated next to the trail.

While the precise wandering route of Donn Fendler may never be traced, what is known is that after he dropped off of Katahdin to escape the weather, he passed between The Owl and Katahdin, then found and followed Wassatoik Stream to his rescue. The first two days he was out are approximated by the arrow.

Thoreau said, "We had to console ourselves with the reflection that this view was probably as good as that from the peak, as far as it went; and what were a mountain without its attendant clouds and mists?"

One souvenir Thoreau left on the tablelands was his name. The highest flowing water source on the mountain is a spring located near the spot where he turned back. Today we know it as Thoreau Spring.

A 12-year-old boy named Donn Fendler got lost in the boulders in July of 1939, when Katahdin was suddenly enveloped in clouds, mist and sleet. His cousin implored him to stay with him in the lea of a boulder until Donn's father and uncle came up the trail, but the boy had other ideas.

He soon got off trail and thus began one of the most inspiring tales of survival in Maine history. Over the next 9 days, Donn worked his way down off the mountain and into the wilderness, where he logged an estimated 80 miles or more among rocks, brambles, streams and clouds of insects. His sneakers disintegrated on Day Two, so he made most of the journey barefoot.

When he staggered out of the woods 9 days later to his rescue by a sporting camp owner, he had lost 16 pounds (he weighed only 58 pounds as a result), had only a torn jacket on, and was exhausted to the point of periodic hallucinations.

The story of Donn Fendler's survival became a national sensation. The book that resulted, titled *Lost on a Mountain in Maine*, was read to and inspired generations of Maine schoolchildren. I am one of them.

In 2014, seventy-five years after Donn Fendler became lost on the slopes of Katahdin, I had the honor of meeting him at a lecture. I told him there were two people I thought of every time I climbed Katahdin, Henry David Thoreau and him. Donn flashed a big smile to the audience and said, "Yeah. Thoreau didn't make it to the top either."

Even at age 87, it's clear that Donn Fendler never lost a step.

Bad weather wouldn't be our challenge on this autumn day. We wound our way through the boulders, past where Donn Fendler got lost, up onto the gorgeous open tableland, where we could see the summit ridge laid out before us, then onward, gently upward to the sign marking Thoreau Spring.

Not far to go now.

In a little over an hour, we stood on the summit, overlooking the famed Knife Edge Trail traversing the very spine of the mountain from Baxter Peak to Pamola Peak, looking down on Chimney Pond, surrounded by the giant cirque of the mountain and out over the wild lands between The Owl, extending north into the unknown where a 12-year-old boy wandered for days on end.

We stood at the northern terminus of the Appalachian Trail. We had been on it all day and would return to our cars by the same route.

At the time, none of us had the remotest idea that two of us on the scene were actually starting a hike that would not last a mere day, but 28 years and over 2,100 miles. It would take a few more trips until it dawned on us that something big was taking shape beneath our feet simply because we shared a love of mountains and couldn't wait to explore new trails.

CHAPTER 2

Vermont

In 1986, Wayne and I began hiking the length of the Green Mountain State, which inadvertently kept our Appalachian Trail adventure alive.

SECTION 1

Forest Service Road 21 to Vermont Route 9

TRIP STATS
October 11 - October 13, 1986
40.1 miles
North to South

The fabled Green Mountains of Vermont form a nearly continuous spine, starting in the southwest corner and extending beyond the Canadian border. Appropriately enough, the first long distance hiking trail conceived and built in America—the Long Trail, traversing the length of Vermont for 273 miles—also established the very vision for the existence of the Appalachian Trail. It was the same with Wayne and me.

Wayne brought the Long Trail to my attention. As would become the norm, as soon as I heard the mention of a new trail, I went out and bought the guide book. (In this case, I bought two different ones—the official Green Mountain Club trail guide and a profile map series published by an independent publisher.) The seed was sown and we made plans to hike the "LT" in a series of 3-day weekends over the next few years. It so happened that in doing so, we would be continuing our Appalachian odyssey

(the southermost 100 miles of the Long Trail are also the Appalachian Trail).

According to the first Long Trail Guide, published in 1917, *"The Green Mountain Club was organized in 1910 for the purpose of bringing the mountains closer to the life of the people, not only of Vermont, but of the entire country. It is building the Long Trail over the Green Mountains from Massachusetts to Canada, affording a high, scenic, mountain pathway where everyone who wishes may enjoy health and recreation at a reasonable expense. It is hoped that those who tramp the Club trails will come to have a keen personal interest in the preservation and upbuilding of our forests."*

I turned into the Long Trail trailhead parking lot just east of Bennington on Route 9, a state road that cuts across the bottom of Vermont, on October 11th of 1986. The ride from Maine was almost six hours and I did most of it non-stop. As usual, my mind locked in on one thing—getting to the trail. Bathroom or fuel stops were the only reasons I took breaks.

My legs were screaming to become unbent. I was eager to see Wayne and jumped out of the truck to greet him. There were two cars in the trailhead lot. One of them was Wayne's faithful VW Rabbit. He saw me drive in, leaped out, stashed the "Hartford Courant" he was reading behind the seat, and walked over to high–five my arrival.

"How was the drive buddy?" he asked.

"Not bad. Good weather for a hike," I said, glancing at the high cirrus clouds. "Good for today at least. Supposed to get pretty nasty. Paper says maybe rain tomorrow and Monday."

There was no time to talk here. There would be plenty of time for that in the tent – especially if it poured. We had to make some headway today and tomorrow before the rain arrived. Every minute counted. Rain can dampen more than your gear. It can throw you into a myopic funk as you slip and slide your way along the path at half your normal pace.

We tossed Wayne's gear into the back of my truck and drove north. The trailhead at Forest Service Rd. #21 is my favorite trailhead in New England. Standing in this dirt parking area, far removed from the nearest paved road, you immediately feel the presence of the trail. It's not like other Long Trail access points where you pack next to a speeding whirr of cars and eighteen wheelers that you can't wait to escape. Here the woods surround you. It's just you, your companion, the trees, the birds, the squirrels and yes, the porcupines——but that story was yet to come.

We dumped three day's worth of food on the tailgate and the negotiations began. "I'll take the cheese and pepperoni, if you take the bagels and cream cheese" and so forth. This is the only communal aspect of packing and it always amuses me. Everything else in your pack is there because you decided to bring it along. But after the food ritual, you can find yourself hiking up a mountain chastising yourself for agreeing to carry a package of cheese fondue (yes, it tastes great, but it weighs a ton).

The other aspect about packing that amuses me is that I'm a mule. On any given trip I probably have 5 pounds more of gear with me than I absolutely need. For example, I have a nylon journal cover with zip pockets that adds a few ounces of weight, but I wouldn't dream of leaving it home. It's been part of my traveling road show for decades now. Then

there's the ThermaLounger®—an ingenious gizmo that turns my ground pad into a recliner. Wayne owns one, too. You can't underestimate the ability to sit comfortably in the tent for hours on end. I've lived out enough storms leaning on an elbow, thank you.

I walked across the dirt road to an old water pump and start cranking the handle. With 10 strokes, the water gushed from the spout and splashed about my feet. I filled my water bottles. Wayne slung his pack on and walked over with my camera. I took a shot of him standing by the Long Trail north sign. Someday we would walk out of the woods from the north to arrive here, but this time we would be going south.

I walked to the truck, took a last look to make sure we were not forgetting anything and locked up. My pack was on. The sun was out. We were on our way, immediately climbing the 2.5 miles to the summit of Bromley Mountain. There was no chance to warm up. My calves were tight as hell. I cursed myself for not stretching out before we left the trailhead.

"No...sense...in...stopping...now." I said to myself as I slabbed the first ridge. "Got my pack on. Have to keep going." Those eight words were powerful motivators and old friends even though I wasn't yet 30 years old.

One hour into the hike, I broke out of the trees and onto a ski slope. The payoff for the climb was spectacular. I turned around and looked east. Nothing but blue sky, Vermont farms and New Hampshire mountains. Wayne popped out of the trees and onto the scene. "Even better up there, I bet," he said between breaths nodding toward the observation tower on the summit.

A quick scramble to the top of the tower yielded the desired result—views extraordinaire. We didn't take our packs off. We had a long way to go and couldn't linger. The sky was sending mixed signals. No clouds to the east, high cirrus on the western horizon.

"Rain in 24 to 48 hours." I announced, as if it was necessary to prod Wayne along. I should've known better. He was already calculating our progress. After all, he was an

Wayne (left) and the author on the summit of Bromley Mountain, 1986.

analyst by trade. "2.5 miles into a 40-mile trip," he said, right on cue.

We climbed down the tower and onto the ski slope. Open summits are euphoric, a rare chance to look around as you walk, as opposed to concentrating on almost every single step. As we descended, I stopped to take one last look at the unobscured view before plunging into the trees again.

The leaves were down and filled the trail, making footing extra tricky. I couldn't see where the roots and rocks were underneath them. On a descent, it's even more dangerous than on a climb. My full pack reminded my shoulders and knees that I volunteered to carry the cheese fondue again.

Once we hit Route 11 at the ten mile mark, we had bottomed out and only had two miles to go. I successfully lobbied for eating the cheese fondue when we made camp. At the 11.5 mile mark, we junctioned with a side trail to a shelter.

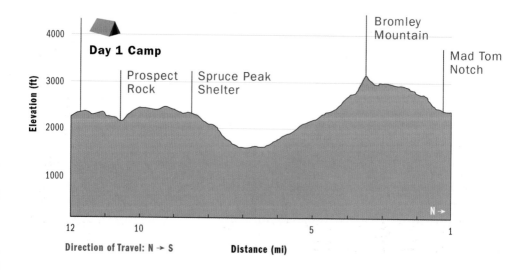

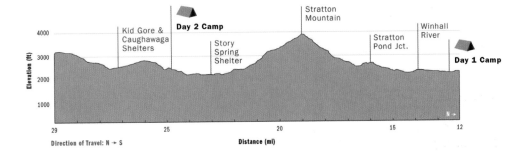

It didn't hold any interest. We had declared a general moratorium on camping in shelters. For one thing, the wooden floors were unforgiving, even when you used an inflatable ground pad. For another thing, they attracted mice and other rodents. (I've spent one too many nights in shelters with mice running over my sleeping bag all night.) Shelters certainly came in handy when it was pouring and you could duck in for a while to plan your next move, but for the most part, we avoided them these days.

We found a flat spot high on a ridge, set up the tent, sat outside on the loungers and ate crackers and cheese. The cheese-fest concluded with the fondue (also served outside) and a discussion about where we were and what lay ahead.

When you are on the trail, you need to constantly be aware of your progress. For me, it's a running dialogue in my head that I can pull into the foreground when needed or keep running in the background, like a computer's hard drive. The inputs are dynamic. Mileage covered, current pace, food and water intake, weather conditions, terrain, clothing choices, my physical and mental states—they each jockey for position in order of importance. You can't last out here unless you are constantly paying attention and weighing the ramifications.

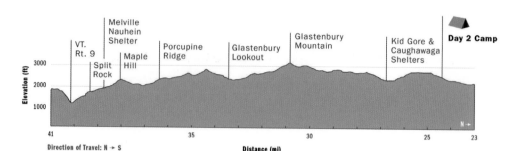

Direction of Travel: N → S   Distance (mi)

"Twenty-eight miles to go." said Wayne. "Would like to cover at least 10 miles tomorrow. Hopefully, most of it before the rain gets here. We can do a 15-miler on Columbus Day. The packs will be lighter."

"Agreed."

At 7:00 a.m., we woke up to cloudy skies and the prospect of 10 or so miles of relatively flat trail to Stratton Pond and beyond. One thing about the Long Trail is even when it's not raining, there are a lot of muddy sections. By 10:30, we were sinking above boot level on the approach to the pond. When we got there at 11:30, it still wasn't raining. We celebrated by eating a massive lunch. Once it started raining, we weren't going to want to stop again.

At 1:40 p.m., the drizzle began. Now it wasn't just cold; it was cold, windy and wet. Our pace slowed to "just fast enough to stay warm"—about 1.5 miles per hour.

Nonetheless, we covered 11+ miles by the time we pitched the tent at 5:00. Just stopping to set up the tent made me start shivering. I was so glad I had double wrapped my dry clothes in a nylon stuff sack then a sturdy plastic bag. Dry clothes and hot soup would be my salvation.

It poured all night long and didn't let up until 8:30 a.m., when it returned to a drizzle. I was certain there would be no views from the Glastenbury Mountain tower on our way out.

It was hard to leave the warm, dry shelter of the tent to step out into the rain and fog. We heated another round of coffee water on the stove instead.

In the midst of the 16+ mile hike out to Wayne's car, we climbed the Glastenbury Mountain tower anyway.

"Wish you could see the view," said Wayne. "It was awesome when P.H. and I were here," he said, referring to a mutual friend he did a day hike with a few years ago.

"We'll be back," I said.

"Yeah. When we do the Long Trail from end-to-end in one shot." he was quick to reply.

I looked out at the tops of the fog-enshrouded spruce just below us. The thought of doing the Long Trail in one trip was compelling. I had been yearning for another major trip.

We still didn't know we were already on one.

SECTION 2

Sherburne Pass (Rt. 4) to Forest Service Road 21

Appalachian Trail

Section hiked in
this chapter

TRIP STATS
May 28 - June 1, 1987
42.5 miles
North to South

I met Wayne at J.J. Hapgood's store in Peru, VT. It was the Thursday before Memorial Day.

Wayne had arrived only 3 minutes before me.

"A good omen for the trip," he said.

We were about 4 miles from the trailhead on Forest Service Road #21 (the same place where we started our trip from Bromley Mountain to Glastenbury a few years before). We were closing in on finishing the Long Trail, but we now realized that we also had our sites on a goal ten times its size—the AT.

On this 40+ mile trip, we worked toward achieving both. For 24 of the next 26 years, we hiked a section of the AT. The only years we took off were 1989 (when we headed to northern Vermont to finish the Long Trail) and in 2000 (when Wayne was recuperating from a motorcycle accident and we went kayaking in Maine).

Once again, we were racing the daylight. But this time it didn't matter. We were "car camping" tonight, which meant laying the ground pads out close to the car, where all of our gear would be within reach.

When we got to the gravel parking lot, there was only one car there. We tucked our vehicles into the corner and set up our ground pads. I placed my backpacking stove between us, fired it up and threw some hot dogs in the pot for dinner. The whole process took less than 10 minutes. We had done this before.

I was exhausted from the lead up to the trip and the 5 hour drive it took to get here. Judging from the snoring that started next to me an hour after dinner, Wayne was, too.

I got up to throw the cook pot in the truck and grab my portable radio. The Boston Celtics were playing in the NBA Eastern Conference Finals. I tuned in the game from my sleeping bag, and turned the volume down so I could just hear the play-byplay.

The clouds screaming by under the full moon became my visual entertainment. I started thinking about tomorrow. "The first 6 miles will be the toughest of the trip. We will climb up to Pico Peak, then over to Killington. I'd better call it a night." I said aloud, even though no one else could hear it. I shut off the radio, rolled over and, as was my habit, fell asleep in under two minutes.

I didn't sleep long.

I was awakened by a persistent scratching noise that sounded like sandpaper being rubbed against metal. I turned on my headlamp and shined it in the direction of my truck. The noise stopped. I kept my light fixed on the scene. A porcupine ambled out from behind the front passenger tire and made his way back into the edge of the woods.

By now, Wayne was awake.

"There was a porcupine under my truck. He's gone now."

"Man, that's weird." he mumbled, followed immediately by rolling over and starting Act II of a spirited return to "World Class Snoring for Humans in F Minor".

Despite the syncopated gasping fest (I was used to it) I also drifted off to sleep, until the porcupine came back. We continued our game of "you come back, I turn on the light and you go away again" deep into the night.

I was determined to outlast him. My pig-headed attitude prevented me from simply moving the vehicle, which I briefly considered, but rejected because (A) I was comfortable in my sleeping bag and (B) I was not convinced that moving my truck a few feet was going to accomplish anything. I figured there was nothing of interest under my truck except maybe a warm engine that would yield temporary comfort, and eventually the porcupine and me would go our separate ways to live out our lives as nature intended without any real harm done.

Sure enough, we both gave up the game eventually. I slept solidly for the last two and a half hours before the birds started chirping and the sky lightened. The clouds were still thick, but it hadn't rained yet. I walked to the truck to grab the coffee and my stainless steel percolator. Great coffee is another benefit of car camping and one I needed at the moment. (On the trail we've tried every freeze dried coffee there is, and they are all poor substitutes for a percolated pot.)

While the pot of French Roast brewed on the trusty Svea camping stove, we split up the food and loaded our packs for the hike. This way, if the rain started before we got to Route 4, we wouldn't be packing outside of Wayne's car and getting wet. We could just hoist our packs and go.

I also had another, more selfish motive. The trailhead on Route 4 is huge and almost always busy. It's a popular hiking spot and a lot of people also pull over there to take photos.

When I get to busy trailheads like this, I want to keep my socializing to a minimum and get up into the woods as quickly as possible. Milling about the vehicle to pack while cars speed by and people come and go raises my anxiety by the second. It grates against me worse than the sound of the porcupine under my truck.

The reason I so dislike noise and potential distraction is that packing must command every bit of my concentration. I have learned from experience that the decisions I make up front can either pay dividends or come back to hurt me many days and miles down the trail. So, as I pack, I keep running tabulations on everything: the number of meals I'm carrying and what they are, sets of clothes, cooking implements, spare batteries, number of water bottles, etc. This is a strange and beautiful ritual that has its own order

and rhythm, much like conducting a symphony. Every note has been considered. Every instrument has its place. And when there's an interruption, like someone in the audience having a coughing fit, the orchestra has the discipline to keep playing. That's certainly what I try to do, unless or until the incessant noise disrupts my perfect symphony.

Whether I need to pack in a crowded trailhead or not, I always regain my serenity by stepping into the forest, where I can return to the reassuring, steady rhythm of my feet turning over on the trail and the welcoming sounds of birds and breezes.

Thankfully, we didn't carve out a trip that would require big mileage days for a change. Forty-two miles in four and a half days was a pretty leisurely pace. If we got to the summit of Killington on day one (only 5.4 miles into the day), we'd be happy. From there, the terrain would mellow out.

True to form, when we got to the trailhead, we grabbed our packs, locked the car and were on our way.

I always love the challenge of an ascent, but today we had the added incentive of trying to make it to the shelter near Pico Peak before it rained. There was no way I was going to stop until I got there. Wayne knew it. I heard him say something about meeting me there as I bolted up the trail.

When we got to the shelter (Wayne was only minutes behind me), it started pouring. We ducked in to stay dry. In 15 minutes, the sun was blazing down and the rain clouds were gone. We rested on a boulder in front of the shelter and checked the map.

The 3.5 miles to the summit of Killington were an absolute blast. It was a long winter (you could still see remnants of snow high on the mountain's slopes). I was so happy to be out in the mountains, I practically flew across the ridge.

We set up shop on the summit lodge roof and watched the afternoon and evening unfold over Vermont. Once again, no tent required. There was no chance of rain now and the summit breeze kept the bugs away. We were fortunate because we were living

on the cusp of bug season. Any day now could be the one that brought the invasion. We brought the heavy artillery with us—bug dope containing DEET. I hate to use it and will only do it as a last resort, but it's the only thing (other than constantly smoking cigars or standing in the smoke of a fire) that keeps mosquitos and black flies away. Yes, there was also the mesh head net option, but hiking in one is worse than getting thousands of bug bites. It's like wearing a portable sauna on your head. What's worse, you can barely see out of it. In a sport where footing is essential, it's not worth the risk.

On Friday, a mostly descending 9.4-mile day put us on top of Beacon Hill. The views here were pretty satisfying, although not what we had on top of Killington. But Beacon Hill did have a feature that was unusual and appreciated—an old phone pole that made a great back rest. As an added bonus, the breeze was again our friend. Not a single black fly or mosquito all night.

Everything changed on Saturday. We descended from Beacon Hill to cross Vermont Route 103 and the impressive Clarendon Gorge on a "hikers only" suspension bridge. Then it was into the evergreens and up onto the ridge. Unlike yesterday, today was mostly climbing. Our target was White Rocks, a high point about 10 miles into the day. We were hoping it would bring a third straight night of great views and no bugs. We arrived at 6:00 p.m. to discover a completely forested summit with no views at all.

We walked another 3.7 miles down from the ridge to set up camp near Homer Stone Brook, we found we were stone out of luck. In a matter of hours, bug season was in full bloom.

The black flies were relentless. We swatted at them all the way through the tent setting ritual. Wayne graciously offered to go fill the water bottles while I got situated in the tent and started digging through the dinner bag. I zipped the door shut and looked through the screen at the swarming flies. Finally, I was on the right side of the equation.

I am an unbelievable target for black flies. I used to think there was something in my chemistry—literally something in my blood—that made me their preferred target. What I have come to believe is that it has nothing to do with my chemical make-up and has to do with the amount of heat I give off. I throw an awful lot of heat. In fact, I'd be a terrible fugitive. If NASA took an infrared heat scan from outer space, I'd bet they could they'd pick me out. They might mistake me for a volcano, but they'd definitely hone in on me.

One thing that supports my heat theory is the fact that the few black flies that follow us into the tent never bite us. Instead they congregate in the peak of the tent where heat collects. They just crawl around up there all night, unless we scoop them out with a potato stick can. But even that risks inviting more flies in than you're escorting out.

On Sunday, we stepped out of the tent and into the swarm. It was as if they waited for us out there all night. "Maybe they'll subside when we get back up on the ridge, away from the water and back into the breezes." I thought.

Yeah, right.

I couldn't have been more wrong. It was officially bug season in the north woods and that's all there was to it. The only defense was to slather on bug dope, keep moving and keep exhaling. This is when you needed to change your style to nose breathing as much as possible. It is risky to open up your diaphragm to take deep breaths, like you normally do on ascents, because there is nothing more disgusting than deeply ingesting black flies. They get lodged against the back of your throat and cause eye watering and guttural hacking fits that make you stop in your tracks and make you hope no one on earth is around to hear.

There was no stopping today, even for lunch. We decided that we'd rather keep walking for a few more hours and call it a day. When we topped Baker Peak (2850') in mid-afternoon, we met a day-hiking couple that just arrived from a side trail. They sat on the ledge for under a minute, then headed right back down. "The bugs!" they said,

flailing their hands and disappearing in a trot.

The bugs, indeed. They were so fierce that tonight we set up the tent and dove in packs and all. No time for an orderly unpacking ritual. This was our chance for escape and respite and we were taking as much of it as possible.

Memorial Day, 1987.

We were underway by 8:00. Only seven miles to go. We should reach my truck by noon, maybe faster given the black fly situation.

Two miles into the day, we reached the shores of Griffith Lake. It started raining. Usually this had an effect on the black flies, but not today. Nothing would defeat them. A half-mile later, we reached Peru Peak Shelter, where a couple was talking to the caretaker—a seasonal employee charged with making sure this area doesn't get too overused. The woman turned to me and asked where we were headed.

"Forest Service Road 21." I said.

"Oh, we stayed there last night. You must be the red pick-up from Maine. There was a porcupine making noise under your truck all night."

"The little bastard is more persistent than I gave him credit for" I replied. "He was under there most of last Wednesday night, too."

The day hikers stepped out of the shelter and disappeared down a side trail. We stayed with the caretaker long enough to chat and eat one orange each in the shade of the shelter. Normally, the black flies wouldn't come into the shelter with us. But today there were still a few buzzing about our heads. I guess they couldn't wait for winter to end either. As soon as they hatched, they were on the hunt for food.

We had two more peaks to climb, Peru and Styles. The last part of the Peru climb was steep, and my sweat washed away the bug repellant. The only defense was to keep moving.

I slowed down on the summit of Styles just long enough to take a quick look around. Only 1.3 miles of downhill trail to go. It's was knee and toe basher. I hadn't started carrying ski poles yet. I was a few years away from the discovery that would take the pressure off my knees and quads on descents and make it possible for me to enjoy hiking into my later years.

I dropped off the granite summit and into the woods. As I plummeted down through the trees, just in control of my footing, I thought, "what if that little creep damaged the brakes on my truck and I lost them at the bottom of a hill on the way home?" I laughed at

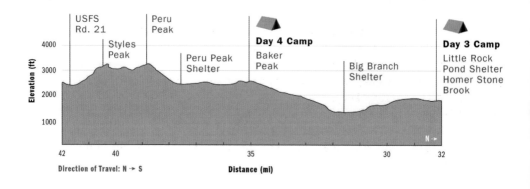

the absurdity and got back to carefully picking my route down.

I got to my truck about five minutes before Wayne, threw my pack into the back, grabbed my keys and wallet out of my pack's top pocket and jumped into the cab.

"Let's run down to that little store and get something cold to drink!" said Wayne, as he hopped into the passenger side.

"Perfect."

I started the truck. It immediately stalled. We were rolling backward and I stepped on the brake. It went right to the floor. We kept rolling backward, now picking up speed. I frantically pulled on the emergency brake. We stopped just short of the opposite edge of the lot, where the edge dropped off into the woods.

Wayne jumped out of the truck and stuck his head underneath.

"I can't believe it. Come look at this. He chewed through your brake line."

I got out and looked. There were quills everywhere—where we had parked, in the engine compartment, everywhere.

"Well, at least the hand brake works," offered Wayne. "We can limp down to a gas station."

I got in to re-start the truck. Now the gas pedal felt funny. The engine was cranking, but it seemed like there was no gas getting to the carburetor. We looked under the truck again, this time back by the gas tank.

More damage. The porcupine ate through the gas line, too. There were quills stuck in my spare tire as a signature to the act. I hastily pulled them out in disgust.

We stood up, brushed the dirt off our clothes, looked at each other and laughed.

"I can't believe it. A porcupine. A friggin' porcupine. This will go down as the all-time excuse for not reporting to work" I said, knowing that this problem wasn't going to be solved before I was due back at my desk the following morning.

We got back in the cab and away from the bugs to discuss our plight. It was noon on Memorial Day. The only things tubular we had were pack frames and tent poles. They wouldn't fix anything. We were four miles from the nearest store. It was time to start walking.

We loaded a day pack with a water bottle, our wallets, spare clothes, bug repellent and our remaining food, then started trudging down the dirt road toward the store.

I turned to Wayne and said, "The adventure continues."

We made good time on the road and because we didn't have to pay attention to roots and rocks underfoot, we were free to walk side-by-each and talk.

"Man, it's a good thing we got to the truck by noon," said Wayne. "We stand a prayer of getting out of here today, as long as that general store is open."

My road map of New England had "HELP" printed in big orange letters on the back. With three miles behind us and the intersection with another dirt road ahead of us, we saw an Isuzu truck approaching. I held up the "HELP" sign. It worked. The driver was totally amused by our story and gave us a ride to the store. It was open!

I dashed in and asked, "Do you have a garden hose, or any other kinds of tubing?"

"No. We don't have anything like that," said the uninterested woman behind the counter.

"Well, you see, a porcupine ate through my gas and brake lines," I said, hoping for a little empathy.

"These things happen," she said.

OK. That didn't work. Back to the pragmatic approach.

"Do you have any duct tape?"

She led us to the end of the store and pointed to the bottom shelf. Nothing but transparent tape and masking tape. They wouldn't do the job.

"There's a hardware store in Londonderry. That's about five miles that way," she said with a fully extended arm. "Sorry I can't help."

OK. At least now we had broken the empathy barrier.

"That's alright. What time do you close?" I asked, in case we needed to return.

"Around six."

"The adventure continues." I said as I turned to leave.

Wayne met me outside with an ice cream sandwich and a Boston Globe. We split the sandwich and started walking toward Londonderry.

"The adventure continues." he said.

Out on paved and busy Route 11, we were plunged into the twentieth century. No dirt roads or country stores out here, just noise, pavement and speed. It was a jarring re-entry after being on the trail for four days.

Memorial Day drivers were in a rush to go wherever they were going. Wayne and I took our sunglasses off to increase our chances of getting a ride. After five cars went by, I made a bold prediction.

"That white convertible will give us a ride."

It stopped and we hopped in. The driver, from Massachusetts, gave us a ride all the way to Londonderry. As we got out he even asked us if we wanted a ride back to the truck.

"Yeah, that would be great if it wouldn't be too much of an inconvenience." I said.

"No problem. I'm just cruising around."

"All right then. We'll be right back."

We started to walk away from the car. The driver yelled back toward us. "On second thought, I think I'll just get going."

He pulled out into traffic and disappeared. Miraculously, there was a hardware store across the street from where he dropped us off. Even more miraculously, it was open! We walked in and the woman behind the counter immediately said, "May I help you with something?"

She led us to the "tubing and clamp section" of our dreams.

We grabbed three clamps, two pieces of tubing and a roll of duct tape.

Next stop; Food. The adjacent IGA had everything we needed to create a Memorial Day picnic. We went across the street to the cool shade of a cemetery and powered down some sandwiches and chips.

Our luck going back to the mired truck was terrible. We had to walk all ten miles. Our only stop was at J.J. Hapgood's store (again) for 2 quarts of Gatorade. We got back to the truck at 7:00 p.m. We had walked seven miles before noon (on the trail) and 13 more (on the road) after the porcupine disaster was discovered. Wayne attacked the gas line problem with gusto and was done in minutes. After pushing and coaxing, the truck finally started. I jumped into the back and saw Wayne's ear-to-ear grin in the rearview mirror.

Wayne drove the truck back to Route 4 with only a hand brake and low gears to slow us down. There was a parking spot right next to his car, so he grabbed it. It's 8:30 p.m.

For me, driving the five hours back to Maine after dark with just a hand brake was out of the question.

Wayne had to get back to Hartford, Connecticut. He didn't have any vacation or sick time to spare. He felt bad about leaving me at the trailhead, but I told him not to worry about it. There was no sense in both of us missing work. He wished me good luck and disappeared down Route 4. I grabbed my pack and the radio, found a flat spot back in the woods and set up the tent. I was too wired from the day's events to go right to sleep. I made another sandwich and tuned in the Red Sox game for a few innings.

I was up before dawn. The pressure was on me to drive the 20 miles west to Rutland (the nearest town capable of taking on a truck rebuilding project) before the traffic picked up. Going down 6% grades using only a hand break and low gears wasn't for sissies and in retrospect, might have been for idiots.

When the terrain and my heart rate both flattened out on the outskirts of Rutland, I found a garage and pulled into the lot. I wasn't going to drive anywhere else until my truck was fixed.

I walked into town, slid into a diner booth and bought the cheapest breakfast on the menu. I didn't know what this adventure was going to cost me, but I was willing to bet it would be at least a week's vacation plus two paychecks. I was a 30-year-old, three years into learning a trade (writing) and most everything I earned went toward food, rent and gas money for hiking trips. I was bracing for the impact.

Back then, when I faced situations that hit my wallet hard, I only knew one formula; Spend less, earn more. It wasn't my fault that the porcupine went after my truck, but I believed it was my responsibility to suffer the financial consequences and to make the money back as quickly as I could. After breakfast, I called into work to explain my situation. Thankfully, my boss was sympathetic. She said I could use my remaining vacation time while I waited for my truck to be repaired.

Back at the garage, there was a party going on under my truck. It was up on the lift and the whole shop was pointing, shaking their heads or laughing. Finally, the

Why Porcupines Love Working on Cars

When I got back from my expensive foray into Vermont, I poked around for stories about porcupines attacking cars and trucks. I learned that vehicle damaging porcupines are not a Vermont-only phenomenon.

There are reports of porcupine damage in the Catskill Mountains of New York, in the backyards of Maine (where one porcupine spent the winter eating the tires off a boat trailer) and throughout North America.

Particularly notable is that hikers and climbers in the Bugaboo Mountains of British Columbia need to encase their trucks in chicken wire to deter the porcupines in that region, who also have an insatiable love for rubber automobile parts marinated in road salt.

Chuck Holmer©

head honcho came into the waiting room to deliver the verdict.

"We've never seen anything like this." he said. "Everything rubber has been destroyed. You'll need all new radiator hoses, clutch cables, rear electrical harnesses, brake line and gas line...and that's what we've discovered so far."

I told them to do what they had to do, then I set about doing what I did best; I grabbed my pack and went for a walk.

I considered getting back into the woods, so I wouldn't have to pay for a hotel. These were the days before cell phones. I had to stay in touch with the garage in case something came up that required my go ahead. So, I found the cheapest hotel within a 20 minute walk of the garage, bought hot dogs, buns and mustard, then set out to find a book store. I wasn't going to waste money on just any book. I wanted the thickest book for the money—something capable of entertaining me for a week. There on the bottom shelf, I found it—the full account of Admiral Peary's polar expeditions. It was hundreds of pages to consume at my leisure.

I spent three nights and four days in the hotel waiting for my truck to be repaired. I maintained my austerity diet of hot dogs, prepared on my camp stove set in the bathroom sink. I spent most of my time reading about how the men on the polar expedition almost died from breathing the fumes from their camp stove. At least my makeshift kitchen had a window I could open.

On Friday morning, I made my daily walk to the garage and got some good news. My truck would be ready by noon.

The damage was more severe than I had imagined. The bill was close to $900. According to the U.S. Bureau of Labor Statistics, the same repairs would have cost more than $1880 in 2014). But that doesn't matter to me the moment I finally turned the key and drove out of Rutland. I was headed home.

As I neared Sanford, Maine, my radiator overheated. Steam poured out from under my hood. I pulled over, waited for the radiator and my temper to cool a bit, then threw in the half gallon of water I packed in case the only rubber hose they didn't replace had a porcupine hole in it.

As I drove the last 45 minutes to my house, I pondered how important it was to have that jug of water along. It made me think of how I always packed rain gear, even though on some trips, I never used it. I wondered, "If I planned a trip expecting everything to go perfectly, never needing to rely on the gear I always brought along for the unexpected, what kind of trip would it be?"

"It would be frigging miserable," I said out loud.

Because it's the unexpected that fills life with excitement, joy and gratitude. When you let go of your expectations and allow journeys to unfold before you, you discover they are filled with wonder—clouds screaming past the moon, climbs to summits with vistas beyond belief, hoards of black flies that send you into the tent, porcupines that eat vehicles and strangers that give you a lift to the hardware store just when you need it most. I wouldn't trade one bit of it—not even the black flies, the forced vacation or the $900 repair bill—for a more predictable and less fulfilling walk through life.

SECTION 3

Williamstown Station, MA to VT Route 9

Appalachian Trail
—— Section hiked in
this chapter

TRIP STATS
November 25 - November 27, 1988
17.7 miles
South to North

On the day after Thanksgiving in 1988, I parked on the wide shoulder of Vermont Route 9 across from the trailhead and wondered why Wayne hadn't shown up yet.

"Man, this is weird. I swore I told him I'd be here by 7:00 p.m. OK, I got my usual late start from work and it's closer to 8:00, but he wouldn't have bolted already, would he? Maybe he just went to Bennington to get dinner or something. At any rate, I'd better go back across the street and check the trailhead parking lot one more time."

I drove across the street to check the parking lot. Sure enough, there were still three cars parked there—two were from Vermont and one was from Connecticut.

"Right state, wrong car," I said out loud. Wayne lived just north of Hartford, but he drove a black VW. This Connecticut plate was on a silver Honda.

I went back to the other side of the road and backed in, so I was facing the highway. It was a better vantage point in case Wayne showed up. If I didn't spot him first, he'd surely spot my truck.

I shut off the engine and got out to stretch. I'd been behind the wheel most of six hours. It was 0° out, so I didn't want to stay outside for long.

"Might as well wait in comfort," I thought.

I grabbed my 0°F-rated sleeping bag, hat and gloves from my pack. I also took 2 beers, cheese, salami and crackers from the food bag. I put the food on my dashboard, which now became my refrigerator. I shook the down sleeping bag to puff it up for extra warmth, then threw it across the bench seat and climbed in. I couldn't fully stretch out across the seat, so I sat with my back against the passenger door. The arm rest dug in just above the small of my back. That wouldn't do, so I rolled up my fleece jacket and stuffed it behind me.

Crackers and cheese for dinner. Wasn't the first time. I wished I had stopped somewhere along the way to eat something more substantial, but I didn't because I was an hour behind schedule. Going somewhere now didn't make sense. What if Wayne showed up and I wasn't here? The problem would only get worse.

I turned the radio on and tuned in the Boston Celtics game. That would keep me entertained until it was time to go to sleep.

10:30 p.m. I moved my head and my hat didn't move with it. It was frozen to the window. Every window was completely frosted over, creating a strange glow every time a car went by, and making me feel a bit claustrophobic. If Wayne drove up now, I wouldn't be able to tell if it was him. The Celts were winning in the fourth quarter. I shut the radio off and went through a round of scenarios that ended with me doing this section of trail by myself if Wayne didn't show up by morning.

1:00 a.m. A car pulled in. I couldn't see a thing except the eerie glow. Two guys got out of the vehicle. They were laughing and walking around. They sounded drunk. I got the feeling that they were here to rob cars and were going to smash out one of my windows. My heart and brain were racing. I grabbed a full beer off the dash. It was the only thing handy I could throw at them.

I heard two doors slam and the car peel out from the dirt and onto Route 9 again. Man, it's amazing what stories you can tell yourself when you are reduced to hearing things. I put the beer down and went back to sleep.

3:00 a.m. Another visitor. This time, it was an eighteen wheeler. Probably just stopping to see if his load straps were still taut. Yup. He was back on the road in under 10 minutes.

6:30 a.m. The sun was up. I couldn't take life in this frost lined-cocoon much longer. I needed a cup of coffee. The question was whether to fire up the backpacking stove here or drive to Bennington. I kept thinking that if I left, Wayne would show up, not realize I had ever been here, and go home.

A knock on the window nearly makes me have to peel myself off the ceiling. I rolled down the window and saw Wayne standing there with a huge grin.

"Good morning, Captain!" he said.

"Where were you?"

"I camped in the woods, just up the trail a bit. I figured you'd see me."

"I looked for your car. Where'd you park?"

"I forgot to tell you. I got a new one."

Oy vey. The silver Honda was his. "You mean I could have slept in the tent in total comfort after all?"

"I need coffee. Let's throw your gear in the back of the truck, then go to Bennington for breakfast." I said. "Just give me a minute to defrost the windshield."

In 1988, the only way we could stay in touch on the road was to find a pay phone and hope for the best. Fortunately, on this trip, our lack of communication didn't get in our way. We still had more than a day and a half to cover less than 18 miles.

We also had the weather on our side, at least initially. While we were driving south, the temps were climbing into the 50s under bright sun, meaning we could repack food and gear outside comfortably when we got to the trailhead in northern Massachusetts.

Packing next to your vehicle is a luxury, especially when the weather cooperates. It's one more opportunity to lay out your gear, assess whether you need it all (in this case, the milder than anticipated weather and forecast let me leave my super-insulated gloves and winter hat under the driver's seat) and finalize the menu. We've now done this so

The view climbing out of Williamstown Station, Massachusetts. Here the trail winds through and over "cobbles", blocks of quartzite estimated to be 350 million years old.

many times, it goes quickly. We are usually repacked and ready to go in under 45 minutes.

When we started hiking sections outside of New England and relied on public transportation to get us to the trail, this luxury was replaced by dozens of e-mails confirming menu choices, who was responsible for shopping for which items, and so on. There was no leaving excess items under the driver's seat. Whatever you walked out the door with was what you carried into the mountains. I would spend many hours leading up to each trip going over my gear on the living room floor instead of on the tailgate or the ground. It was as far away from a 45 minute packing job as you could get.

It was hunting season, so packed one thing we normally didn't—blaze orange hats and vests. We didn't think we'd see any hunters on the trail, but if they were around, we want to make sure they could see *us*.

By 10:00, we were heading up the Pine Cobble Trail, which junctions with the AT a mile or so south of the Vermont border. The trail was named for the blocky piles of boulders that formed the open summits in this part of the world.

Five hundred million years ago, these mountains that seemed such a permanent part of the landscape hadn't even formed yet. In fact, geologists widely believe that almost all of what we know as eastern North America was once under water. Over a period of 150 million years, sediment collected on the ocean floor and became sandstone and quartzite. The rocks were thrust upwards, riding on top of granite formations over a billion years old. The resulting ridges and ledges are incredibly weather resistant, and can be seen on the Appalachian Trail as far south as northern Virginia.

A mile and a half into the hike, we stopped and sat on the sunny summit of Pine Cobble for a quick break. The bright quartzite blocks of stone that surrounded us are unlike anything we had seen on the trail. They were so randomly placed it almost looked like they were unloaded here by a giant dump truck. It was hard to imagine the force that was required to push them up from below the earth's surface.

We looked over at Mount Greylock, just a few miles to our south. The summit tower of the highest point in Massachusetts was framed against the sky. The AT went right over its summit. Some day we would be heading in that direction, but now, we had 16 miles of northbound trail to cover. It was time to go.

We stepped off the cobble and into the woods. Near the top of East Mountain (the last peak in Massachusetts), the sign for a view of Mount Greylock had fallen down. I grabbed a rock and pounded the sign back into its rightful tree trunk.

We crossed into Vermont and spent the afternoon hiking through moderate forest terrain.

The easy terrain meant we could make good time. It also meant that the area was accessible and popular with hunters. We had seen close to a dozen of them already. Part of our "being seen" strategy called for making deliberate headway and not deviating from the trail. I'm glad I brought my blaze-orange hat.

The clouds had been moving in all day. They obscured the sun around 3:00, and the temps dropped into the 40s. I was glad to see the cloud cover. It meant the temps wouldn't plummet tonight. Just like blankets on a winter bed, they would seal today's warmth in. If the skies were clear, there would be no stopping the heat loss.

We bagged a hilltop site just above a thicket of brush. As we set up the tent, we got a dusting of snow. We were happy to be stretched out in a warm sleeping bag and drinking soup. After last night's struggle to find comfort and quiet, it was quite the treat.

Before I drifted off, I replayed the day in my mind. Thinking about all the hunters we saw today, I was glad we were only 5 miles from the car.

"I hope we don't see any more hunters tomorrow," I said. "Tomorrow's the last day of deer season. We should try to get to the car by mid-afternoon."

I woke with the birds at 6:00 a.m. to a light mist falling on the tent. Boy, did I sleep! Ten hours straight through. I fired up the coffee water and pulled out my journal to jot

down some notes. By now, I had a growing collection of the same brand of wire spiral bound journals filling my office shelves at home. They were the perfect size for my occupation. When they disappeared from the supermarket shelves, I called the manufacturer and had them send me a case of them—enough to capture a full lifetime's worth of stories.

We were underway by

10:30. It would be a quick hike out. We didn't want to travel through hunting territory in anything less than full daylight. We only made two stops on the way. One at Congdon Camp Shelter, where we ducked out of the mist to make coffee, and one just two miles from the car, when the mist turned to steady rain and we put our rain gear and pack-covers on. (Why we even bothered with pack-covers was a good question. In 40 years of hiking, I've never used one that works more than a few trips. The waterproofing wears off and you end up carrying a soggy, wet nylon cover.)

We bolted for the car. There was only one small ridge left to climb. I reached the top and looked ahead down the trail. There was a hunter standing right in front of me, looking away from me. Should I yell? Should I dare to move?

I stood still, but moved my left hand out to the side—to signal to Wayne that something was up ahead and to walk slowly. Usually, it meant I've spotted wildlife. He understood and moved up beside me.

"Hunter," I said, just loud enough for Wayne to hear.

The hunter's head and rifle both turned our way. The rifle pointed safely toward the ground.

He walked toward us until he was standing five feet away.

"Any luck?" asked Wayne.

"Nope. Been out here three days and haven't seen a thing." He shook his head, flinging raindrops from the brim of his hat to the ground. He grunted a "good bye", stepped around us, and continued his walk down the trail. In three hours, his hunting season will be over.

"In case I forget next November, please remind me that we shouldn't be on the trail during hunting season," I said before we start heading down the hill toward Wayne's car.

"Roger that."

We walked less than 100 feet when there was a loud noise to our left. A giant doe crashed through the brush, crossed the trail just a few feet in front of us, then zig zagged down the ridge and into the deep woods.

I turned around and looked back at Wayne.

"Timing is everything." he said.

I thought back to all that had happened in just two days. Sleeping in my car because I couldn't find Wayne, tiptoeing through a minefield of hunters, the rain not arriving in force until the end of the day, and our send off by the doe. Yes, timing was everything indeed.

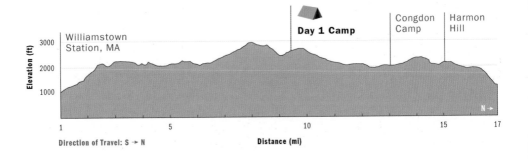

CHAPTER 3

The Boot
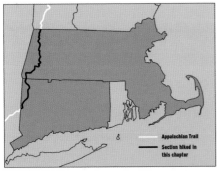 # Fiasco

"For that trip by road or rail
For extra grip on those rocky trails
You're gonna need a quality shoe."

— Mark Knopfler *From the song Quality Shoe*

North Adams, MA to Pawling, NY

TRIP STATS
May 25 - June 5, 1990
141.8 miles
North to South

One of the great things about being on the trail is it places you firmly in the present. There are no ambiguities. There are clouds in the sky or there aren't. You have eaten all your oatmeal or you haven't. You are behind schedule, on schedule or ahead of it.

The decisions you made to get to the here and now come into play in small ways ("I wish I hadn't eaten all of the chocolate") and in big ones—as was the case on this ten-day adventure.

There were a lot of moving pieces that had to be sorted out before we could step onto the Massachusetts and Connecticut sections of our path. First, there were the logistics: the big ones were buying and packing food and getting cars spotted on both ends of the trail section. Then there was an added twist; People were joining us on the hike. Four of Wayne's friends were driving up from Connecticut to spend two days climbing up and over Mt. Greylock with us, then heading back home on Sunday. What a godsend having the extra crew turned out to be!

While preparing for the trip, I noticed that the trail went right through the town of Dalton, Massachusetts the day after we would descend from Greylock. I called up Wayne.

"Hey, what if we mail a food box to Dalton to avoid having to carry an additional 8 days of food up and over Greylock?" I asked.

"Friggin' genius." he replied.

I was used to the food box scenario. When I did my Mexico-to-Canada trip in 1983, I spent 6 months drying and packaging food, then packing boxes to be shipped to post offices in towns along the way. Back then there weren't many dehydrated vegetable options in supermarkets, so I dried onions, zucchini, tomatoes, spinach, potatoes—and a whole farmer's market worth of other varieties—ahead of time, mostly using a food dehydrator.

We'd hike into a town we'd only heard of in a guide book, find the post office, grab the box awaiting us, then go to the supermarket to buy whatever else we needed to create menus for the next several days. (I wrote everything contained in the box on the inside box flap so we wouldn't have to take inventory when the box arrived.)

This time, I threw everything we'd need for 8 days of meals into the box. We wouldn't have time to go to the supermarket. We wanted to grab the box on the Monday we'd be ambling through Dalton, load up our packs, and go.

The North Adams caper

My day began in Falmouth, Maine. I drove to West Hartford, CT to meet Wayne at a preferred burger joint. Then we drove our cars to Pawling, NY to drop his car off at the southern end of our planned trip, then up to North Adams, stopping only for antipasto and pizza along the way. We rolled into town at around 11:00 p.m., exhausted and ready to catch some z's.

There are no places to park or camp near where the Appalachian Trail enters or exits North Adams, Massachusetts (the closest spot to the northern end of the AT in the state and the starting point of our trip). The closest "sanctioned" parking spot is at a community center a fair distance from the trail. And the closest place to camp was on the trail itself.

We drove around North Adams until we saw an industrial type building that was closed for the night. Driving around back, we discovered a section of abandoned dirt road. It extended about three car lengths before it was blocked by boulders.

"Perfect," we said in unison.

I parked the car, leaving just enough room in front to spread out our ground pads and sleeping bags. After 750 miles of driving, I was more than ready.

The bowling alley, circa 2014

At 2:30 a.m., I awoke to a car cruising slowly behind the building. It slowed down and then pulled in behind my truck. Next, a spotlight came on and started scanning the scene.

"Damn," I muttered under my breath. "We're bagged."

"Do you know you're on private property parked behind a bowling alley?" announced the stern voice of the policeman.

"Well, no." I said. "It's been a long day."

"Can I see your drivers licenses?"

In minutes, our licenses were being radioed in and a back-up unit was on its way. After brief discussion, we were allowed to stay put, as long as we promised to vacate the premises at sunrise. No worries there.

I don't think the North Adams Friendly's restaurant ever saw anyone arrive, dine and depart as quickly as Wayne and I did. By 7:15 a.m., we had day packs on and were bolting north to the Vermont border and back (an 8.2 mile round trip). We didn't want to end this trip with 4.1 miles of Massachusetts trail left to do.

Ready to roll

The most important piece of equipment you have on the trail is your mind. You can't walk tens of miles, let alone thousands, if you aren't wired for perseverance. You either have it, develop it, or go home.

The second most important piece of equipment you have is your boots. You can get yourself out of almost any situation by walking your way out. But if your boots fail, you are in serious trouble.

There's a lot riding on your boots. They have to be supportive, protective (soles, toes and ankles) and have more-than-decent tread. Many a hike has been cut short because the hiker was trying to squeeze one more trip out of his or her old boots, with soles so worn that the first rainstorm effectively turned them into ice skates.

In my experience, boots almost always failed over time. I had never known boots to fail quickly. One reason for this was that I was that I was working for an outdoor company that carried boots from highly regarded manufacturers. Because I did so much hiking, I was often asked to put hiking boots to the test. That was the case for this trip. I had been given a pair of new hiking boots manufactured in Europe. When I put them on for the first time, I was impressed. They were supremely comfortable. As with most above-the-ankle styles, they had two sets of "speed hooks" above the eyelets. Speed hooks are basically posts with a metal tab folded over the top. You slip your feet into the boot, wrap the laces around the speed hooks, tighten them up, tie them—and presto!—you're ready to take on the trail.

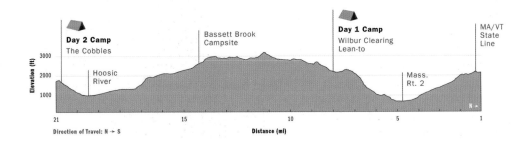

At least in theory.

Coming down off Mount Greylock (elev. 3491') on Sunday morning, where the granite summit monument would serve as a recognizable landmark for days, I stopped at a rocky trailside overlook. I set my pack down and leaned over to cinch up my boot. I gave the lace a tug and the post and tab of one of the speed laces popped off and went flying over the cliff.

I couldn't believe it. I looked back at my boot. It couldn't have been worse; There was nothing left on the boot to wrap the lace around. If it had been one of the top speed laces, I could have gotten by. But this was one of the ones just above the grommets that was critical to locking your heel down in the boot and preventing blisters.

"Well, that sucks." I announced to the crowd. "Eight days to go and my boots are screwed."

Wayne and I briefly discussed options. Fortunately, I had another pair of boots stashed behind the front seat of my truck. Unfortunately, they were day hikers—more sneakers than boots. The notable difference was lack of integrity in the soles. Unlike me, they weren't built for scrambling over roots, rocks and roads for days on end.

"I know," said Wayne, turning to the other four members of our hiking party. "You guys are headed back to your car at the next paved road anyway. Why doesn't Jeff give you his truck key and you can bring his day hiking boots back to us. That way, Jeff can resume the rest of the trip with fully functioning boots."

They readily agreed.

It wasn't an ideal footwear scenario, but I would make due. I was happy we had decided to drive my truck to the northern end. If we had left my truck at the southern end, my spare boots would have been 150 miles south.

It was late afternoon when the foursome returned with my boots, then departed. Now there were two of us. We climbed to the top of a hill called "The Cobbles" with a stellar view of the Greylock ridge with the village of Cheshire below. We had covered a solid 12 miles, so we set up camp. There was enough of a breeze to keep the bugs at bay, so we just unfurled our ground pads and sleeping bags and watched the sun go down as the lights came on in the valley below.

One of our nods to civilization was bringing a small radio and speakers along for the ride. Between songs, the DJ mentioned "the Memorial Day forecast for tomorrow." My stomach immediately sank.

"Did you hear that? Tomorrow's Memorial Day."

"So?"

"So, no food from the post office in Dalton tomorrow."

"So much for brilliant planning."

We were seven miles from Dalton. We'd have to do a short day tomorrow, hit the post office as soon as possible on Tuesday and make up serious mileage daily to have a prayer of making the New York border and Wayne's car by next Monday. The once-brilliant food drop mailing idea was defeated by a critical detail.

Five miles into a leisurely day-three woodland stroll, we found a beautiful spot to camp in a pine grove. It's a good thing we had such an easy day. The rest of the trip would be insane.

We were so far behind the 8-ball a mere 26 miles into the trip that we needed to string together some high mileage days. Years later, I would look back and be amazed that we never considered any option other than walking all the way to Wayne's car, nearly two states away. But it never crossed our minds that we would do otherwise. One undeniable reason, is that when it comes to things that matter to me, I have a level of perseverance (some would say stubbornness) that must be in the top quintile. I made a pact with myself to do this hike, and damn it, I was going to see it through. Over the years, my relationship with perseverance evolved. My first inclination stayed constant—I always wanted to see things through. It's what kept me moving forward. But I became more willing to accept outside input—to see things as they were (not as I wanted them to be). And that kept me moving forward with sanity. If I needed to alter the plan as a result, so be it.

That mentality would kick in on future trips. But in 1990, under the Massachusetts pines that formed our 14-hour home, we only considered one option: walking 100-plus miles to New York.

On Tuesday morning, we were on the trail by 7:00 and at the Dalton P.O. by 9:00. What I remember most about downtown Dalton was the noise. There were trucks rumbling everywhere, and I couldn't wait to get away from the hubbub and back onto the trail. We attempted to find a cash machine—these were the days long before they were ubiquitous— and found out that the nearest one was 4 miles away. We stopped at a diner and spent $7 of our last $7.85 on two breakfasts of 2 eggs, home fries and toast, then escaped to the woods under thickening clouds.

By mid afternoon, it was pouring. The trail was muddy anyway. The rain made it worse. My glorified sneakers soaked through and the footing got treacherous. Some sections of trail had been turned into wide quagmires by people on foot and on horseback. There was no stopping, even though I took a fall off the end of a bog bridge that stunned me for a second. One absolute about hiking: When it rains, you must be diligent about stepping over logs and roots. Otherwise, you are going to fall.

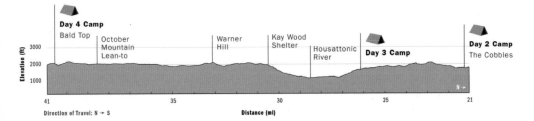

Day 4 Camp
Bald Top
October Mountain Lean-to
Warner Hill
Kay Wood Shelter
Housattonic River
Day 3 Camp
Day 2 Camp
The Cobbles

Elevation (ft): 3000, 2000, 1000

Distance (mi): 41, 35, 30, 25, 21

Direction of Travel: N → S

Wind joined the rain as the low pressure system moved in with a vengeance. At times like this, I imagine looking at the overhead view of the weather map with there being sun everywhere on earth except this little spot where we are hiking, then a scene of someone holding voodoo dolls of us directly under a kitchen faucet.

The wind and rain never let up, but neither did we. At the 15 mile mark, we topped the wooded summit of the ironically named Bald Top Mountain (2040'). By the time we set up the tent, I was a shivering mess. We had walked 13 miles since our breakfast in Dalton, much of it in the rain, and were starved. A three course meal of wonton soup, pasta with pesto and shrimp, and cheesecake with orange marmalade slathered on top was our decadent reward.

I awoke around 5:00 a.m. It was still pouring. Damn. Almost everything we had with us was soaked. We fired up the stove to make coffee to slug down with the leftover cheesecake for breakfast. At 7:10, we hoisted the packs and started down the mountain in the frigid rain and wind. Water was sloshing in my boots within minutes.

The trail was hardly a path. It was more of a jumble of slippery roots and rocks. As I picked my way along, "London Bridge is Falling Down" stuck in my head. It wasn't the worst "ear worm" I've ever had, but it was easily in the bottom ten.

By the time we came to the edge of Finnerty Pond, the rain had stopped and clouds were blowing out. This was a huge plus.

We dropped down to cross Route 20, then the Mass Turnpike on a double footbridge. To literally pass over "Mass humanity" speeding along in their post Memorial Day hazes left a lifelong impression on me. The 70 mph difference in our speeds was only the beginning. At least temporarily, their world was full of stressful obligations, whereas mine boiled down to roots, rocks, mud, walking and yes, London Bridge.

UPPER GOOSE POND CABIN
AND CAMPSITE, 0.5 MI

CABIN OPEN ←

GOOSE POND RD 2.7M

MT WILCOX NORTH
SHELTER, 14.0M

←

US RT 20, 1.6M

OCTOBER MTN
SHELTER 8.8M

→

"Again, the noise." I thought. "Just like downtown Dalton." I couldn't wait to get up and over the next ridge to get away from it. But I had no idea how rewarding it would be.

Goose Pond Reservation is a 112-acre gem managed by the Massachusetts Trustees of Reservations. There is only one way to experience Upper Goose Pond—on foot via the AT.

What made our arrival at the edge of the pond all the better was that it coincided with the arrival of the sun.

OH…MY…GOD the sun felt good. I didn't even wait for Wayne to arrive on the blessed scene. I pulled everything out of my pack and started hanging it from branches or spreading it out on the ground. Soon he followed suit.

We had already covered 7.5 miles, so we assured ourselves that we could afford to hang out for a while with the laundry and gear. A full blown, 1.5 hour sun worshiping picnic broke out, complete with smoked salmon, cheese and crackers.

It's amazing what a psychological boost the sun delivers when you emerge from a storm. On this day, the wind sped up the gear drying as an added bonus. I later wrote in my journal that the change in mood was the key to the whole trip. Even a muddy trail becomes more tolerable when the sun is shining down upon it.

We needed every advantage we could get. We were 104 miles from the car with 6 days to go. For in shape "through-hikers" that wouldn't sound too bad, but for a pair of 32-year-old desk jockeys (albeit active ones), it was going to be a challenge. I hoped for the best, especially from my day-hiking boots.

The trail gods were kind, just when we needed it. The trail climbed up and away from the pond, then we started a gorgeous and forgiving stretch through pastures with a three-mile road walk mixed in. Road walks are insane. You can make up serious ground (a 3+ mile per hour pace), yet you pay for the gift of not having to lift your feet more than an inch. The pavement is unforgiving and shin splints are a danger, not to mention inattentive drivers.

We were some pleased when the pavement turned to dirt and we got back into the woods. At 7:00 p.m., we arrived at the empty Mt. Wilcox North Shelter. We had covered 19.6 miles, even with our hour and a half lunch at Upper Goose Pond. It was the highest one-day mileage total of our entire 28 year saga.

Usually a high mileage day is followed by a much lower one. Your body wants you to rest. When I go back through my journals, I see it over and over again. A 15 mile day followed by a 10 mile day, a 17 mile day followed by a 12 mile day, and so on. Today was no different. My body was begging me to stay and rest, yet my brain was urging me forward with a large dose of reality. We were 5 1/2 days away and 94 miles from Wayne's car. The deadline wasn't going to move. We both needed to drive home and report to work next Monday.

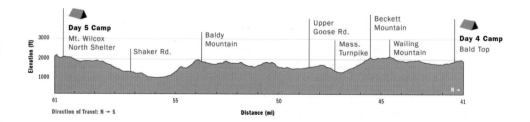

The brain eventually won out (we left the shelter at 9:00), but that didn't mean the body didn't push back mightily all day long.

There's a difference between moving and making time. Today we were dragging ass. By 12:30, we had only covered 5 1/2 miles—a pathetic 1.5 mile-per-hour pace. We needed to get it in gear. We allowed ourselves a 15 minute lunch under the brutally hot sun, then we were off again.

All afternoon, my knees and feet were killing me. It was the first sign that the day-hiking boots were taking their toll. Each time I stepped on a root or rock brought new sensations in pain. I picked my route accordingly. We popped out of the woods for another road walk under the open skies and blazing sun—this one 2.5 miles. The bottoms of my feet were burning up, a combination of the super heated pavement and the wimpy soles between it and my feet. As I walked, a little space opened up to my right, just next to a corn field. A granite slab marked the last battle of Shays' Rebellion in 1787. The sight made me smile. I don't know what made me happier, knowing that this important piece of history was memorialized, or that 203 years after the event the livelihood linked with the uprising— farming—was still thriving right alongside the monument.

I'm guessing that those of us who remember Shays' Rebellion from grade school may have hazy recollections of a story about a rural insurrection that was quickly quashed. But many constitutional scholars believe that Shays' Rebellion contributed mightily to America's survival.

Only 10 years after the Declaration of Independence was signed, our young nation was struggling to survive. The government was deeply in debt. New England's merchants (based mostly in Boston and other seaport cities), sought to pay down the debt and establish trans-Atlantic trading as a way to ensure the nation's survival. One of the ways they raised money to fill the government's coffers was to levy land taxes on farmers.

The farmers saw things differently. Many of them had fought in the Revolutionary War and had never been paid for their efforts (despite promises). Many more of them had seen their neighbors lose everything they had (sold at below market value), then hauled off to debtor's prison because they couldn't pay their taxes.

A reluctant leader (and former captain in the Revolution), Daniel Shays was among the farmers who couldn't take it anymore. He and an estimated 1500 followers marched on the Northampton courthouse to prevent the debtors' court from going into session. This and similar insurrections worked for a time.

Then in January of 1797, Shays' band marched on the military arsenal in Springfield, Massachusetts. This time, four men were killed by a single cannon shot and Shays' men scattered into the countryside.

In the aftermath, a few men were hanged and most of the others were offered clemency. Shays himself escaped to Vermont, then New York, where he resumed farming and died in relative obscurity. But the effect of the rebellion that bore his name was both immediate and historic. It strengthened the movement for a government that balanced federal and state powers. The issues raised by this band of farmers created a sense of urgency and vigorous debate during the summer of 1787. It culminated in the adoption of resolutions which addressed the relationship between state and federal rights being written into the Constitution of the United States the following September.

By 7:00 p.m., we were back in the woods and facing our own resolution; To begin the steep climb of the end of a ridge known as Jug End. Saner people would have camped at

Panning from north to northeast. Mount Greylock can be seen on far end of range.

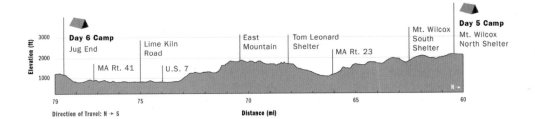

the base. We climbed the 1100' in a mile instead. It took some doing, but we found a flat spot wedged between blueberry bushes at 8:00. We vowed an early start tomorrow. That was a crazy way to cover 17.8 miles to be certain. My feet ached so much that I didn't want to stand on them again until I needed to step back onto the grand stage.

As soon as the sun rose over Jug End in the morning, it got oppressively hot in the tent. I volunteered to go outside and remove the rain fly from the tent. There was no way I wanted to put those painful boots on for the task. I crawled out of the tent opening. There was barely enough room to stand up next to the blueberry bushes that encircled us. I "Ow, ow, ow-ed" my way around the hexagon tent, unclipping the rain fly at each corner, trying to avoid falling onto the dome the whole time. My poor feet.

With everything freed up, I pulled the fly off with one tug, magician style. The tent could breathe now, giving us at least a 10 degree cooler advantage for breakfast. There was no way we were going to make anything that required cooking. The stove would push the tent temps back up to the "unbearable" setting. We wolfed down granola with powdered milk and were moving again by 7:45.

View wise, it was a five star day. We undulated along the range all day as we closed

Bear Mountain Tower, Salisbury, Conn.

in on the MA/CT border. The summits of Mount Undine, Mount Everett and Race Mountain all brought spectacular views, with the half-mile ridge walk along Race being a special treat. The only downside was that the downhill sections between the summits each brought wincing pain. My knees and feet were screaming. (As it would turn out, this was one of the last trips I would do without hiking poles—a discovery that saved my hiking career.) Nonetheless, the roller coaster ride along the ridge yielded plenty of exhilaration, and by mid morning we had covered 6.7 miles. We sat at the end of Race Mountain and looked over to our next target, Bear Mountain (2316'), the highest mountain summit in Connecticut.

The highest summit and the highest point aren't necessarily the same thing. That's the case in Connecticut, where the highest point in the state (2,379') is actually on the side of Mount Frissell, which is 1.3 miles west of Bear Mountain and not on the Appalachian Trail. (The summit of Mount Frissell is in Massachusetts.)

The story of Bear Mountain's place in Connecticut lore is pretty interesting. Toward the end of the 1800's, a Norfolk, Connecticut resident named Robbins Battell took issue with the Encyclopedia Britannica's claim that there was no point in Connecticut over 1,000' above sea level. Battell had the local hilltops in the region (known as the Litchfield Hills) surveyed and declared Bear Mountain as the state's highest peak. But he didn't stop there.

Battell signed a long term lease to the summit of Bear Mountain and the surrounding land and hired a stone mason named Owen Travis from nearby Salisbury to build a summit monument that could be seen for miles.

Over the next three years, Travis hauled over 350 tons of stone to the mountaintop and constructed a dry laid (using no mortar) tower that was 20 feet square at the base, 10 feet square at the top and 22 feet high. For good measure, he placed a 17' lightening rod on the top. Travis placed a tablet in one side of the monument that declared the spot as the highest in the state.

Befitting of Travis's skill and Battell's vision, the tower could indeed be seen for miles—at least until nature and time took their inevitable tolls.

What became of Owen Travis is unknown. Robbins Battell, however, went on to become a renowned doer of good deeds and significant benefactor of both his home town and Yale College (as it was known before it became a university), which still holds its summer school of music and art in Norfolk, thanks to his vision.

The legacy of the Bear Mountain monument is less of a shining beacon. In 1972, almost 90 years after it was built, a private donor stepped in to have it repaired and had a cement top added. That effort and a few others bought it another 6 years. In 1978, one corner gave way and the tower completely collapsed. The plaque, although inaccurate in its claim that Bear Mountain is the highest point in Connecticut, was placed in the rubble. It is a fitting monument to the two men behind its construction.

I'm pretty sure the mountain was named for the animal, but it is fittingly a bear of a climb as well—1000' from where the trail peels away from the waterfalls of Sages Ravine to the crumbled monument in a little more than a mile. We ate lunch beside the ruins and baked under the June 1 noon day sun.

That afternoon was a splendid mix of traversing the end of the range, dropping down through the woods, a 2 mile road walk, a pasture crossing and a 500 foot climb up onto a ridge known as Barrack Mattif, where we pitched the tent on an old woods road. 16.6 miles by 6:00. Not bad at all.

As usual, I crawled into the tent just enough to keep my feet outside while I pulled off my boots—no need to bring leaves and dirt in with me. I couldn't wait to get those things off. My feet were the sorest they've ever been. Now it wasn't just the roots and rocks that were causing distress during the day, it was every step. The boots just weren't made for the high mileage and heavy pack weight I was putting them through. The layer of cushioning foam in the midsoles was completely compacted. It was barely better than walking barefoot. I looked at the guidebook. Fifty-nine miles left to go in 3 1/2 days. "We've already done over 80 miles," I said to myself. "I think I can make it to the car." It certainly helped to have 13 hours for the soles of my feet to recover.

In the morning I could tell it was going to be another hot day. The earlier we started, the better off we'd be. We managed to be up and out of the campsite by 7:30 and cranked out five miles along the top of Wetauwanchu Mountain before another road walk, this time along the Housatonic River. The good news: It gave some flat terrain relief and the ability to quickly cover three of the remaining 54 miles in about an hour. The bad news: It was

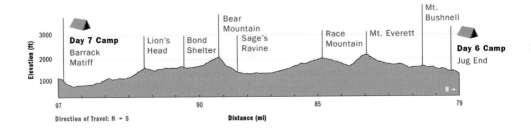

sweltering hot (85° and unrelentingly humid) and my feet were in agony. The pavement felt more like 1000°F and my soles begged for relief. I alternated between the softer shoulder and the pavement where I could.

There is no question we looked bedraggled. At one point, a suburbanite watering his lawn took pity on us and offered us his garden hose to cool down and top off our canteens.

Here began a wild interspersion of nature and humanity I can best describe as disconcerting and disorienting, particularly after spending many days in relatively tranquil woods and pastures.

As we walked along the Housatonic River, there were several canoeists out enjoying the day. Most of them drifted past us without ever noticing we were in their midst. It was nice to see others out having fun on this early June day. As our road walk ended, and we started climbing up Sharon Mountain, we experienced quite a different manifestation of people out having fun. The sound of race cars and the announcer's sound system emanated from Lime Rock Race Track in the valley below. We spent the afternoon walking in the world between canoeists and whitewater rafters to our east and race car fans to our west—a world punctuated with views of farms and mountains, and tranquility-piercing sound.

By the time the sound died down, we were taking a one hour late afternoon snack and rehydration break under the shady roof of Pine Swamp Brook Shelter, 14.2 miles into the day.

"The last 2.8 miles of the day felt like 208." I wrote in my journal that night. "Another long uphill ridge walk that tested my stamina and mental toughness. No doubt, this wouldn't be as difficult on me if my feet weren't complaining every step of the way. Finally heard the brook and began our descent to Caesar Road and Campsite. So happy to get situated and rest the soles."

As we sat in the tent, I looked up to see four people wearing backpacks and animal masks walk by. I wondered if I was seeing things, but I glanced over at Wayne, who was laughing. You absolutely don't know what you are going to see out here.

Early the next morning, one of our animal-masked people came over to our tent and said, "You guys didn't get to see our arrival in full regalia, so I thought I'd tell you what we are all about."

They were hiking with masks to raise awareness for an endangered species bill and ask for support. It all made sense now, although I wondered how many supporters they were going to find in backcountry campsites. There was only one other camper here and he had left at 6:00 a.m. Our game plan for the day was to hike 14 miles to the village of Kent, Connecticut, find the nearest cheeseburger, then cover another mile on the AT, leaving us a 10 mile walk to the car tomorrow.

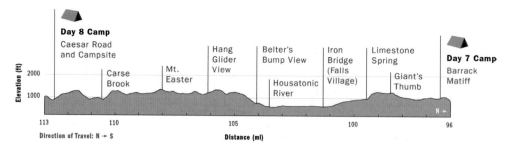

Boots of choice

The trail can be punishing to your knees, joints, feet (and likely your demeanor) if you don't have the proper footwear for the trip. There are two basic choices: wear "day hikers" (lightweight with modest support) or wear backpacking boots (heavier with superior durability, ankle and arch support).

The conventional wisdom is that if you're carrying a light pack and stopping often for resupplies, day hikers will serve you just fine. My personal preference is to wear backpacking boots on almost every trip, because I prefer the extra support and the added ankle protection from roots and rocks.

Day Hikers

Backpackers

Photos courtesy of L.L. Bean, Inc.

The plan went nearly perfectly—a 3-mile hike up and over Pine Knob, followed by a 5-mile walk on a dirt road along the edge of the Housatonic, featuring a huge stand of red pines. It was like walking through a cathedral. From there, the trail climbed steeply up St. John's ledges, via 90 rock steps installed by an Appalachian Mountain Club trail crew from the White Mountains. (From my journal: "God, what a grunt! I was hot as hell, I was dripping with sweat and my bandana was soaked. One step at a time. Umph. Umph. Umph. The view was worth it though.")

Visions of cheeseburgers drove me through my incessant foot pain. We spent all afternoon following what I described in my journal as a "nearly endless ridge." In retrospect, I don't think this section would have been as interminable if my feet weren't aching and a cheeseburger wasn't waiting at the end.

As we finally neared the end of the ridge and began descending into Kent, we heard the

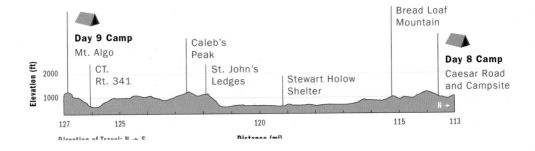

sounds of an announcer over loudspeakers followed by periodic cheers. It was the Kent School's graduation ceremony.

We stepped onto the pavement for the final leg of our quest for a cheeseburger at 3:30. Fourteen miles down, 14,000 calories to go! I think I could have eaten a whole supermarket's worth of food.

As we passed the prestigious Kent School, where there was a Lear Helicopter and fields full of luxury cars parked for the event. We entered town, where there were several restaurants that didn't accept credit cards and no ATMs. (As unbelievable as it seems today, in 1990, it was hard to use credit cards in small towns.)

As always, perseverance paid off. The Fife and Drum restaurant pulled through. We propped our packs against the wall out back, changed into our least offensive shirts and went inside.

We still must have smelled awful, because we were seated in a room all to ourselves. What a feast! Nachos, house salads, cheeseburgers, fries and endless pitchers of ice water followed by chocolate cake and coffee.

Satiated, we walked out back to get our packs, which were right next to the screen door to the kitchen.

"Did you know those two guys were on the Appalachian Trail?" asked the cook.

"No. But I did know they needed showers." said the waitperson.

We got back on CT Route 341 to walk back toward the trail. It was a hot but quiet evening. The Kent School festivities had wound down when we walked past for a second time. Soon we turned back on the path and into the woods for the .7 mile ascent to the Mt. Algo shelter.

We decided to stay in the shelter this last night out. Usually we didn't like to sleep on the unforgiving wood floor, but if we did, we'd save some tent dismantling and packing time in morning.

I took my day-hikers off to give my feet some freedom and fresh air. It had been a demanding week for my hard working feet. I vowed I would never subject them to that treatment again. I decided to pamper them a bit by dipping them in the cool stream near the shelter.

"No need to put the boots on." I reasoned. "Just a short hop on round boulders between here and there."

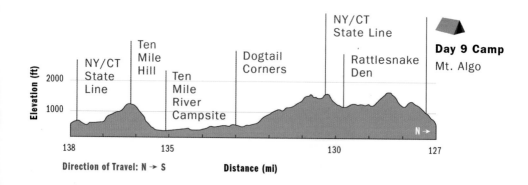

Not a good call. On the way back to the shelter, I grazed my right big toe on a rock and blood exploded everywhere. I was stunned.

When I got a closer look, it wasn't nearly as bad as I had feared. Because my feet were so tender, what amounted to a quarter inch cut was the source of all that blood.

I wrapped it tightly with a clean bandana, elevated it on my stuffed sleeping bag, pulled out my journal and pencil and enjoyed nightfall from the shelter.

Even though I didn't need to write them down, I felt compelled to capture the two lessons driven home this week—ones that would stay with me for the rest of my hiking career:

1. Don't be so aggressive with daily mileage estimates. Just because it is possible to average a certain amount of miles per day, you need to account for rest time and the unexpected (weather, etc.).

2. Never head out of town with an unproven pair of boots. You should always give them a prudent test drive/break-in.

I then turned my attention to writing about the events of the day, ending with the splendid scene that played out all around me.

"The trip was winding down. I looked out of the lean-to periodically as the sky darkened and tried to absorb the beauty around me forever—the rushing water, large pines silhouetted against the sky, whispers of wind making the high boughs sway."

I drifted off to sleep knowing that only 11 miles separated us from the New York border and the car that would speed us back to our livelihoods.

Two states down. One dozen more to go. Where would we go next?

CHAPTER 4

Vermont Part II

A Thanksgiving weekend hike brings the opportunity to be thankful for food and friends we hadn't met.

Dartmouth, NH to Route 4, VT

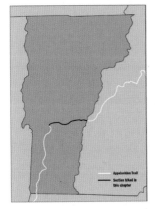

TRIP STATS
November 23 - November 25, 1990
42.7 miles
North to South

Five months after we stepped off the trail in Pawling, New York, Wayne and I were ready to fit one more hike into the 1990 schedule.

Time was running out, so we focused on the long Thanksgiving weekend and started casting about for likely 3-day hikes. I suggested a few in Maine, but Wayne presented a more compelling option.

"Let's finish Vermont and get another state under our belt. Then we'll only have eleven to go."

I didn't need any more encouragement. I pulled out my New Hampshire-Vermont Appalachian Trail Guide and started making plans. The trail looked friendly through this section that connected the White Mountains of New Hampshire and Green Mountains of Vermont, never to reach over 3,000'.

Two days before the trip, my employer gave me the chance to product test a new piece of equipment. This time it was a nifty cooking pot designed to nestle down over my Svea stove.

To my mind (and that of many hundreds of backcountry explorers that came before me), there will never be a stove that compares to the Svea (a.k.a the Optimus 123). It is

one of the most reliable pieces of camping equipment ever made. Designed to burn white fuel (purified liquid petroleum also known as camping gas), yet capable of burning good old unleaded gas (cheaper, sooty and not recommended), this solid brass beauty lights up every time, has a controllable flame and an unforgettable sound that we have dubbed, "the roar of the Svea." When you hear this stove going to work on a pot of water, there is no doubt that dinner will be served soon. But, diner beware! Wolfing down whatever you're having could cause third-degree burns on the inside of your mouth.

The Svea typically gets covered in soot. For this reason, I usually carried mine in an old coffee can with a plastic lid. The stove fit perfectly inside. However, for this trip my new toy to test was a cooking pot that nested down over the stove. The idea was you could leave your cook set (and coffee can) at home. Sounded good to me. My pack is usually loaded to the gills when we first set out. This time, I pleasantly fit everything inside, instead of having to lash a few items to the back. The only extra thing I brought was a huge stash of leftover Thanksgiving turkey, which I figured we would tear through in the first few days.

When I rolled into Hanover, New Hampshire, I was psyched to see Wayne, to have a new cooking pot and to get back on the beloved trail.

We rendezvoused in the huge trailhead parking lot on VT Route 4 (just west of where the AT and Long Trail converged), right on schedule. I tossed my gear into the back seat of Wayne's car, and we drove off with our sights on Hanover, NH,—home to Dartmouth College and the Appalachian Trail, which passed right through the center of town. My recollections of that part of the stroll include a sign in a barber shop window proclaiming that they didn't shave beards (too many hikers stopping by, no doubt) and the beautiful campus of the Ivy League college itself.

It was a foggy, late fall day, yet the trail (when we finally stepped onto it after our road walk) wasn't wet enough to slow our pace much. We arrived at the Happy Hill Shelter with enough daylight left to select a preferable spot.

This was a particularly good turn of events because the Happy Hill Shelter was living up to its claim as the oldest shelter on the AT. Built by the Civilian Conservation Corps in 1933, it had seen too many winters, too many driving rains, too many insects that thrived on rotting wood and too many campers that left the place a mess. The porch was still in good shape, however, so we opted to lay out our ground pads there instead of putting up the dome. If we set it up, we'd have to deal with drying it out at some point tomorrow. Either we'd get a late start because we would be waiting for it to dry or we'd carry a heavier, rain soaked tent for 12 miles. Sleeping under the roof would be the perfect solution.

I broke out the new cooking pot, set it on the porch and filled it with water. I poured some white fuel on the stove and lit it, an event we called "the flame ball." The purpose was to heat the fuel in the tank below enough to make it vaporize as it exited the nozzle below. If you timed it right (like I did tonight), you could turn the stove key just as the flame ball died down and you wouldn't need to light another match.

As I was setting the pot on the burner, I noticed that a three leaf pine needle cluster had stuck to the bottom.

"It'll just burn off," I thought. I had seen this happen so many times. The flame would burn the needles in two seconds and everything would be fine. Except this time, it wasn't.

The pine needle cluster did burn off quickly. What I couldn't see was that the base of it, a ball of pitch lodged on the other side of the pot, heated up to a glowing red dot. The company that invented the Svea was primarily a blow torch manufacturer. And now the stove's heritage came glowing through. Just as the first tiny bubbles indicating an approaching boil started to form on the base of the pot, I heard a hissing sound. I lifted the pot off the stove. Sure enough, the flame had gone out. I relit it and set the pot back on. More hissing, followed by an extinguished stove. I lifted the pot high and observed a tiny stream of water escaping.

"I'll be damned," I said. "The pot has a frickin' hole in it! The pitch ball burned right through the bottom."

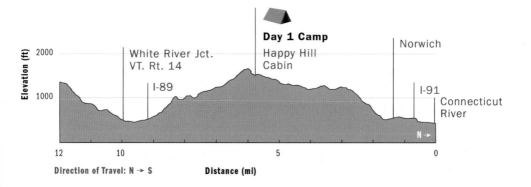

Now we literally didn't have a pot to cook in. It was time for Plan B. We took inventory of the foods that didn't need to be heated, then dined on crackers and cheese. We could have bagels and cream cheese in the morning.

I checked the guide book to see if there might be a town where we could get to a store. Even a coffee can would do. We just needed something we could heat water in.

"Eureka!" I said. "In 3.7 miles, we pass through West Hartford. The guide says there's a store." We "high-fived" our good fortune and made plans for an early start.

In the morning, we slathered cream cheese on bagels for breakfast and scampered down the trail. We were in shape and practically flying up and over the hills that stretched between us and West Hartford. Soon the wooded path turned into a paved road that led right past the West Hartford store. When we strolled into the lot, a sign in the window pronounced our fate: "Out of Business."

We slid our packs off and took out the guide and maps again. What to do?

As we looked at the map spread out on my pack, a local stopped his truck on the other side of the road, rolled his window down and said, "Are you looking for the trail?"

"Nope. We're actually looking for a cooking pot."

"Say what?"

I explained what had happened, and the man, who introduced himself as Ben, offered to help.

"I'm a camper and fisherman," he said. "I have a bunch of cooking pots. Why don't I give you a ride to my house, you can pick one out and I'll give you a ride back here."

Sure enough, in less than 15 minutes, I was staring into a closet full of camping gear, choosing a cooking pot to serve us the rest of our trip. I insisted that Ben give me his mailing address, so I could send back the pot when I got home. He grudgingly obliged. "I really don't need the pot," he said. "As you can see, I've got a few of 'em."

Soon Ben was dropping me off at the defunct store for my reunion with Wayne. We shook hands with Ben, patron saint of our hike through eastern Vermont, and he drove away to resume his weekend chores.

While Ben and I were gone, Wayne made a new friend who would become the second patron saint for the trip—a big, happy Samoyed. It looked like this puppy was just under a year old and quite taken with the prospect of joining our hike. Despite our pleas, she insisted on following us out of town and up the trail. Periodically, we would stop and point back toward town, saying, "GO HOME."

We might as well have been yelling to a tree. She would wait until we got a ways ahead, then come bounding up the trail to rejoin us.

"Eventually, she'll give up and go home," Wayne said. "Just ignore her."

Five more hours and over 10 miles later, it was clear that our new friend was going to be with us for a while. Moreover, she decided that my side of the tent was the place to be. She'd hopped into the tent and plopped right down against my left leg for a good night's sleep.

"It's a good thing we always bring extra food," said Wayne.

For the next two-and-a-half days, our new unnamed friend was our faithful companion. She certainly loved to hike. I was glad we were not going above tree line on this trip, that we would be in the woods and below 3,000' the whole way. Long stints on granite can do a number on a dog's nails and paws.

The low hills that connect the White Mountains and the Green Mountains are a great place to acquaint yourself with New England's flora and fauna. In a single day, you can walk through stands of red pines, maples, oaks and birches, then climb through green pastures to arrive at vistas that let you trace in your mind's eye the path of where you've been, and where you are going.

Yet the vistas of today are nothing compared to those available in the late 1800s—for a different reason than you might expect.

When looking out over expanses blanketed in forest it's hard to imagine that Vermont's landscape has seen some of the most dramatic changes of any state in America. In fact, from the 1760s to the dawn of the 1900s, Vermont went from 90% pristine forest to 70% deforested. First there was a Merino wool craze and subsequent bust. By 1837, farmers had cleared enough land to support over one million sheep. Within a decade, the price of wool collapsed, leaving them destitute. Many farms were abandoned and, by 1870, more than one-third of Vermonters had moved to other states.[1]

It wasn't just farming that claimed forests. Logging overtook agriculture as Vermont's leading industry in the 1850s and in its wake, Burlington became the third largest lumber port in the nation.[2] The lumber that was cleared was nearly all virgin softwood, such as pines. The trees that regenerated abandoned farms and clear cut forests were hardwoods, such as oaks and maples, which now fill the landscape. Today the pastureland punctuates the hillsides, allowing you to take in views of a 78% forested

state. To think of a time when the tables were reversed is nearly unfathomable, unless you look for clues.

In addition to the presence of hardwoods, which are particularly spectacular in the verdant spring and golden autumn months, you can't help but notice the hundreds of miles of stone walls that the former sheep farmers left behind. Mother Nature may have reclaimed the pastures, but their borders are capable of outlasting any tree that will ever shade them.

It is interesting to consider that the same forests that reclaimed much of the landscape in the last 100 years play such a strong role in generating the state's income today. Vermont is a leading producer of maple syrup, thanks to the stands of sugar maples that flourish on the hillsides. The brilliant fall foliage showcased by maples, oaks and birches is an important contributor to the state's tourism industry, drawing people from around the world every autumn. The forests and mountains also draw vacationers year-round who enjoy hiking, skiing, cycling, fishing and simply relaxing.

And then there are the farms. Farming is once again a vital part of what it means to be a Vermonter. There's a reason Ben & Jerry's ice cream started in the Green Mountain state and Vermont cheddar is synonymous with great cheese. The pastures that now dot the landscape make this section of trail a varied and fun hike where you periodically emerge from shaded woodland landscapes into bright, sunny pastures with expansive views. No wonder the dog wanted to join us!

I was trying not to get too attached to this goofy dog, which for some reason found me interesting. I didn't even want to give her a name, thinking it would only make dropping her back off in West Hartford even harder. I began thinking of that mission in terms of putting a fledgling back into the nest.

"Maybe I can just cruise by her neighborhood, drop her off and everything can go back to normal." I thought. "That would be ideal."

But, as I looked at the funny, loyal and determined pup sleeping next to me, her tummy filled with handfuls of turkey and paws stretched out against the tent wall, I realized she deserved a better name than "the dog."

"Part Samoyed, part German Shepard," I said to Wayne. "And a fugitive, to boot. I think we have a winning name: Sam Sheppard," I said, referring to the doctor that inspired the tremendously popular TV series "The Fugitive" in the 1960s.

"It's a she, " said Wayne.

"OK. The Sam stands for Samantha then."

"Two days and 26 miles to go, " said Wayne, looking up from the guidebook. "Pretty doable, especially in this terrain. Just need to get an early start."

The story of our lives.

We wouldn't be able to take long breaks, that's for sure. November hiking means early darkness. You need to keep making miles until you reach your goal. Then you can relax. It's not that you don't see anything. You're observing every step of the way. It's just that the long, sit-on-a-rock-and-look-out-at-the-world-for-a-while opportunities are off limits. We certainly couldn't help but take a break when we arrived in the pasture that gave us a stunning view of Killington and Pico Peak to the west. We would be completing this hike in the valley just short of reaching them—in the same parking area where the porcupine adventure began.

Our last day in the woods was a spectacular November treat. Fifty-five degrees and full sun, perfect for making the 16 remaining miles to Route 4. Despite an early start, it was a race against the light.

We were trying to reach my truck, parked across the very busy Vermont Route 4, and the last few miles were testing us. We couldn't stop for fear we'd be returning "our new dog" to her West Hartford home in the darkness. I didn't want to be driving around the village knocking on doors in the dark. The last climb made me curse a bit. I couldn't believe we were climbing to a gap, but we were.

I heard the constant whirr of traffic and knew we were almost there. I grabbed the dog's collar and held her close by until we were safely on the other side of the highway and she was in the cab of my truck.

It was barely light when I arrived in West Hartford. I pulled into the store "parking lot"—a dirt turn-out really—and saw a little boy playing in the yard next door. I rolled down the window and yelled his way.

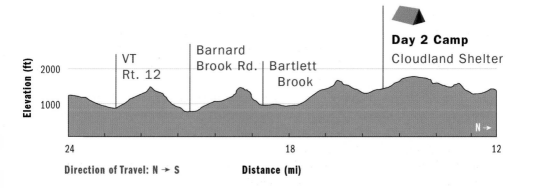

"Hey. Do you know whose dog this is?"

"Yes." He pointed toward a house a hundred yards down the road. "She lives over there."

I drove up next to the house and tried to let the dog out of the cab.

She didn't want to go.

I felt horrible making her leave, but I couldn't just drive off with a new (to me) dog. I opened the passenger door, got back behind the wheel, then pushed against her back side until she had no choice but exit the passenger side.

"I'm sorry, " I said as she half fell out, "But you need to go home."

Quickly, I closed the passenger door. I was just hitting the gas to leave when she got a running start and threw herself over the tailgate into the truck bed. The poor girl didn't want me to leave.

Now I felt even worse.

I got out of the truck, put the tailgate down and urged her out of the back.

"I'm sorry. I'd like to take you home. But I bet there's someone in that house who's worried sick about you."

This time, I sped out of the lot with tears in my eyes. I watched in the rear view as she finally tired of running after me, then turned and slowly walked toward her real home. Perhaps her owners looked out the window, saw what was happening and popped out to call her name. That's what I'd like to believe happened. I liked the sound of that ending, so I held onto it as my truth. It was easier to leave her that way.

Over the years, every time I heard a story about a dog that travelled hundreds of

miles to reunite with their owner, I thought of that incredibly loyal dog. I also thought about why I never knocked on that door and introduced myself to her owners. At the time, I thought that I was simply doing the right thing—finding out where she lived and reuniting her with her owners. But it might have been a better thing to tell them that their dog hiked 30 miles of the AT with us and that she was well cared for all the way.

As for Ben, I mailed his cooking pot back to him, along with a gift certificate and an L.L. Bean Fly Fishing catalog.

I went back to West Hartford, Vermont in October of 2014. The defunct store building still stands. Most recently, it was a pizza restaurant that also went out of business. The sign in the window now says, "Building for sale."

The home where I dropped off the dog exists in my mind's eye, but none of the two homes next to the defunct store match my memory's description. Three buildings down from the old store is the West Hartford town hall. There's a huge, relatively new dirt lot behind it. Perhaps that is where the family once lived.

Wherever they went, I wish they knew that their beautiful white dog who walked with me for three days will stay with me forever.

1, 2. *The Forests of Vermont: Here Today, Gone Tomorrow: A history of Vermont's Forested Landscape.* Kyle Adelman. University of Vermont. www.uvm.edu/landscape/.../forestsVT.ppt

CHAPTER 5

Shenandoah

The mountains of Virginia present a whole new state of mind.

Rockfish Gap to Front Royal, VA

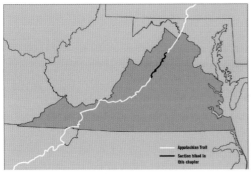

Appalachian Trail
Section hiked in
this chapter

TRIP STATS
May 22 - June 1, 1991
106.6 miles
South to North

I began my writing career creating product descriptions for mail order catalogs. My ability to generate story lines has always been my bread and butter. But, every compelling product story also includes a compilation of essential details, such as colors, sizes, price and "how to order".

At the time of this journey to Virginia (and to this day), the writers at the company where I worked were responsible for providing accurate information for several hundred products at a time. The information came from a variety of sources and would be fact checked before the pieces were published, but it was the writer who was responsible for investigating discrepancies and keeping things on track.

Managing the process wasn't too difficult, as long as I was available. But I knew that when word got out that I was leaving town for a few weeks to hit the trail, I'd be chased down by the whole production team. And who could blame them?

For weeks leading up to the trip, I was busy getting details for new products (has anyone made a decision regarding zip or button pockets?), verifying changes to existing products (we're dropping fuchsia and adding sky blue) and writing versions for the various catalogs. I would gather information by day, then after everyone went home, I'd write deep into the night. It was the only way my welcome back would have any true measure of "welcome" in it.

On top of my work duties, I also needed to handle the personal and shared logistics of pulling the hiking trip together. Putting a pack on and walking out the door is a lot different than throwing a reasonably assembled pile of gear into your car and fine tuning your packing job at the trailhead.

Then there's the prospect of leaving a vital piece of gear behind. If you are driving to the trail and forget something—say your water purifier—you can also drive to an outdoor store and buy one along the way. If you are on a series of trains and buses, as we would be, you lose that spontaneity. And you'll end up spending part of your precious trail time finding a store, waiting and paying for a cab and all the hassle that goes along with that.

I've found it's far better to make lists, assemble gear piles and keep fine tuning right up until the day I leave.

I did have one slight hedge going for me. I'd drive from Maine to Connecticut to stay at Wayne's house the night before we left. If I had any excess gear, I could leave it there.

On May 21, I fielded one last request from a co-worker, walked out into the fading light and turned the ignition key to my little red truck. The passenger side was filled with an overstuffed expedition sized backpack, a small duffle of clothing and a cooler of perishables. I stopped at Maggie's Sunoco to top off the tank and grab a soda and chips. This vehicle was making no unplanned stops between Freeport, Maine and Tolland, Connecticut.

I should have been exhausted when I got there, but I was full of two-weeks-on-the-trail-itis and there was no cure except to let it run its course. We stayed up until 2:30 a.m. food shopping, going through the menus and gear lists and listening to/watching Red Sox baseball on TV in the background.

Four-and-a-half hours of sleep was all we could afford. I awoke to Wayne scrambling all over the house in search of something. Turns out he had lost his credit card. Couldn't find it anywhere. The phone rang. It was the credit card company. A guy was apprehended trying to use Wayne's card. The tip off? The dude had his own name (Mike) tattooed on his knuckles. With the card found and cancelled, Wayne dashed off to his bank to get cash for the trip. I stayed put and did one last repack. My pack was so full, that the hood floated above my head like the Grinch's sled on top of Mt. Crumpet. I practically had to duck going through door frames. But after a day or two of eating, I knew it would settle back down to manageable form.

Next stress test, please.

Wayne was driving us to the train station in New Haven, where he would hand the keys over to his friend, "P.H.", who offered to help with shuttling duty. We left Tolland in plenty of time, except for one thing. A car accident had us practically stopped on I-84 about one-third of the way into the trip. There was no way we were going to make our train without pulling a drastic move. We pulled into a rest area, bypassed about 20 cars, then sped back onto the highway, which now miraculously opened before us. Wayne was doing his best Formula One driver imitation. The only thing going faster was our adrenaline.

"Five minutes from the station. Six minutes 'til departure." announced Wayne.

"The adventure begins." I said.

"Damn." said P.H. "We've got a blue light."

I turned around to see the cruiser in the far distance.

"Hold on." said Wayne.

We pulled off the highway at our exit and made the traffic light. Seconds counted.

I looked out the rear window. The cruiser passed on the highway, lights blazing and siren blaring. He saw us take the exit. He obviously had been off to handle a more pressing crisis all along.

Wayne pulled right up to the station. We grabbed our gear (it took some extra tugging to get my overstuffed pack out the rear seat passenger door), yelled good bye, ran through the front door and up onto the platform. A conductor waved us on yelling, "Hurry up!"

The sight of us sprinting with full expedition packs must have been some sight for him and the passengers. We just made it inside the train door before it started moving. The alcove in the very back of the car was the only place that would fit our packs. We shoved them both in there and collapsed into the two nearest seats to catch our breaths and wipe the sweat off our brows. Phew. Finally, the challenges of the morning were behind us. Now we could relax and enjoy the commute.

As was the case when I arrived at Wayne's house, I was too charged up about the hike to miss anything. I stayed awake the whole ride down to Charlottesville, reading the Appalachian Trail Guide to Shenandoah National Park and taking in the scenery.

When we got to Charlottesville at 9:15 p.m., we were facing a four-hour layover before our short bus ride to Waynesboro. We quickly found the Blue Ridge Brewery restaurant, where we made quite the impression. A couple of 30-somethings walking in with humungous packs on apparently didn't happen that often. We leaned the packs against the end of the bar (they were almost tall and wide enough to warrant their own seats) and ordered up a couple of burgers. A number of the college kids that packed the place stopped by to ask us what we were up to. They were intrigued for sure. Over the years, this fascination with our exploits would only increase with our ages. By the time we hit ages 55 and 56 and people discovered we'd been on the trail for nearly three decades, we were drawing questions and accolades from people all along the way.

By 1:00 a.m., we'd had our fill of food and conversation. It was time to catch the bus to Waynesboro, VA, the closest public transportation stop to the trail, less than 5 miles from Rockfish Gap. There we would jump onto the path.

At 2:00 a.m., we shouldered the packs and started walking away from the bus stop via US Rt 250. We were still operating on 4 hours of sleep and soon realized that we were crossing the line into insanity.

"Let's find a place to crash." I said.

"Here in suburbia?" asked Wayne.

"Anyplace. I'm beat." I said.

In a quarter mile, we came to an abandoned gas station on our right. We scooted behind it as fast as we could, found a place to set out our ground pads and called it a night at 2:30 a.m.

Less than four hours later, we were up again. With memories of our illicit bowling alley campsite fresh in our minds, all we could think about was getting back on the road before someone spotted us.

That lasted about 100 yards.

A man who introduced himself with a hearty handshake as "Jack" came bounding out of his driveway and asked us if we wanted a ride to the trail. Who were we to say no?

"I'll be right back. You just stay put." he said.

Jack disappeared up his driveway, which wound around the back of his house.

I couldn't believe what we saw next.

A hearse came out from behind the house and pulled up alongside us. The electric window went down on the passenger side and Jack said, "I think there's enough room for your gear in here. Who wants to ride in the front?"

He was laughing hysterically. The look on our faces when he pulled out from behind his house must have been something. No wonder he didn't want us to follow him up the driveway.

Sure enough, there was plenty of room in the back for two overstuffed packs and Wayne. I sat up front with Jack, one of the many people I met on this journey that I could have chatted with longer. All too soon we were at Rockfish Gap, where there was a Howard Johnson's restaurant serving breakfast. We got quite the stares from the diners in the windows as we pulled our packs out of the back of the hearse.

Finally, on day three, fueled by massive breakfasts and less than eight hours of sleep total, we took our first steps on the AT in Virginia.

Skyline trail

Shenandoah National Park extends 80 miles from Waynesboro to Front Royal, Virginia. The park's approximately 300 square miles encompass remarkable scenery and ecological diversity as well as Skyline Drive (a paved two-lane road with numerous scenic turnouts) and the Appalachian Trail.

Because both routes place a premium on scenic beauty, the AT and Skyline Drive are seldom far apart (the AT crosses Skyline Drive 28 times). But it's not as if the trail is crossing over a busy highway. The windy layout, a 35-mile-per-hour speed limit and an entrance fee help ensure that people in the park are there to enjoy the beauty, so it's a peaceful coexistence.

Even under extreme sleep deprivation, it was easy to feel the difference Virginia trail made beneath my feet. It was wide, well-groomed and an absolute joy—like walking barefoot on a shag rug compared to New England trails.

The mountain trails of New England have "up and over" in their DNA. Most often, you ascend peaks via old rock slides or stream beds. Here in Virginia, the trail generally traverses long ridges where you ascend via switchbacks and cruise at elevation for miles on end. An added bonus is there are much fewer roots and rocks to contend with. From Pennsylvania to Katahdin you need to concentrate on your footing because you are almost always placing your feet on roots or rocks. More precisely, you are trying to avoid stepping on roots (particularly when they are wet) and in between or on top of rocks. On wide, well groomed trails like this, you can look up and take in the surroundings as you hike with occasional glances down. It's like driving a high end sports car vs. a sub-compact.

And today was the perfect day to let my feet fly. I was so amped up to be on the trail and exploring a new part of the country that sleep deprivation took a back seat. Our only detour was a short dash down a side trail to get a backcountry camping permit from the ranger station.

It was springtime in the mountains. Hiking through the woodland sections was like walking through an impressionist painting. Thickets of enormous, deep green rhododendron created a surreal backdrop for their bursts of pink and white blossoms. And when we popped out onto open summits, they were covered with yellow phlox and white daises.

By early afternoon, my exuberance couldn't quell the effects of my lack of sleep any longer. The temps had climbed into the 90s, we were sweating like crazy and were tapped out. It was time to look for two things: a place to top off our water supply and a nice camp spot.

At the junction for Calf Mountain Shelter, we took the quarter-mile side trail down to a flowing spring and broke out the water filter. Water borne illnesses are a constant threat, even in mountain streams. The rule of thumb is to treat all water. One of the most well-known parasitic diseases is giardiasis. If you've ever suffered the effects, as I have, you don't think twice about carrying a filter. Sure it weights a bit and takes time to use, but what's that compared to crippling stomach cramps, terminal diarrhea, mind-boggling weakness and a hospital stay?

While we were filtering water at the spring, we were joined by a through-hiker that hailed from Pennsylvania. He was hiking solo, hadn't taken a day off since he started at Springer Mountain, Georgia, was averaging 20-23 miles per day and was having trouble as he put it, "staying up mentally". He said that his cure was simply to "walk through it".

Yikes.

I am very much a "to each their own" person. But in this case, I couldn't help myself.

"Maybe a day off is in order," I offered. "I've done a through hike, and there were times when a day or two off really filled my tank again."

"No. I think I'll just keep going." he said. "Nice meeting you guys."

Oh well, I tried.

As we were just topping off the last bottle—which involves one person holding the filter input hose in the stream and the output hose in the bottle and the other person setting the filter on a rock, the side of their boot or something else stable and pumping the water through a microscopic membrane filter—another solo hiker showed up. This guy had taken a day or more off, and was in much better spirits.

"Hey, are you the guys from New England?" he asked. "The ones who got a ride in the hearse?"

I burst out laughing. "That would be us." I said. "How did you hear about that?"

"Jack gave me a ride to the trail from Waynesboro in his 'regular car'. He's still laughing about the looks on your faces. He got quite a kick out of it." The hiker stuffed his water bottles in his pack, then nodded up toward the ridge. "Well, gotta make some miles. I'll see you guys down the trail."

"Gotta make some miles." Those four words took root in my brain. Maybe it was because in this place and time, on a hot Virginia afternoon, under the relative shade of tall trees with cool water flowing past us, "making some miles" was something we didn't have to do.

"What do you say we down a few quarts?" I asked Wayne, which he would come to know over the years as code for "Let's take a long break and sit here for a while."

"I'd rather find a flat spot up on the ridge and call it a day." he said.

"OK. But, I vote for the first one."

As we would learn, finding flat spots along this hundred mile stretch could be a challenge. The first good one wasn't high on the ridge, it was almost all the way down to Jarman Gap, some 1.5 miles away.

About 90% of the time, I am hiking out in front. I tend to have a slightly faster pace than Wayne, which almost always means I am 20 minutes (or about one mile) ahead of him from mid-morning until lunch and from mid-afternoon until we stop to choose a campsite.

Our site selection routine is amusing. When we have agreed that we should start looking for a camp spot (or when I have decided that I've had enough), I start scanning the landscape for suitable spots. I'm pretty good at quickly deciding whether a place makes the cut or whether we should keep going. As with everything in this team, all decisions are negotiable. There have been hundreds of times where we have urged each other to keep going ("there has to be a better site up ahead"), put down our packs to make short reconnaissance missions to see if there are better options or in rare cases, go back up the trail to a spot we just passed.

The general criteria are:

Flat terrain - Sleeping on a slope is awful. You either slide down into a tent corner or your gear all congregates there. Even worse is trying to sit for extended periods. You are constantly fighting gravity with your leg muscles precisely when they are begging for rest. If

it rains, you inherit even more problems. Water loves to pool up in the tent's lowest spot.

High terrain - The views, breezes and water drainage are at their best.

General location - How does the spot jive with our itinerary? We have passed by some spectacular spots because to stop would give us practically no chance of completing the section in our allotted time. Conversely, there have been many trips where on day one or two we have stopped early because the site is so spectacular and we are in position to make up miles over our remaining days.

Here on day one, 7+ miles into the day, we were absolutely ready to stop. Fortunately, the trail crossed a well-used woods road just before we reached Jarman Gap. I looked back up the trail. Wayne was right behind me.

"Man made flat spot." I said. "Let's climb up the road a little and see what we find."

Just over the first rise, we found a car turnaround spot on the road that looked barely used. I slid my pack off and let it hit the ground with a thud.

"Good enough." I declared.

By 3:15, we were in the tent. By 5:15, Wayne was snoring. I wouldn't be too far behind. I only fought sleep long enough to look out the front door to appreciate the beauty that surrounded us, jot a few notes down in my journal and go outside to hoist the food bags into trees as a precaution against ransacking bears. At last, after three frantically paced days, there was only one entry left on my "to do" list: sleep.

We awoke to overcast skies, but no rain in the forecast. With 12 hours of sleep, it was easy to get up and out into the world, and we were hiking by 8:30 a.m. It would get to 88 degrees today, so water would again be key. There would only be one spot to tank up in the next 12 miles—Upper Fork Moorman's Creek—at the base of the hill we were on. It was muddy, but we had the filter on our side. (It eliminates sediment, too, although it becomes a lot harder to pump with clogged pores, despite rinsing.)

We climbed up through blooming rhododendrons to enjoy some of the nicest hiking anywhere. The trail stayed faithful to the ridge and was remarkably root and rock free, allowing us to hit a nice three mile per hour pace.

We were sitting at the Sawmill Overlook enjoying the view, when the third through-hiker we met on the trip (another soloist) came through. I asked him how he was doing.

"Not too great, man. I've got the Virginia Blues. They're really bringing me down."

We'd heard about the Virginia Blues, an affliction that apparently hits a number of through-hikers. The theory goes something like this: Hikers leave Springer Mountain, fueled by ambition and a sense of adventure. Sure enough, they cover the 76.4 miles through Georgia quickly—one state down!

Then they encounter North Carolina (95.5 miles), which they can also hike through in a similar timeframe, with a commensurate feeling of accomplishment—two states down!

Now the going gets tougher. The Tennessee section is almost 288 miles long. The mountains are more formidable and the reality of trail life sets in. Some get homesick. Some yearn for the finer things in life—better food in greater variety (perhaps cooked by someone else for a change), a mattress and box spring underneath them, feet and joints that don't hurt, water that comes out of a faucet whenever you want it, no bugs—to most folks, those things start pulling at them. By the time they approach the Virginia border—if they've gotten that far—a huge number of hikers have already decided that through-hiking isn't for them (there's a 75% dropout rate among through-hikers).

Those who remain have three states behind them and are looking ahead at one long and amazing walk across Virginia. Because the Appalachian Mountains cut a diagonal path across the state, almost exactly one-quarter of the entire AT (550 miles) is within it. If someone has any doubts about whether their head, heart or body are committed to completing the trail, this is where they find out.

When the guy disappeared up the trail, I turned to Wayne and said, "I give him a 50-50 chance."

"It's work out here." he said.

It was a strange phrase to hear, and I almost dismissed it as quickly as he said it. Up until this point, I'd hiked close to 4,000 miles. And while some of them were difficult, I never thought of them as being "work". I thought that they were the short bursts of effort that were required to gain a more meaningful appreciation of the whole. In my mind, the payoff (grand vistas, a sense of satisfaction, introspection/deeper meaning) were the rewards for the pact you made with yourself to be out here in the first place—always making progress, always listening, always looking and yes, always appreciating. "If you can do that," I thought as I tugged on my waist belt and shoulder straps to continue the journey, "the Virginia Blues can never take hold."

The blues were something I didn't want to think about at all. What I was slow to understand is that they were already traveling with me.

Just because you hike hundreds of miles with someone doesn't mean that you know them. Hiking is a solitary activity, even when you are on the journey with someone else. You can experience long stretches of isolation, where it's just you, the path and your mind. Even when you stop for a break, there's no guarantee that your hiking companion will be joining you soon. Maybe their leg muscles hurt more today and they're off to a slower start. Maybe they stopped at a different viewpoint for a while. Maybe they've got the Virginia Blues.

There's a saying that popped up in the trail community a few decades ago that I wholeheartedly embrace: "Hike your own hike." The idea that you can experience the same journey with someone else and both see and feel completely different things is powerful and healthy.

In this sense, hiking is like white water kayaking. You can travel down the same river together, yet your approach to paddling through a set of rapids can be completely different. Perhaps you take a line to the left of a boulder in the center of the rips and your paddling companion takes a line to the right.   When you emerge from the fast water and hit a gentle stretch of river again, you regroup and continue on.

The takeaway is there is no right or wrong way to paddle (or hike or travel through life). There's only your way and everyone else's. Once you see the journey this way, you are free to fully enjoy it.

Is "hiking your own hike" the same thing as utter self-absorption? Certainly not. At least by my definition. There are dangers in listening only to the voices in your head and not getting another person's perspective. (I wonder how much of the solo hiker's case of the Virginia Blues could have been avoided if he wasn't hiking alone.)

In the thousands of miles I had hiked to date, there were several instances when I needed encouragement and a dose of level-headed thinking.

One such time was on the Pacific Crest Trail. My trail mates and I were completing a stretch of trail that crossed the Mojave Desert (where daytime highs routinely hit 120°F) and water was obviously scarce. The only known place to tank up on this day was a windmill fed cattle trough called the Butterbredt Well. The conditions for us were dire. We had less than 3 quarts of water when we set out on the six mile hike to the well that day, and the trail (a jeep road in this section) suddenly became a slog in deep sand. Without good traction, it was taking even more effort than usual to make headway. Stepping off the road and walking around the sand wasn't an option—sagebrush and rattlesnakes abounded. There was only one thing to do—make it to the well.

Uncharacteristically for this hiking trio, I was out in front. I had one thing going through my mind, "Get to the well. Get to the well. Get to the well." Those four words drove me all the way there. I couldn't wait to drink quart after quart when I arrived.

I was cranking right along when I eyed the prize. The windmill on the well was barely spinning, but spinning it was. I could already envision the water flowing forth beneath it.

Only it wasn't.

The windmill's shaft was broken and there was no water coming out of the ground. There was only a huge puddle on the ground with a few cattle standing in it. Even the most delusional, water-craved individual knows better than to take on cow pie infested mud water with iodine pills. (We didn't have a filter back in those days.)

The other guys arrived and we weighed our options. They weren't great. We had to drink something, so we passed around our water bottles until we had half a quart left. The guide book indicated there was a reliable stream four miles ahead, so we set off again.

The key landmark would be a well-travelled road. When the trail met up with the road, the stream would be on the other side. I took the lead, spurred on again by water laden fantasies. When I arrived, I yelped with joy. I peeked over the edge of the road to discover a completely dry stream bed—not even a teaspoon of standing water.

Just then, I heard the sound of dirt bikes. Three guys came screaming around the corner and stopped. "Can you take me to water?" I asked.

"Yes. Hop on."

I grabbed my water bottles and iodine tablets and jumped on the back of the bike. In three minutes, I was standing next to another cattle trough. This one had water flowing in from a pipe. I couldn't wait any longer. Trusting the water source, I chugged down two quarts before I knew it. The guys asked me if I wanted a ride back to my pack, but I declined. It was a short walk and my hiking companions would already be there.

I drank some more water, filled my bottles (dropping a few iodine tablets in each for good measure, then walked back to my friends.

Two days later, I began suffering from my impulsiveness back at the trough. I had contracted Giardia. Suffering is hardly enough of a word. I had never known stomach cramps that painful. Without getting graphic, there were other side effects, too. At its worst, I was taking my pack off every few hundred yards, experiencing an event and shouldering my pack again, only to have to start the process again. My mind compelled me to move on, but my body wanted nothing of it.

Finally, my friend Mick came down the trail toward me to deliver the news.

"We're several miles ahead of you. We can't keep going this slowly. You need to get off the trail and get better. Let me grab your food. We can meet up at the next town."

I was crushed. It was the hardest message I ever received on the trail. Missing part of the journey was something I never wanted to consider or face. But it was what everyone needed at the time.

"You're right." I said. It was all I could muster just then without bursting in tears of frustration. I set my pack down, opened the top and dug out the food bag.

"I'm sorry, man." said Mick. "But it's the right thing."

In ten minutes, Mick was disappearing up the trail and I was on my own. I felt a stunning sense of loss because for the first time in almost two months—since we left the Mexico border— I felt the adventure was continuing without me.

I spent the rest of the day working my way back down the trail to a paved road and hitchhiking to the town of Lone Pine, in the eastern shadow of the High Sierras. Here I convalesced for four days and three nights at the Dow Villa Hotel.

What I thought I needed most was a medical check up and a diet of salad and yogurt. I

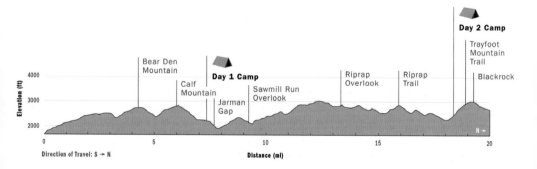

got all those things, which helped get my body back on track. I also got something I didn't even know I needed—a different look at the world.

A handful of retired men called the Dow Villa their home. They were possibly lured to Lone Pine by the temperate climate, views of the eastern face of the Sierras and low cost of living. I was just thankful they were all in my presence. The stories they told! One had been a gofer for a number of Alfred Hitchcock movies. One had explored the High Sierras in the early 1930s, sleeping out with only a horse blanket to keep him warm. It was the perfect symbiotic relationship. I was filled with inquisitiveness, they were brimming with decades of stories, ones I would carry forward for decades to come.

As it turned out, the adventure didn't continue without me as my friends wound through the mountains I could see from the sidewalks of Lone Pine. The adventure was with me all the time. I was simply hiking my own hike.

Eight years later, as I ambled along the gorgeous Shenandoah Trail, I wished the ridge, Skyline Drive and my friend Wayne could continue to be my only companions. The gnats and mosquitos had other plans. "Damn. They found me again!" As the week wore on, we wondered how we again managed to pick a late spring week for our hike. The bugs and heat were both intense. It was one of the last times we would tempt such a fate.

I stopped at the 5.8 mile mark where the trail popped out into the Wildcat Ridge Parking Area. It was time for lunch. Wayne was only 5 minutes behind me. It was now obvious he was in a foul mood. I figured the oppressiveness of both the heat and the bugs were getting to him, too. We bolted down the trail a few hundred yards, set up the tent and dove in to eat lunch.

In under five minutes, the positive of having a completely bug free luncheonette was nearly overcome by the sauna effect of being inside of it. It was almost 90 degrees outside and our bodies were throwing off heat and sweat to boot. The fine mesh nylon of the tent couldn't let heat out fast enough. (This was a good feature in cold weather when we were seeking to retain heat, but not so much at the moment.) Yet, even though we were baking inside, it was better than being dive bombed by bugs all the way through lunch hour.

I sat akimbo in the tent across from Wayne and watched as he set out crackers, sun melted cheese and pepperoni on a pan lid that now doubled as a serving tray. As funny as it sounds, I had hiked around 500 miles with Wayne, yet I still hardly knew him. One reason was the long stretches of hiking our own hikes—making headway at our own pace to meet again somewhere down the path. And even though we had spent many evenings in the tent, most of them were after high mileage days that demanded long hours of sleep after the fact.

There were two other elements at play. One was that we were practical opposites. I was a verbally oriented extrovert. Wayne was a numerically oriented introvert. I was conceptually inclined. He was mechanically inclined. I was "go with the flow". He was "go with the plan". In the early years of our hiking together, the common ground we shared was occupied by hiking, cheeseburgers, pizza and baseball (and even there it was Red Sox vs. Tigers).

The other element at play was time. Relationships are nurtured through shared experiences. We simply didn't have many to draw on yet, although the catalog of adventures was certainly starting to build. As the decades and trail miles passed beneath our feet, we could draw on a wealth of material that could make us alternately laugh or shake our heads in a "what were we thinking?" kind of way.

Then there were the changes we went through as we got older. Over the years, Wayne became less introverted and I, dare I say it, got a little more analytical. I would never reach his mythical status of being able to retain mileage and elevation numbers from the guidebook without having to refer to the pages, but I at least I grew to understand and appreciate how his mind took things apart and reassembled them.

Those days would come, but they weren't here yet. For now, I was walking with someone I instinctively knew I could trust, but didn't know well enough to understand.

Thus, earlier in the day, back at the overlook, when Wayne said, "It's work out here." he really meant that he was having a rough go. It should have been my first indication that he was carrying more than his pack on this section of trail.

I completely missed the signal and kept making headway in my Virginia bliss.

When he caught his breath, Wayne said that the heat and bugs only exacerbated what was actually eating at him, a bunch of stuff that had been going on at work.

So that was it.

The bugs we could somewhat control with bug repellant or the tent. The heat at least dissipated after it got dark. But carrying the mental stuff—well, I was hoping that a few days of walking would be the cure.

One of Henry David Thoreau's lesser known quotes addresses this concept. He said, *"I cannot preserve my health and my spirits, unless I spend four hours a day at least—and it is commonly more than that—sauntering through the woods and over the hills and fields, absolutely free from all worldly engagements."*

As Wayne went into greater detail about the work situation, I found myself thinking of Thoreau's quote. On this trip, I had been able to leave work behind. I thought about saying something to that effect, but reconsidered. Maybe whatever was bringing him down would

stick around for a while like the oppressive heat in the tent, but eventually it would work its way out and slowly dissipate into the mountain air. I wasn't convinced that saying anything would speed up the process.

I switched gears and looked out the screen window. These little tent breaks were a stroke of genius. I carried the tent poles on the outside of my pack and Wayne carried the tent wrapped inside his ground pad on the outside of his. This meant that we set up the tent quickly without having to rummage through our packs. It made packing up just as easy. We could be back on the trail in under 5 minutes.

As I hiked along after lunch, I made the inevitable comparison to the late spring hike through Massachusetts and Connecticut, when the heat and bugs were also unrelenting. But this hike already had substantial differences all the way through. The most important was that we only needed to average ten miles per day. The need to be covering so much less ground daily was an enormous benefit. We didn't have to be moving during nearly every daylight hour. Instead of taking short lunch breaks that were spent shooing away bugs between bites and weren't at all restful, we could set up the dome, dive in and take a meaningful break.

Water was an incredible challenge on this trip as well. We had to plan our days carefully around where we could find reliable water sources. On this day, it meant that we'd have to bypass the AT for 1.5 miles, paralleling its path on Skyline Drive. The Trayfoot Overlook had a fountain that was permanently on. The idea of camping near an infinite water supply wasn't just compelling, it was necessary. The 90°F heat and incredible humidity turned us into sweating machines. We had to stay hydrated. Heat exhaustion was a real concern.

We celebrated our arrival at the Trayfoot fountain as if I had discovered a working Butterbredt Well. No filter necessary! We chugged and chugged until we were full,

then filled our water bottles (six one-quart bottles in all), then bushwhacked up the embankment on the other side of Skyline Drive to set up camp. We wanted to stay within easy reach of the fountain.

Known water sources (as highlighted in the trail guide's descriptions) would dictate our stops and our campsites for the rest of the trip through Shenandoah National Park. This was an important benefit of carrying a guidebook. Without it, we would probably bypass some of the lesser known water sources (that are sometimes located down relatively obscure side trails only frequented during periods of drought. Some of these trails are only marked with blue blazes that are easy to miss).

Then there were the through-hikers. When we hiked through Massachusetts and Connecticut in this time of year, we may have seen one or two through-hikers. This time, we were far enough south to be meeting the "North-bounders" that left Springer Mountain in March and the beginning of April. (The Virginia Blues dude was one. The guy who had taken a few days off in Waynesboro was another.) In the two days we had been on the trail, we'd already met more through-hikers than in the six years we'd been section hiking.

We started the next day with a visit to the fountain to quaff more water and top off the water bottles, then we backtracked down Skyline Drive to rejoin the AT. After a steep climb of Blackrock Mountain, we dropped down to Brown's Gap to hike in the footsteps of history.

In the spring of 1862, Confederate Maj. Gen. Thomas J. "Stonewall" Jackson led one of the most daring and successful campaigns of the Civil War in the nearby valleys and hills. In 48 days, Jackson marched his force of 17,000 men 646 miles, keeping the Union troops playing defense and diverting troops that would have been dedicated to the Peninsula Campaign—a plan to capture the Confederate capital of Richmond, Virginia. The well-traveled low point in between Blackrock and Loft Mountain known as Browns Gap was a natural choice for moving large numbers of troops from one side of the Shenandoah

Mountains to the other. It played an important role in Jackson's strategy to keep the Union Army from discovering his troop's whereabouts.

As we bottomed out in the gap and started our three mile ascent of Big Flat Mountain, I became aware that my strategy of waiting for Wayne's foul mood to lift would require more patience on my part or perhaps something to change the dynamic.

"We've all been there." I thought as I chugged upward in the 90-degree heat. "Sometimes it's hard to change the station that's playing in our heads." I had been stuck on countless bad trail songs (London Bridge is Falling Down anyone?) and other less trivial things for mile upon mile. I certainly knew the drill. I also knew that changing the story can sometimes be a simple as encountering something that jogs us out of it and resets the dial.

We planned to camp at Loft Mountain Campground, just over the summit of Big Flat Mountain. There were showers there, as well as a store. Maybe the combination would be a mood changer.

When we got there just after noon, Wayne grabbed his water bottles and went on a reconnaissance mission. The look on his face said it all. The showers were mobbed. We'd have to wait. But the store certainly hit the spot. We bought 2 pounds of hamburger meat, buns, mustard and cold drinks, then set off to set up camp.

We found the perfect site—within easy walking distance of the store and showers—then indulged in burgers and ballgames on the radio, followed by scrambled burger casserole for dinner.

Sometimes it's the simple things that help us reset the dial. This time for Wayne, all it took was a couple of non-standard trail fare meals and an 18-hour hiatus from hiking in the heat with a 55-pound pack.

"I think I'm out of my funk. But no more hot weather hikes for me." he said. "I'm more of a early spring, fall and winter hiker. These temps bring me down. This is supposed to be fun."

"No problem there." I said. "I can hike anytime."

I awoke at 5:00 a.m. with a start. There was a bear outside the tent making wheezing sounds. We'd bear bagged the food, but it obviously wasn't enough.

I sat bolt upright. My heart was pounding. Wayne was fast asleep, snoring with his back to me. I looked at my gear. The best I had to attack with was a full water bottle.

I zipped the front door of the tent open and looked out.

What a relief! It wasn't a bear. It was a large doe, looking at me, wheezing and stamping her front hoof. Apparently, we were occupying one of her favorite spots.

"We won't be here long." I said. "Please come back in an hour."

Wayne heard me talking and woke up.

"What do you say we take turns staying with the gear and taking showers, then walk the one mile to the Loft Mountain Wayside for breakfast?" I said.

At last, a full bore smile. Wayne was back!

Down at the Wayside, we ordered breakfasts to eat outside on the deck, where the views were equally fulfilling. A woman who had been journaling at an inside table cracked the door to the deck open and asked if we were through hiking.

The next thing we knew, we had spent four hours talking with Suzanne, who was hiking southbound from New York with her dog named "Ben".

The trail community is astounding. It takes a lot to put your boots on every morning with the intention of making headway on a path that leads you to places you've never seen, both mentally and figuratively. And almost all of us need outside support to make it happen. Fortunately, there are many ways to find it.

Every year, AT through-hikers that are on the trail form a kind of traveling support group. They learn each other's trail names, run across each other at various times and pull for each other all along the way.

Then there are the hostels, restaurants, outfitters, laundromats, grocery stores and other businesses that support the hikers. Their generosity is legendary. Offers for rides back to the trail and other such gestures are common, even when it might be more convenient for them to go back to work.

The clubs and Appalachian Trail Conference chapters that keep the trails in good shape and keep updated guidebooks and maps available are also important, often unsung, sources of support.

Finally, there is the fraternity of hikers, AT and otherwise, who are willing to sit down and "talk trail" with anyone of their ilk. It's a strange and wondrous lot of us that enjoy hiking to the point that we'll do it for hundreds, let alone thousands of miles. It does us good to spend time with others who have done the same or better yet, may be inspired to do so.

Suzanne was one of us. Talking with her on the deck was like reconnecting with a long lost friend. She told us what to expect of the trail when we hiked the sections between New York and here and we told her what to expect between Katahdin and New York.

Interestingly, she brought up the subject of keeping your spirits up.

"I think it's important to have a safety cord back to civilization rather than just floating along the trail disconnected from society." she said.

I thought back to the "Virginia Blues" dude. "I guess you're right. I don't have enough solo hiking time to weigh in on that, but it does seem to me that you also need to disconnect from society enough to learn to be comfortable in your own skin. I think sometimes people are afraid to disconnect at all."

"Amen." said Wayne.

We could have sat on that deck and talked all day if it weren't for the slight issue of being only 21 miles into a 106 mile hike. The "running behind schedule" scenario sounded familiar. Maybe this hike was more similar to the MA-CT hike than I thought.

As we bid our goodbyes and headed in opposite directions, I hoped our paths would cross again someday.

It was scorching hot again. We turned onto a fire road that looked like it junctioned with the AT and climbed up into the woods until it dead ended. No turning back. We bushwhacked up a steep embankment and back to Skyline Drive, where the heat coming off the pavement felt like 120°. Fortunately, it was a quick scoot to Ivy Creek Overlook, where we could jump back on the trail.

The afternoon was a series of "up and overs". When we sat in the tent that night on top of Flattop Mountain with the hint of breeze thankfully speeding the evening cool down, we marveled that we had covered almost 10 miles despite our 4 hour chat with Suzanne.

"There's something to be said for shorter mile days and keeping your sanity." I said, reflecting on our chat with Suzanne.

"I don't know how sane this afternoon was, but I get your point." said Wayne.

"Early start tomorrow." we said in unison, then laughed.

The next 1.5 days were more of the same—hot, humid days, undulating trail and a dependence on mostly human supplied water sources (picnic areas and campgrounds).

The proximity of the AT and various side trails to Skyline Drive also create chances to meet with people from all over the world. We met people from Germany, Japan and about 15 states. Invariably, someone would be parked at an overlook or out for a short hike, see us come out of the woods and ask us what we were up to. This aspect of popping in and out of human contact made traversing Shenandoah National Park the most unique section we hiked in all of our 28 years. Your safety cord to society was certainly never too far away here. But as we learned, that only matters if you're willing to use the safety cord.

Big Meadows Campground was our next goal. We had a food box waiting at the lodge (we hoped). We had mailed one there containing meals for the last 4 days, so we wouldn't have to carry them all the way through the park.

When we strolled into the campground, I went into the lodge to verify our food box had arrived. It had. I'd come back to get it when we were situated in a campsite. First things first. Showers and laundry. That done, we secured a campsite, then fetched the food box.

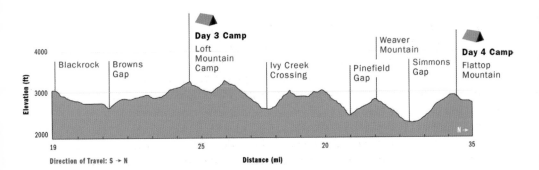

Hawksbill Mountain

Washing the sweat and bug dope off and putting on clean clothes had a therapeutic effect for both of us. Even though it was still hot out, we'd have another laid back afternoon ahead. We were on schedule and didn't have to make up ground.

The next two days we covered 22 miles in 95° heat. The highlight of the first day was a short side trip off the AT to the summit of Hawksbill Mountain (4050'), the highest point in Shenandoah National Park. It was worth the trip.

So was the air conditioned lunch at Skyland Lodge, where we indulged in salads, burgers, fries and blackberry ice cream pie! One thing about hiking, you can certainly rationalize eating as much as you want. It all gets burned off—at least when you have a young person's metabolism. One other nice thing about the stop was they kept the pitchers of ice water coming. We even filled our water bottles with the frosty liquid.

The highlight of the next day was also a summit. Mary's Rock, located right on the trail, is a boulder formation that has presided over a spectacular view for over one billion years. Billion year old rocks actually form the backbone of the Appalachian Mountain range all the way from southern Virginia to Katahdin. But there are few places the billion year old rocks are exposed. In most places, they are covered by sandstone or granite.

The second best highlight on the next day was—you guessed it—cheeseburgers. This time, an 11:00 a.m. treat at the Panorama Restaurant at the six mile mark for the day.

It may seem to some that we were on more of a "Tour de Cheeseburger" than an AT hike. But when you are on the trail, food becomes an obsession. Your body craves it because you need the fuel to keep you moving. And your mind is willing to oblige, creating fantasies of tables filled with every food imaginable—BBQ ribs, chocolate shakes, pad Thai, pizza, lobster rolls, chicken wings, ice cream and, of course, big, juicy cheeseburgers.

The Shenandoah section of trail put many of those obsessions within easy reach. The campground stores and restaurants that were built to serve the "Skyline Drivers" were never far from the AT. There wasn't another section of trail like this, where—for several days in a row—we could exit the trail, eat a decadent lunch and get right back on again. Once we discovered this, there was no way we weren't going to take advantage.

The Panorama Restaurant had another restorative amenity—air conditioning. After our plates of cheeseburgers, fries and blackberry ice cream pie disappeared, we stayed inside for an extra hour to digest our food and two newspaper's worth of world events.

An hour and a half diversion was all I could take. I needed to get back on the trail. Wayne was on the same wavelength and said he'd be right out.

When I pushed open door to walk outside, I was hit by a wall of 95°F heat and humidity. I grabbed my water bottles and went back inside to top them off.

As I climbed out of the gap, I was powered by something more powerful than food and water—my resolve. Yes, it was hot and humid, but I wasn't going to let it ruin my trip. I looked at the positives. It wasn't raining for one.

I've hiked through 17 days of rain (most of them with snow beneath my feet). Believe me, it sucked. My gear and clothes were always wet, the footing was treacherous and the summits I reached didn't even offer any views. This Shenandoah stretch was uncomfortable, but all it took for me to make it less so was thinking of that two-plus week slog through central and northern Oregon.

I never sweat more than on the 700' climb up Pass Mountain in Shenandoah National Park. When I reached the wooded summit, it was loaded with deer in search of shade and perhaps a cooling breeze. The shade was all they would find. The humidity, heat and still air enveloped even the mountaintops.

I had just left the summit when I met a south-bounder, cursing the heat and swatting black flies away with a bandana.

"You picked a hell of a time to hike through these parts." she said between gasps for air.

"Yeah." I said. "It's pretty buggy."

"Buggy? Where are you from, somewhere down south? It's hotter than hell out here!"

"Well yeah. That, too." I replied.

I asked her about upcoming water supplies and camping spots.

"Take the half mile side trip to Byrd's Nest #4. There's water and no one ever stays there because it's off the AT. You'll have the place to yourself. Further down the AT, Gravel Springs Hut has water, but it also has termites and a giant rat living in it." she said.

We wished each other luck and said our "so longs". As soon as she disappeared over the ridge, I stopped and turned to Wayne.

"A giant rat? Out here? It's probably a chipmunk or something that's taken on legendary status. I've never heard about rats living in the woods."

"I concur." said Wayne.

We had one more steep climb ahead to get to Byrds Nest #4 (one of four day use only shelters named for Senator Harry Byrd Sr., who donated four of these shelters to Shenandoah National Park). I turned off the AT onto the Neighbor Mountain Trail and blasted up the hill toward the shelter, fueled by a cheeseburger, blackberry ice cream pie and the vision of having a prime mountaintop campsite to ourselves. People almost always create campsites near shelters. I was sure there's be a great spot up there and maybe an evening breeze to cool us down.

"There's a reason people don't use the shelter." I thought as the terrain got steeper. "This ascent weeds out everyone except people as crazy as us."

I made a hard push to the top and could see the stone hut up ahead. I couldn't wait to call it a day. I entered the clearing to discover the south-bounder had given us bad advice. There were two twenty-something year-old guys sitting in the back of the shelter with gear strewn about them on the dirt floor. They had been here for a while.

"How long are you staying?" I asked.

"Until our food runs out." one guy said.

I considered saying something about the "day use only" designation for the shelter, but let it go. Instead I wished them good luck and started down the other side of the ridge toward a reunion with the AT again.

I'm not sure why I did this. There was no reason for Wayne and I not to camp near the shelter as we had planned. But something about finding the place occupied made me want to move on. I went about a quarter-mile down the trail and waited for Wayne in the heat and swarms of black flies.

When he arrived, he wasn't pleased. "Why didn't you stay up there?" he asked. "We could have found a flat spot in the shade and been near the water. Maybe we'd get some evening breezes."

"Something about those guys threw me off." I said. "Maybe it was the guy who looked like Axl Rose. He said something about hanging out until the food ran out. Between that

The view from Mary's Rock, May 30, 1991.
The Panorama Restaurant, visible in the cloverleaf below, was demolished in 2008.

and finding the place occupied in the first place, it made me want to scram. I'll go back up if you want."

We both looked back up the trail.

"Or we can go a little further." I offered. "Once we get through this rhododendron, there might be a flat spot."

Wayne gestured down the trail. "After you." he said.

I could tell he was still irritated, but surely the ridge would yield a flat spot before long.

I should have known better. The trail slabbed through rhododendrons for what seemed to be an eternity and they were so thick we couldn't pitch a tent among them even if there was a flat spot.

Finally, we topped a ridge and entered a great stand of oaks. There were views to east and west, a slight breeze and even a flat piece of ground. At last, I could stop eating crow.

The breeze wasn't enough to keep the bugs at bay, so we dove into the tent. We checked our food situation. Because we had been stopping for lunch every day, we had a cheese surplus. And because it was so hot outside, our cream cheese had already spoiled. We needed to eat up the block of cheddar before it did the same. We also had a tin of smoked oysters, so we made a snack plate for dinner. But eating the oysters brought its own problem.

I was still feeling guilty about not staying at Byrds Nest #4, so I volunteered to deal with it.

"I'm not too keen on having that oyster tin and the spoiled cream cheese in our midst with bears out here." I said. "I volunteer to take a trash run down to Skyline Drive. Based on what we've already seen, there's got to be an overlook with a trash can near here."

"If you want to do it, I'm not complaining." said Wayne. "I'll stay here and do some journaling."

I left the tent at 6:15 p.m. and dashed down to Skyline Drive. It was pretty wild to be hiking without a pack and I made fast time. Good thing, because the first 3 overlooks didn't have trash cans. I passed the Thornton River Trailhead. No trash can there either. The traffic on Skyline Drive was practically nil, so I walked in the center of the left lane. I began wondering if I'd make it back to the tent before dark.

"There's gotta be one at the next overlook." I thought. "I'll walk to one more." No trash can. Same as the one after that.

Two-and-a-half miles after I left the tent I arrived at Elkwallow Picnic Area complete with trash cans and a water fountain. I drank my fill and started race walking back toward the campsite. No time to lose.

The late time of day brought the deer out in force. They came out of the woods to browse the picnic area and the grassy shoulders on each side of Skyline Drive. It was a pleasure walking back to the tent with so much company. I stopped a few times to talk to them long enough to make them lift their heads, then tilt them to the side. They didn't

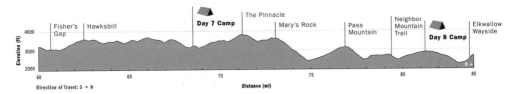

quite know what to make of it when I laid on a thick Maine dialect.

At 7:45, I arrived back at the tent.

"5 mile trash run." I said.

"I was about to send out the search party." said Wayne, meaning the search party of one.

"Glad you didn't. I bushwhacked up to the AT from Skyline. You probably would have walked right past me."

At 8:15 the next morning, someone walked right past us—another north-bounder. Actually, he was half running up the trail with no gear except a hip pack with a water bottle in it. He waved toward us, then he was gone.

"Must be training for a marathon or something." I said.

Later that morning, when we arrived at Elkwallow Picnic Area (this time via the AT), we saw a truck from Maine parked in the lot. I went over to find out if it was someone I knew. The woman introduced herself as the support team for a speed hiker. The guy that passed us earlier in the day was him. He was shooting for a 45 mile day today in what was forecast to be nearly 100°F heat. And I thought we were crazy!

We only had two days left to go. After today's 8.5 mile walk to Gravel Springs Hut (the alleged home of the rat), we'd have a 13 mile hike out to Front Royal, Virginia, where an old friend of mine would be picking us up.

We were in trail shape and our packs were nearly as light as they'd get. Even though we took our time, we still made the side trail to Gravel Springs Hut by 3:15 p.m. We were greeted by a rattlesnake basking in the trail.

"There's someone who likes the heat." I said as I took a ten foot detour to the left. "Watch your step."

"Maybe he ate the rat." said Wayne.

There was no one at the shelter. I looked at the sky. Over the last few hours, thunderheads had been building. We were hoping that a storm would move through to cool things down. If it did, it would be better to be in the shelter. Our tent would stay dry. We could move back out after the storm.

We broke out the last of the cheddar and crackers.

"Lots of food left." said Wayne. "We can eat up."

"I'm not carrying that instant cheesecake out of here." I said. "We finally have a stream to cool it in."

This was the last time I brought an instant cheesecake on the trail. They were a fun

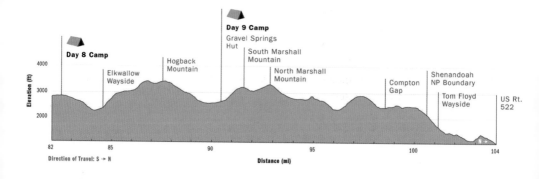

novelty to have, but weighed too much to carry up and over mountains for a week.

I lined the bottom of the large cooking pot with graham cracker crust, mixed the filling and poured it on top. I secured the pot lid with the spring action handles, so no varmints would get in, then set the pot in the nearby spring to cool. This was going to be good!

Around 7:30, I heard something down by the steam, where the cheesecake was. I thought it might be a bear until I heard the handles on the pot snap open, then shut. It was a human.

A minute later, he appeared in front of us.

"Which way are you headed?" he asked.

I took a look at his attire. A faded navy blue cotton t-shirt, red nylon shorts and a falling apart pair of nylon/leather hiking boots.

"North," I said. "What's your name?" I asked, expecting him to give us his trail name.

(Almost every AT through-hiker adopts a trail name, a pseudonym they use within the trail community. It's not uncommon for someone to put out their hand and introduce themselves as "Greybeard", "Sweet Magnolia", "Dances with Flies" or whatever moniker they've adopted for life out here.)

"My...name...is...Bill*." he said, with painfully long pauses between each word.

It was evidently important to Bill that we knew he was on his fourth through hike of the AT and that he'd also done the Pacific Crest Trail twice. He mentioned it several times. I harkened back to the "keeping contact with society" conversation and wondered if Bill had been disconnected from society for too long.

Bill pulled out his food stash—Ritz® Crackers, cream cheese, jelly and something that completely grossed me out—a half-empty one-quart jug of milk. I had to look away when he put it to his lips. There was no way it was still safe to drink after carrying it for days through 95°F heat.

I whispered "tent" to Wayne and we started making our move.

"We're going to move." I said. "There's supposedly a big rat in this shelter."

"Oh. Most hikers don't know the difference between a mouse and a rat." said Bill. "I've come across these stories in lots of shelters and never seen a thing."

"Nonetheless, we're going to play it safe." I said. I didn't think there was a rat in there either, but I didn't want to be in the same shelter with a 95°F milk chugger. I couldn't fathom a happy ending.

We set up the tent within sight of the shelter and tuned in a baseball game. Wayne quickly fell asleep. I stayed up and watched the greatest firefly show I'd ever seen from just inside the tent's front screen window. The fireflies were so thick they bounced off the tent like raindrops. It was stunning.

Bill was reading by flashlight in the shelter. He shut the light off at 10:10 p.m. At 10:20, all hell broke loose.

"A rat! A rat!" he cried. His screams and bouncing flashlight beam said it all. Looked like Bill was going to need his tent, too.

When we broke camp in the morning, Bill was eating a breakfast of cereal and "putrid milk a la trail" at the picnic table.

---

* Not his real name.

I stopped at the junction of the Gravel Springs Hut side trail and the AT and turned around to talk to Wayne.

"Yikes." I said. "I know it's none of my business, but I still can't get over the 95-degree milk thing."

"I'm guessing we won't see him again." said Wayne.

At the 9-plus mile mark, I came to a sign marking the northern border of Shenandoah National Park and waited for Wayne.

"Congratulations, man." I said. "We made it through the park. Only 3-plus miles to go."

"The Tom Floyd Wayside is just up the trail and we need to kill a half hour, so we can meet your friend right at 2:00. Let's stop at the shelter for a few minutes." said Wayne. "I'd rather wait there than next to a busy road."

"I'd rather wait there, too." I said. "One last chance to wind down before we need to start making our way home."

We took the spur trail down to the shelter. It had a feature most shelters didn't—a deck in the front. We sat under a suddenly angry sky and drank a quart of powdered lemonade mix to celebrate our trip. With thunder rumbling and dark clouds gathering, we knew we'd get soaked in our last three miles.

We were packing up to leave when we heard someone coming down the trail. It was Bill.

"Which way are you guys headed?" he asked.

"Still going north, Bill. Just stopped for water." I said.

He didn't say anything.

"We were at Gravel Springs Hut last night." I said. "Same as you."

He looked perplexed, but still said nothing. Instead he started heading steeply down the blue-blazed side trail to the spring, presumably to get water. We never saw him again.

On the rainy hike out, I gave thought to the many people we met on this trip. Some were on the Appalachian Trail for the long haul like us—section hikers, repeat hikers, six month hikers and speed hikers. Some were on the trail for a morning or a day, perhaps to sit on a mountaintop and look out at the farms below. Others still didn't know this 2,100 mile national treasure existed until a couple of guys with huge packs on walked into their midst.

Normally when I was on the trail for more than a few days, my mind would wander ahead of me, urging me to stay out here as long as I could. But something shifted on this hike. I was content to finish this section and to look forward to the many more long hikes we'd have to string together to complete the AT.

Who knew if we ever would—at this pace, it would take decades. But we were both fine with that. All we needed to do was to stay healthy and keep making progress. If Wayne was up for doing more, I'd be right along for the trip.

"So, where do you want to go next year?" he asked.

"How bout doing another section in Virginia?"

"Fine with me, as long as it's in the fall." he said.

"Three words." I said. "The adventure continues."

Epilogue

I visited Shenandoah National Park in 2014. It was the first time I'd been back since our 1991 hike. Many things are the same—notably the overlooks, the trails and the natural features of the park such as the mountains.

But there have also been significant changes. The Howard Johnson's restaurant at Rockfish Gap is long gone. Surprisingly, so is the Panorama Restaurant, where we indulged in cheeseburgers and blackberry ice cream pie. Over the years there weren't enough people stopping there to make it a viable restaurant. There was some talk of turning it into a museum to honor the Civilian Conservation Corps, but that vision never took hold. The building was leveled in 2008. Unless you were one of the several thousand visitors, you would never know it was there.

Another vanishing feature: the water fountains at overlooks. I don't know what we would have done on our heat-filled traverse of the park without them. But now they have been removed and paved over without a trace. Hikers now need to rely on natural sources, campgrounds and stores, which isn't bad as long as you aren't walking through a heat wave as well as a National Park.

CHAPTER 6

A Granite State of Mind

The mountains and valleys of New Hampshire are a feast fit for any insatiable hiker's appetite.

SECTION 1

The Presidential Traverse

TRIP STATS
June 21, 1988
24 miles
South to North

Set foot on any stretch of trail in New Hampshire and you'll soon understand why it's known as, "The Granite State."

Rock formations are ubiquitous and responsible for the state's unforgettable vistas. It is a hiker's paradise, treating you with long stretches along mountain streams and my favorite—above tree line—where you can scamper above the valley fog and delight in views that span hundreds of miles.

Yet, the same scenery that draws thousands of yearly visitors can be treacherous to the unprepared. New Hampshire's most popular destination, the Presidential Range, has clocked incredible wind speeds, due to its 6289' elevation and its sheer exposure. On one April day in 1934, the wind speed on the summit of Mount Washington was clocked at an astounding 231 mph — still the highest ground speed recorded on earth.

The weather can change rapidly in the expanses above the trees and with few places to take shelter, hikers can quickly get in over their heads.

The Appalachian Trail leads over the spines of three impressive ranges — the Franconia Range, the Presidential Range and the Carter-Moriah Range — before crossing the Androscoggin River and entering Maine.

Starting in the early 1990s, we hiked the three ranges in separate trips, then filled in the rest of the miles in between.

The Presidential Range

Because the Mountains of New Hampshire are so close, I have spent hundreds of days exploring their trails and peaks. The Presidential Range and the northern portion of the White Mountain National Forest, in particular, were always magnets for me. I would pore over maps and guidebooks, planning loop hikes that would take me to new destinations and help me get as much time in the backcountry before I needed to be back at my desk on Monday mornings.

In the mid 1980s, I heard the phrase "Presidential Traverse". The idea was to hike the entire Presidential Range in a day. In going through the guide book descriptions and maps, I figured it may be a hike even too crazy for me to attempt. It would be a 24 mile day, most of it above tree line and chock full of climbs and descents. The only way to pull it off would be to start out with headlamps before dawn on the solstice (the day with the most daylight of the year) and have a campsite within a few hundred yards of where the hike would end, so we could just eat and sleep when we got there. The weather would have to be perfect and we'd have to keep a close eye on our pace.

It was so much fun, I did it 5 times. Wayne was with me for two of them, including the first.

We put considerable planning into the one-day, 24-mile traverse. It was likely that we'd need every bit of daylight to cover that kind of mileage over what was essentially a massive pile of rocks. Scrambling up and over boulders all day is both exhilarating and exhausting. We would focus on traveling light and making time.

Traveling light at elevation is relative. You still need to carry a wind shell, a fleece pullover, a winter hat, a first aid kit and a few other things you hope you won't need. The weather above 5,000' on exposed summits can change in minutes, even in the summer months.

To maximize our hiking time, we plotted a route that would end in a campground and grabbed a spot as close to the trail as possible — only a few hundred yards. When we got off the trail we expected to be exhausted. We didn't want to have to drive anywhere.

We wanted to keep the cooking easy, too. I bought a few big steaks in anticipation of a celebration and had them marinating in a cooler in the trunk of my car. All we'd have to do is toss them on my gas grill.

We went to bed early and set the alarm for 3:30 a.m.

We were up and out of the campground by 4:00 a.m. (I'm sure that made us popular with the other campers.) We drove west to the Webster-Jackson trailhead and started up the trail by 5:00. The Webster-Jackson Path intersected with the AT and cut a few miles off the trip. We thought that adding even more miles to the day would really be pushing it.

The feeling of being above tree line for me is indescribable. Spending a full day up there brings me immense joy. The Presidential peaks create an inspiring set of milestones before you: Jackson, Pierce, Eisenhower, Franklin, Monroe, Washington,

The Presidential Range as seen from the summit of Mount Hight. Even on this late May day, the peaks were still holding onto the previous winter's snowfall — just one indication of the weather on this very exposed northern range.

Jefferson, Madison, Adams and Quincy Adams. It was a sensational blue sky day. The cumulus clouds would occasionally paint large parts of the mountainsides in shadow, then disappear as quickly as they arrived.

As with any trip across mountain tops, we needed to keep tabs on our physical conditions and our timing. Our first obligation was to get down safely. That meant if we fell too far behind schedule, we'd opt for another trail down.

All day long, our only stops were for snacks and water. The summit of Mount Washington (the highest peak in New England) was just short of the halfway point. When we got there, it was jammed with tourists that had driven up there on the auto road. As soon as we walked into the summit lodge to use the bathroom and get some water, we wanted to leave. It felt like we were in a shopping mall at Christmas time. I couldn't wait to put some mileage between me and the frenzy.

By late afternoon, the granite was taking a toll on our shins and knees. We had one more peak to go before making our steep plunge down the mountainside and through the woods to reach our camp spot. I was so looking forward to getting off the granite and finding some relief on woodland trail.

When we arrived at our campsite at Dolly Copp Campground, it was nearly pitch dark. We were so famished that we were barely able to stay awake for the grilling of the steak.

The next morning, we slept in late, then drove straight to Gorham, New Hampshire and Wilfred's Restaurant, which featured an all you can eat breakfast

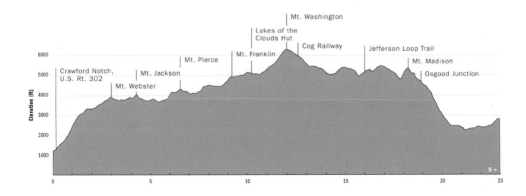

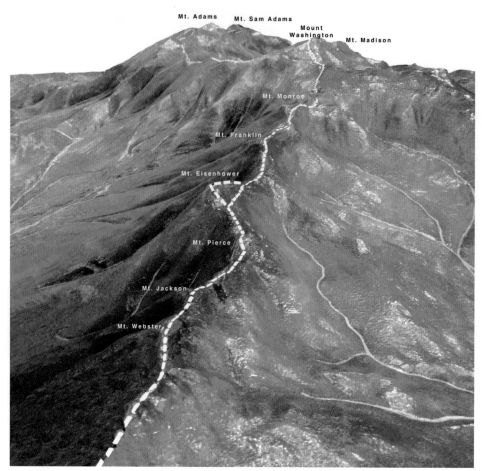

Presidential Traverse Profile

buffet. We sat at a table for two hours reading the newspaper and making periodic trips for refills. These days, the restaurant is long gone. I sometimes wonder if our post Presidential Traverse pig outs were partially responsible for their demise.

Every year I did the Presidential Traverse, my legs would rebel for days. The worst was always day two, when I would make the long walk from the parking lot to my desk and try to stay seated as much as possible. By day four, my legs would be back and I would be planning the next great adventure.

Funny thing, but the one little piece of AT we bypassed at the southern end of the Presidential Range ended up being one of the last sections of the AT that Wayne completed on our 28-year hike. I had climbed it several years earlier, but Wayne had never gotten around to it. So on December 10, 2011, we scampered up there. The valley below was punctuated by the arc of the Maine Central Railroad tracks above and Route 302 traveling through the base of Crawford Notch below.

SECTION 2

Franconia Ridge

TRIP STATS
September 3 - September 6, 1993
24 miles
South to North

The Franconia Ridge is second only to the Presidentials in hiking popularity.

Whereas the Presidentials run generally west to east, the Liberty-Lafayette Range (as it is more commonly known) runs north to south, looming above Franconia Notch. As impressive as it is from ground level, (Rt 16 runs its length on its way to Canada), it is simply spectacular from the open summits above.

Much like the Presidentials, there are long sections of exposed ridge line, where there is no escape from poor weather conditions. You need to choose your traversing days carefully. There is one AMC hut nestled in the north end of the range between Galehead Mountain and Mt Guyot. Other than that, if you need to seek refuge, you need to duck below tree line and pitch a tent.

As far as access points go, there are three ways to approach the ridge: from the aforementioned Rt 16 (there are a number of trailheads including the Franconia Notch Visitors Center) or by two other means that were also established by the need for modern transportation, except these roads were carrying a different kind of car.

In the late 1800s, timber harvesters eyed the virgin forests of central New Hampshire as their next great conquest. Neighboring Maine had only recently lost its title as the largest timber exporter (Bangor was a logging epicenter), and Vermont briefly took over as the leader until that state was 90% deforested. New Hampshire was ready to take its turn.

Franconia Ridge from the summit of Flume Mountain. The AT goes over the summits of (from l to r) Haystack Mountain, Liberty Mountain, Lafayette Mountain and Mount Garfield.

The Zealand Railroad traveled through Zealand Notch along the slopes of Whitewall Mountain. It can be seen here at the base of the cliff in the center of the photo. A view from this trail section is shown on the next page.

One of the most successful logging operations in the state was owned and operated by a man named J. E. Henry. His company bought thousands of acres of woodland in central New Hampshire, then he set about building the means to harvest the trees. Henry built two rail lines of major significance. Built first, the Zealand track ran south from what is now Rt. 302, past Whitewall Mountain. By the mid-1880s, the town of Zealand had sprung up to support the operation, including a post office, a store and homes for J.E. Henry and his company's workers. Yet by 1892, most of the area had been logged and Henry moved the bulk of his operation to Lincoln, where he had built another rail line that ran north into the area next to the East Branch of the Pemigewasset River.

At first, Henry leased the Zealand operation (which was still yielding enough timber to make it viable), but by 1900, operations ceased. The rails were torn up and, with no need for workers and social infrastructure to support them and their families, the town of Zealand subsequently disappeared. The most obvious remnants are a few cellar holes located next to modern day Route 302. Some logging continued in the Zealand area until the land was acquired by the U.S. Forest Service (in part in 1915, then in full in 1932).

While the rails in Zealand Notch and Lincoln Woods are long gone, the wide, gentle trails that remain in their stead provide exceptional access to the mountains deep within the National Forest's boundaries.

For this trip, we'd be heading in on the old Zealand railroad bed. We carved out a nice 27-mile section between Route 302 and Route 3 (Franconia Notch) that would take us over the Liberty-Lafayette Ridge, plus allow a few short side trips to Mount Hale and

The view from the AT along the base of Whitewall Mountain. Here the old Zealand Railroad line has been least disturbed by more than 100 years plus of history. In other places, rock slides and vegetation have made much greater impacts.

Mount Garfield. We figured we'd bag two additional summits listed on New England's 100 Highest Peaks while we were in the area.

The railroad bed was such a great warm up compared to what we had encountered in other sections of trail (say Pennsylvania, or parts of Vermont). We were hiking in the mist and made really good time all the way to the ascent of Mount Hale. On the way up in the mid-afternoon, we encountered a number of day hikers on their way down mumbling about no views. By the time we made the summit, the clouds were lifting off. As they were hiking down through the undercast below on the way to their cars, we were enjoying far flung views of mountaintops piercing the clouds. By sunset, the clouds completely vacated the valleys, whooshed out on the last of the afternoon breezes.

The next morning, we were underway by 9:00, working our way across the ridge (and I mean working). The side trip up Galehead was a beast. But again, we were rewarded. We grabbed the only spot on the summit, not far from inspiring views down to Galehead Hut in the valley. We walked by headlamp down to the viewpoint and listened to the voices of the overnight campers rise from the hut's porch with the mountain stream in the valley serving as background music.

Day three was the real test. We were gassed by the time we summited Mount Lafayette (halfway across the ridge), but we were committed to making it all the way across. We briefly toyed with the idea of going beyond the AT to summit both Haystack and Mount Flume, but we settled for stashing the packs and bagging Haystack alone. Mount Flume would have to wait for another day.

As it was, we arrived at my truck at the nearly dark hour of 7:30 p.m. Our reward was

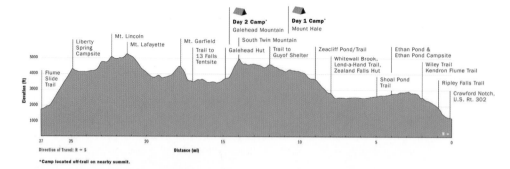

steakhouse burgers and giant salads. We drove back to Wayne's car and found a nice campsite near the parking lot. There was no way we were driving back to our respective states after our traverse. Instead, we awoke at dawn, found a breakfast joint, then drove back home as respective exercises in winding down.

I was at my desk writing by 10:00, with another great escape in the rearview mirror and a newfound energy in my writing. It worked every time.

SECTION 3

Moosilauke

TRIP STATS
September 4-7, 1993
25.8 miles
South to North

I woke up at 6:00 a.m. and immediately wanted to look outside. Our camp near the summit of Mount Moosilauke treated us to spectacular sunset views of the Green Mountains before we crawled into the tent last night. I was looking forward to more of the same.

Instead, I unzipped the front door to be greeted by impenetrable fog. I couldn't see more than five feet. The euphoria of seeing for miles was gone. I was enveloped by a strangely comforting blanket of silence and calm. I walked a few feet from the tent and sat on a nearby rock. There was no wind and scarcely a sound, except Wayne's low grade snoring from inside the nylon dome.

I left Wayne in the tent to get above tree line. It was an early September treat to be here at 4800' among the golden grasses of the open summit with nearly no wind and mild temperatures that let me simply sit out in shirtsleeves and let the day unfold.

As the sun got higher and began slowly burning off the fog, I sat perfectly still and content thinking about the climb up here yesterday and the view that awaited. It is a blessing to sit at elevation and watch the sun set behind distant mountains. Thoreau spoke of the mountaintops with both reverence and fear. It has always felt to me that his sense of giddiness from walking among the clouds was always tempered with the perspective of only having a day pass — that he needed to scamper back down to the safety of the forest.

Some might argue that these days, a little more of that reverence would be a good thing. That the modern conveniences of being able to drive closer to the mountains and being able to wear technical clothing has tempered our respect for nature and put more people in danger.

As I wrote this chapter, we were only a few weeks removed from a winter tragedy on Mount Washington. A 32-year-old woman attempted to climb up and over three of the presidential peaks in February 2015. She was traveling light and traveling alone. Her plan was to ascend from the west side, climb the three peaks, then descend the east side of the range to meet her husband in Pinkham Notch. When she left the trailhead to begin her ascent, the weather was reportedly near zero degrees Fahrenheit with 40 mile per hour winds. By the time she got above tree line and started her traverse over the wide open summits, a winter storm had arrived. The temperature plunged to an estimated -30° F and 104 mph winds buffeted the range. There was no place to take shelter. One can only imagine what it was like to be trying to stay alive up there. At roughly 3:00 in the afternoon, she turned her rescue beacon on.

A rescue crew based in the valley determined that the conditions were so poor, that they couldn't look for her without risking their lives. The next morning, the rescuers found her body above tree line. It is presumed that she made the summit of Mount Adams and turned back in an effort to get back down.

One experienced mountaineer that was interviewed in the wake of the tragedy summed up the situation by saying that you have two choices in the mountains: travel light and fast or travel heavy and slow. The difference is, if you travel light and fast and make a mistake, it's a lot harder to recover from it and sometimes even deadly.

The woman's death hit me hard. It's tempting to imagine what was going through her mind when she made the decision to turn back or even to attempt the climb at all. But those decisions were hers to make. I consider myself one of the lucky ones who made a few poor decisions in my early climbing and hiking career and successfully navigated out of them. You don't have to be put in harm's way to be a smarter adventurer. But some of those early warnings about my own limitations and "getting real" about what was happening around me, such as deteriorating weather conditions, shined a bright spotlight on all of my decision making ever after.

One thing I absolutely believe is this: you are entirely responsible for your actions in the wilderness. That means constantly assessing everything: your health, your gear, the trail conditions, "plan B" routes in case you need to change plans, your food and water situation, your itinerary (are you still on pace to make your destination without putting yourself at risk?), the current weather and forecast and yes, even what to do if you encounter someone on the trail that needs help.

It's a lot of responsibility. But I believe it's the bare minimum for being on the trail in the first place.

As it stood now, my current responsibility was simply to enjoy watching the day unfold. The tent was drenched from the mist and it would be a while before the sun worked its magic on the nylon. Besides, Wayne was still asleep.

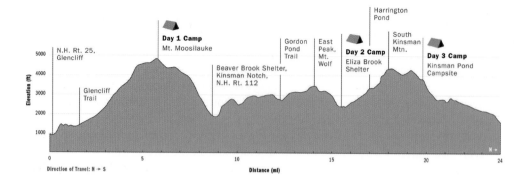

I sat with my knees pulled up against my body and continued to watch the fog lift from the mountaintop. Soon, the peaks around us would poke up through, Stegosaurus like, then the fog would lift from the valleys.

I was content to enjoy the hour. It was rare that we weren't already dining and preparing for the hiking day by now. But, this trip we gave ourselves a generous four days to do the range.

I hadn't had many days off from work since late spring, but I wasn't complaining. I had taken a 24 day vacation in late May and early June with my friend, Ed, to do a trip I planned while on a bus traveling across the California desert in 1983. I hadn't even set foot on the Pacific Crest Trail yet when I started thinking about how fun it would be to traverse the state of Maine. The Appalachian Trail would cover part of it, but the idea of bushwhacking and/or walking woods roads or paved roads for the rest of the way didn't have much appeal.

Then it hit me. What if we combined biking, hiking and paddling to do it?

Thus, we mapped out a route that involved biking from Portsmouth, New Hampshire (just south of the Maine border) to Kingfield, Maine (where Ed's Uncle had a cabin and the AT passed less than a mile away), hiking on the AT to Telos Dam at the head of the Allagash River, then paddling a canoe north on the Allagash and St. John Rivers to reach Madawaska, Maine on the Canadian border.

Now, months later, I was finally back in my beloved woods and mountains, if not quite yet basking in the sun, soaking in the solitude. I knew from experience that being out here on Labor Day weekend meant that peaceful interludes were apt to be interrupted often. Continuously was more like it.

Going up and over the mountains of the Kinsman range for the next two days, we kept running into clusters of 8-10 hikers coming down the trail. This required us to step aside and let them pass. After the fifth group, it started getting a bit old. When you have uphill momentum going with a full pack on, you hate to stop for anything. But judging from the ages of the groups, they didn't have enough experience to know that the downhill hiker should stop to let the uphill hiker(s) pass.

"At least", I thought, "they know enough to travel in groups of 10 or less." (This guideline holds that smaller groups are less harmful to the wilderness experience of others and even potentially, the trail itself, as huge groups tend to fan out and cause erosion.)

Even so, the number one feature of this section of trail was mud. In places the "trail" was a ten foot wide sea of muck that was spreading by the day. I felt like sending smoke signals for Lester Kenway to get his crew over here pronto!

The groups kept right on coming. During our lunch stop at Beaver Brook Shelter, "Mike the Hike" from Britain (left Katahdin on April 3) and "Billy and Sally" from East Hartford (left Katahdin March 21) stopped for 10 minutes to chat. They told us that many more waves of college groups would be heading toward us and we'd feel like the proverbial salmon swimming against the current. They also gave us a lot of credit for our approach of doing the trail in sections, which they felt was a lot harder than doing all 2,100 miles at once.

"Man, I can't imagine having to get your legs in trail shape each time", said Billy. "Not to mention having to stick with it year after year. More power to you." (If only he knew that we'd be at it for another twenty years!)

That night at the Kinsman Pond Campsite, I harkened back to that brief conversation at the shelter about section hiking and wrote in my journal:

"Yes, it does take a while to warm up after you've been desk bound. But it's also exciting to do the trail this way. There are lots of possibilities for trips and the dream factory gets fired up with all of them. I find myself wondering if the rocks on the PA trail are as relentless as they are made out to be or what it's like to hike in Georgia. It's fun to work out the logistics and plan the next phase."

As it turned out, the next phase would take us out of New England, but Pennsylvania and Georgia would have to wait a bit. The Blue Ridge Mountains were beckoning again.

CHAPTER 7

Back to Virginny

With four states completed close to home, it was time to turn our attention southward for an autumn trek.

Rockfish Gap, VA to Daleville, VA

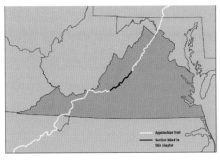

TRIP STATS
September 9 - September 21, 1993
133.8 miles
North to South

Just five weeks after our scamper over the Lincoln/Lafayette Range in New Hampshire, Wayne and I were on an Amtrak train bound for Virginia. It was time to get back onto the path through the Blue Ridge Mountains, this time for thirteen days.

Once again, I had to earn the time off by front loading my department with a whole catalog's worth of product descriptions - hundreds of them. I put in 58 hours of solid writing in the five days leading up to the trip. When I walked out to the parking lot at 6:50 on Friday night, my truck was the only vehicle in the lot other than the security guard's. I drove straight to Wayne's house in Connecticut, then hauled all my gear and food into the living room to begin the packing ritual — a two hour repackaging of food and reconsideration of what stayed behind and what would be traveling with us. This time, I had purchased something new — an insulated nylon cooler designed to be used with a lunch bag. It was just the right size to hold 3 pounds of cheese, a couple of sticks of pepperoni and assorted luncheon meats. I'd carry it separately on the train, so we could easily access our food and avoid paying snack car prices for sandwiches on the

way down the east coast.

By the time everything was packed and ready for our two week adventure, it was 2:30 a.m. A good night's sleep would have been nice, but it wasn't to be. I had to be up at 5:30 to write the intro to a catalog, then we would head into Hartford, so I could fax it into the office before I left. (These were the days before practically anyone carried cell phones, let alone envisioned the day when we could send work anywhere in the world from them.)

We caught the 12:50 p.m. train from Hartford and arrived at Charlottesville, VA at 9:30 p.m. I wish I could have slept on the way down, but I was too full of trail-drenaline to even try. We ate a couple of huge burgers at the Blue Ridge Brewery while we pondered our next move. We found out that there was a payphone nearby, so we paid our bill, hoisted our ginormous packs to the amazement of the mostly collegiate crowd, then went outside.

I set the insulated cooler on top of the payphone, so my hands would be free to make the few calls we needed to firm up our plans. The Charlottesville hotels were booked. We called a cab company and they offered to take us to Rockfish Gap (where the trail and a Holiday Inn both waited) for $50. Sold!

We arrived at Rockfish Gap to realize double disappointment. There were no rooms available and I had left the insulated bag full of perishables on top of the phone in Charlottesville. Perhaps if I hadn't been so sleep deprived, I would have remembered it.

We walked down Skyline Drive in the early morning darkness to look for camp spot. We didn't want to go far. There was a convenience store next to the Holiday Inn that would open in the morning. I was hoping they'd at least have ham and cheese to replace our protein stash and we didn't want to have to backtrack any further than we needed.

The first vehicle turnout did the trick. We half slid down the embankment below until we were below the beer bottles and cans that had been thrown out of vehicles and safely out of sight. It wasn't flat, but it was good enough. We rolled out our ground pads and sleeping bags and slept under the stars.

Now that all the considerable progress to get here was complete, I should have been able to nod right off. But I had to do one more round of beating myself up for leaving the cheese bag behind, then spend a few minutes wondering whether if some drunk guy hurled a beer bottle from the turnout, it would hit me in the head and maim me for life. Every time someone pulled into the turnout (which was steadily), I woke up and listened until they drove off. At last, as a beautiful red sunrise appeared through the trees and over the farms below, it was time to hit the trail.

By 7:30, we were on our way to convenience store, then trail heaven — weighed down by 13 days' worth of food including Oscar Meyer luncheon meats and many packets of cheese. We made a quick stop by the Blue Ridge Parkway sign, where we asked a friendly tourist to take our sun-splashed photo. The 1993 southern swing on the AT was finally underway (or more appropriately "under weigh").

Of all our AT adventures, this would be the longest. To carry 13 days of food without stopping for a resupply is fairly unusual. Most AT hikers stop more frequently to take side trips from the trail. Those side trips are time consuming, which is less of a factor on a through-hike. But as section hikers, we wanted to minimize our side trips and maximize our forward progress. If we could average 12 miles a day, we could complete the section while enjoying as much time on the trail as possible.

Yet carrying 13 days of food up and over mountains is asking a lot of even a body that's in shape. Thankfully, freeze dried foods had come a long way in the past 15 years. Back when I first tried them — on a bike trip through Nova Scotia in 1975 — they were utterly horrific. (To this day, the words "Chicken Tettrazini" are capable of evoking my gag reflex.) But by the 1990s, the two best known makers of freeze dried foods for backpackers were actually turning out some pretty palatable fare. Our favorites were freeze dried scrambled eggs (great for breakfast burritos), chicken stew and a spicy black bean and corn dinner. Choosing these meals to cover 40% of our dinner and breakfast needs saved us considerable weight (and space) over carrying pasta, rice and other fare. But they were also expensive. I was really glad I had a hefty employee discount at an outdoor store!

Even though we had brought the freeze dried food, my pack in particular was ridiculously heavy. Every square inch was stuffed with gear, clothes and food, and I had extra stuff hanging off the back. When some of the food was eaten, there'd be room inside again. But for now, it had the appearance of what my friend Mick once called, "The Beverly Hillbillies' truck", with pots, pans and other junk dangling off the side.

The trail through this part of Virginia often comes close to and sometimes crosses the Blue Ridge Parkway (although nowhere near as frequently as it does through the Shenandoah National Park section to the north). Rockfish Gap, where we now stood, marked the spot where Skyline Drive ended and the Blue Ridge Parkway began.

The Blue Ridge Parkway began in 1935 as a way to connect Shenandoah National Park and Great Smoky Mountains National Park. It runs 469 miles. The last section was completed in 1987 — 52 years after it was started. It is the most visited National Park in the system.

The work it took to build what was originally called "The Appalachian Scenic Highway" is certainly evident when you drive it, but you really get a sense for the skill of the road builders when you walk alongside it.

Nine years into our trip, we started seeing a significant number of section hikers for the first time. This made sense, given the time of year (cool days with many fewer bugs) and the proximity of the trail to the Blue Ridge Parkway, (which offered a number of places to easily get on or off the trail).

There were a few more firsts as well. This trip marked the latest I went for a swim on the trail. On October 12, we crossed the Tye River on a beautiful, relatively new suspension bridge. The river looked irresistible to me. I wanted to wash some of the trail grime off me. I made my way down to the bank, stripped down and plunged my naked body in.

"Holy crap!", I exclaimed. Refreshing to be sure, bur freezing was more accurate. It was WAY too cold to stay in more than a few seconds. This was tremendously fortunate, because just after I pulled my shorts and shirt back on and scrambled back up the bank, four adults and four kids started walking across the bridge from the other side.

This trip was also the first time since Killington back in Vermont, that the trail topped 4,000', when it topped a mountain called The Priest.

The climb up was superb. Just after our walk across the Tye River Bridge, we crossed a road (where the the group of eight had come from). A big old tan Wagoneer with white boot soles strategically painted on it from hood to tailgate pulled up. It was "Rusty" of Rusty's Good Time Hollow, a legendary stopover for through hikers. The Good Time Hollow had no electricity and no shower, but Rusty provided enough southern hospitality to more than make up for that.

The author after his late season dip in the Tye River

He was dropping off a fellow southbounder, who introduced himself with the trail name "Ten Years After".

"You should come back to the Hollow", said Rusty, always the entrepreneur.

"Not today, I'm afraid. We need to keep making miles.", I said.

Ten Years After turned to me and said, "I'm glad I stopped. In fact, wish I could have paid him more."

I held firm. "Next time, for sure.", I said. I wondered exactly what the Good Time Hollow held in store, but not willing to lose two days of hiking to find out.

Rusty drove off, TYA fussed with his gear a bit, and we ducked back onto the trail to start the four mile climb of The Priest.

The trail was awesome. If I could have met the designer, I would have shaken his or her hand. For the first two miles, the path made long, gentle traverses of ridges, with short forays into little valleys to cross streams. At the three mile mark, we emerged on a rocky outcrop. I had come all the way from the road nonstop. I wanted to go all the way to the top, but I wasn't quite in condition for it yet.

Ten Years After passed us here, saying, "See you at the top." We never saw him again.

On the final mile, my legs went lactic. Wayne took the lead, as I dropped back into my lowest gear, the one accompanied by a voice saying, "one…two, one…two" over and over until I popped out into the open and I could grab the shot of adrenaline that would power me to the summit.

We made the top at 2:40. It was everything the guide promised and more. Fantastic views all round. The sun disappeared behind clouds and the arctic air blew over us. I started shivering. We got the hint. It was time to go.

That night, I took a thorough assessment of how things were going.

Mileage: Thirty-five miles in four days. Not bad. I was sure we'd pick it up as the packs got lighter.

Food: Plenty. We actually could start eating more to accelerate the lightening of the packs.

Water: Pretty spotty. Some springs were dry. Tonight was great, because we were camped near a flowing creek. We could rehydrate after today's big climb and descent.

Health: My legs felt really good (the lactic last mile of the ascent of The Priest notwithstanding). It was my back that was acting up. I couldn't sit in one position for long. I took some aspirin, but it didn't make a dent. I hoped that a few days (and six meals) from now, my back would also be thanking my lighter pack.

I rebounded nicely on the next day, a 14-miler through rhododendron, hickory and maple forest, punctuated with beautiful overlooks from the ridges. Of particular note was Wolf Rocks overlook, land of bright red sumacs, granite boulders and gorgeous views.

At 4:30, we ascended into an open meadow that marked the beginning of a series of "balds". The Forest Service burned the summits here regularly to maintain the panoramic views that have been this way for hundreds of years, if not longer.

Right on cue, the sun came out to greet us. We stopped near the top of Tar Jacket Ridge to bask in the heat and the panoramic scene. We could trace our last three days of walking, across the tops of the ranges, which included the pyramidal summit of The Priest, now 17 miles behind us, and Three Ridges, well beyond.

After the balds, we entered the woods for a few days. I was finally in trail shape, and could now go several hours without stopping. It is a spiritual experience to walk through the woods when it's so quiet you can hear autumn's falling leaves hitting the ground. "God, it's fun to be out here.", I heard myself say more than once.

On one afternoon, I stopped at Punchbowl Shelter to rest, drink water and wait for Wayne, who wasn't far behind me. Even in the light of day, shelters are dark inside. Their design, with a hefty overhang across the front makes that a foregone conclusion. It's hard for the sun to get in. In recent years, some of the builders have put opaque panels in the roof of their shelters, to lend the effect of a skylight. This makes a huge difference. But here at Punchbowl, that wasn't the case.

As I waited for Wayne, I reached into one of the dark corners to see if that's where the shelter's register was kept. I pulled out a small black stuff sack instead. Inside was somebody's camp stove.

Sunset over Buena Vista, VA

"Shit.", I said out loud. "Somebody is really bumming."

After Wayne set his pack down, I handed him the stuff sack and said, "Check this out. Someone left it here. Probably last night."

"They'll be pissed when they get to camp tonight.", he said.

"I'm going to take it with me.", I replied. "Who knows, we might catch up with them."

We had walked nine miles with a bagel as fuel, so we fired up our stove and made freeze dried chicken stew to power us up the next ridge.

While the water heated, one of the section hikers we had met earlier in the trip appeared in the clearing. We waved him in to sit down with us.

"When you get to Pennsylvania, give yourselves extra time.", he advised. "The rocks are a real drag."

"So we've heard.", I replied.

That night, we enjoyed the view from the best site of the whole trip, on top of Bluff Mountain. Watching the sun go down over the ridges while the lights went on in the town of Buena Vista was spectacular. It was hard to believe that a place this serene was also a place of tragedy.

In November of 1890, a little boy named Ottie Cline Powell, who was just shy of five years old, wandered away from his schoolhouse in Amherst County, Virginia. He had been gathering firewood with his classmates to heat the schoolhouse when he vanished.

His body was found the following spring, seven miles away, only yards from where we were camped on the summit of Bluff Mountain. When we arrived in the afternoon, I happened upon the bronze plaque in the clearing that was placed in honor of the little boy.

That night, as the temperatures dropped outside, I sat in the warmth of my sleeping bag thinking about the fate of Ottie Powell. A wave of profound sadness came over me. Empathy for parents, siblings and a community I would never know except from afar. But mostly, I felt sad for Ottie himself. I only hoped that slipping into a hypothermic state allowed his spirit to painlessly and peacefully lift off from the mountaintop.

In the morning, the clouds draped over the summit. Before we left, I walked over to the plaque to say good bye to Ottie.

The next two days were cloudy and rainy. We didn't stop much because of it and ripped off big chunks of mileage as a result. The two highlights were crossing the James River and finding the name and address of the owner of the MSR stove in the Thunder Hill Shelter trail register. The guy (trail name "Special K"), lived in New Orleans and was beside himself that he lost his ability to cook.

"I'll mail it to him when I get home.", I said to Wayne, as I wrote down Special K's address.

Theoretically, the last few days out should have been fantastic. The weather was perfect. The storm system had cleared out and the temperate, sunny autumn weather moved back in. We were also in trail shape. I hadn't felt this strong in years. Then a storm system moved into my body in the form of a virus.

By the next to the last day, my body felt like it had gone 10 rounds in a title fight. The sweat was pouring off me on every climb and I was down to the "one...two" pace again. My legs were wobbly and I was nauseated. I had to keep stopping on climbs.

"Damn it. I was feeling awesome two days ago.", I said to myself.

Wayne passed me on one of the climbs.

"Only three miles to go.", he said. "Then we can call it a day."

We were aiming for Fullhardt Shelter. If we got there, tomorrow would be a 5 1/2 mile walk downhill into Daleville.

I stopped again and looked at the ground. The sweat was dripping off my forehead onto the ground. My bandana couldn't keep up with the flow. A shadow moved through the forest and across the trail. I imagined it was the hawk's way of urging me on.

The all-you-can-eat breakfast we planned for tomorrow when we hit town was hardly a motivator at this point. The thought of eating anything was repulsive.

"Just...have...to...keep...going", I said out loud as I kicked my way through the oak leaves that littered the path to the top.

When I arrived at the shelter, there were four people there including Wayne. One guy took a look at me and said, "Holy shit. Are you sweating enough?"

"Yeah. I guess so." was all I could manage for a response.

An hour later, I sat in the tent looking at the water bottle in my hands. I had already downed a quart and a half and I was still thirsty. I was also still nauseated. The idea of another freeze dried dinner wasn't enticing. I munched on crackers and cheese instead.

It was time to get my mind off the turmoil in my stomach. I knew the right prescription. I pulled out my journal and started writing.

Epilogue

When I got home, I mailed the MSR stove to "Special K" in New Orleans. A few days later, I received a package. When I opened it, there was a cake and a note inside. The cake was a "King Cake", a New Orleans tradition. The cake had a plastic baby baked inside. If you got the piece with the baby in it, you were supposed to be the recipient of good luck.

By now, my stomach was well back to normal. (It actually felt well enough on the final day of the trip to take on the all-you-can-eat buffet). I took no chances on getting my share of good luck. Over the next two days, I ate the whole King Cake myself.

CHAPTER 8

Land of Rocks and Hawks

The ridges of Pennsylvania hold a special place for all who venture there

East Stroudsburg, PA to Port Clinton, PA

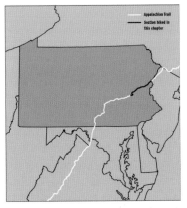

TRIP STATS
October 6, 1995 - October 13, 1995
72.4 miles
North to South

The heat we had endured on our traverse of Shenandoah National Park the year before affected our trip planning for every AT hike thereafter. The first example was this trip — our first in the Keystone State.

The section of AT that passes through Pennsylvania has a horrible reputation for one reason, the rocks. It's hard raise the prospect of Pennsylvania hiking without the subject coming up in the first few words. The legend of how the trail ravages knees, feet and boots is shared up and down the trail and now the blogospehere — something that didn't exist in 1995. If it had, we would have probably been more intimidated about hiking there, though no less committed to doing so.

Putting the legend of the rocks in context requires at least a brief discussion about the forces that put them there.

When viewed from above, the ridges of Pennsylvania look like the symmetric ripples formed when the edge of a rug is pushed violently forward. In a sense, this is precisely what happened.

Over the course of hundreds of thousands of years, a number of geologic events including the approach and retreat of supercontinents, the formation and drainage of inland seas and the eruption of volcanoes formed an amazing series of parallel ridges that extend from north central Pennsylvania to the Shenandoah area and beyond.

The history of these events is written in the types of rock that remained in their wake. In some places, they remind you of walking across a giant slate tiled patio that was hit by an earthquake. In others, you strain to keep your balance across jumbles of loose, fist-sized rock formed by freezing and thawing called talus. And in still others, you traverse giant irregular slabs that make you contort your ankles every which way just to make it across. Almost always you need to pay attention to your footing. Walking through Pennsylvania isn't like walking on a woods road where you can look at your surroundings as you go. That said, these same ridges that cause some people despair also boast rocky outcrops that offer a perspective on the beautiful farms and fields below that is indescribable.

Maybe it's because I'm from New England, where rocks are almost always factored into a hike, but I've never understood the vitriolic banter about Pennsylvania rocks. To me, complaining about the rocks on a mountain trail would be like going sailing and complaining about the existence of water.

For this trip, we knew just enough about what we were getting into to be cautiously optimistic about our ability to make it to Port Clinton with time to spare.

As trips to the trail went, this one was uneventful, other than the fact that we were traveling down through the remnants of Hurricane Opal. This was one of those times I was grateful to be leaving the getting there to someone else. I could just sit back and read while fierce, wind-driven rain buffeted the bus.

By the time we checked into the hotel room we had reserved in East Strasburg at 1:00 a.m., the rain had stopped. Fifteen minutes later, I walked outside to see the last of the storm leave the area. All that was left of the ferocious storm was high clouds screaming past the moon high overhead. Looked like we would be hiking in good weather for at least a few days.

There are days on the trail that I can summon back to relive at any time, even decades later. The morning we climbed out of East Stroudsburg to reunite with the AT is one. The storm had indeed moved completely out, leaving a cerulean blue sky and the clearest views imaginable. The four mile road walk up to the ridge was as pleasurable as they come. As often the case, my steady pace was soon accompanied by a song that pounded the same rhythm. This time, a one-plus hour version of, "My City Was Gone" by the Pretenders. Again, much happiness. It could have been dreadfully worse. Only those who have been stuck on, "A-we-meh-weh, A-we-meh-weh, The Lion Sleeps Tonight" for trail mile after trail mile can fully appreciate my good fortune.

Traditionally we take a break when we reunite with the land of the white blazes again — nothing formal, more of a nod to the importance of the trail as a constant in our lives. An acknowledgment that yes, even after x many years, we are still out here chasing the dream. This time, we turned onto the trail and kept on walking. There was a viewpoint called Wolf Rocks a little ways in that we had scoped out as a better place to celebrate being on the trail again.

There was no breaking in period regarding the rocks. I tried stepping around them, but soon discovered that I would be relying on my dexterity and poles to rock hop my way along. It was the only way I could keep up any sort of hiking pace. Two miles in, we encountered the Wolf Rocks lookout. The views of the Pennsylvania farms was incredible—a giant quilt of fields stretching to the horizon. We would have many gorgeous views from the ridges this week.

You can learn a lot by sitting quietly on a mountaintop and tuning in to your surroundings. One immediate realization was the volume of commercial traffic moving over the land. Pennsylvania's nickname is "The Keystone State", so named because of its location (originally in the center of the country's original thirteen colonies) and its importance to commerce. (In architecture, the keystone is the center wedge in an arch that holds the whole together.) As America spread west, Pennsylvania certainly retained its importance as the keystone. A lot of freight moves through Pennsylvania on its way to and from New York and New England. The dull roar of highways, freight trains and airplanes is a constant reminder of this and can be heard nearly all the way through the state on the AT. I attribute at least part of the noise factor to the fact that it was easier (and cheaper) to build highways through the valleys than through the mountains—the valleys hold the sound.

The ridges and valleys make it easier for other things to move through here by the thousands as well—birds of prey. Every spring and fall, hundreds of thousands of birds ride the thermals of Pennsylvania on their annual migrations, including bald eagles, peregrine falcons and at least eight varieties of hawks.

One of the best and most famous places to witness the annual migrations (different species have different peak migration times) is from Hawk Mountain, located just west of the Appalachian Trail and accessible by a side trail. The area now includes the 1,400 acre Hawk Mountain Sanctuary, a conservation area dedicated to protecting birds of prey and providing a place to view them. But less than a century ago, it wasn't that way.

In 1929, the popular sentiment was that predatory animals were a nuisance to be

eradicated. Accordingly, the Pennsylvania Game Commission put a $5 bounty on every Goshawk that could be killed. Two years later, a recent college graduate and amateur ornithologist named Richard Pough went to Hawk Mountain and witnessed the shooting of hundreds of passing hawks. The photos he took of dead hawks lying on the mountainside drew the attention of a New York conservationist named Rosalie Edge.

In 1934, Mrs. Edge travelled to Hawk Mountain and leased the 1,400 acres that became the world's first refuge for birds of prey, Hawk Mountain Sanctuary.

To sit on a slab of Pennsylvania rock on the AT and watch a hawk rise dozens of feet above you with a simple tilt of a wing, then circle high above for hours on end is one of the greatest thrills I can imagine. And while it's romantic to believe that you are witnessing this majestic spectacle for free, it really came because someone before me was willing to make it possible. Interestingly, I don't see the Pennsylvania Game Commission as a villain in this story. I prefer to believe they were doing what they felt was right for their time and adapted to a new way of thinking. A lesson for the ages if ever there was one.

The next three days required unprecedented concentration on footing. The loose rock on the trail was a constant challenge, often giving way when I pushed off. This was more frustrating on flat trail than on climbs or descents. Theoretically, the trail should have been more settled on the flats and we could have made better time. But not here. Again I counted heavily on my poles to help me stay lighter on my feet.

Water was also a concern. Most of the springs on the ridges are only reliable after heavy rains. Otherwise, the water percolates down through the rocks and into the valleys. At 4:20 p.m. on day three, we dropped into Little Gap to reach a paved road and an unexpected sight, an elderly woman selling apples from a makeshift roadside stand. We must have been exuding hunger and thirst. I started taking off my pack to get to my wallet to buy some apples, but she beat me to it. She insisted on giving us four apples each without allowing us to pay.

We turned east toward the entrance to a ski area, where we thought we might find a water spigot. Better than that, we found a guy painting the lodge.

"I'm cleaning up and getting out of here in 20 minutes.", he said. "If you want to use the bathroom, you'd better head inside now before I lock up."

We brought every empty water vessel we had with us inside: three 1-quart water bottles each and a collapsible 7-quart water bag I'd brought along. In addition to the water faucet, we also found a soda machine. We bought three iced teas and a Dr. Pepper to add to our 13-quart water supply.

We thanked the man profusely and staggered out of the parking lot. I was carrying 20-plus extra pounds in water alone.

"First flat spot", I said to Wayne as we got back on the pavement. "I'm not climbing out of this valley with an extra 20 pounds."

"Ahead of you on that one.", said Wayne.

We turned up a dirt side road affiliated with the ski area, climbed a small embankment and found a nice out of the way spot. In minutes, we were sitting in our loungers drinking cold iced tea and admiring the stash of water we had for drinking, cooking and powering us through the next day. All this and fresh apple slices to put into our morning oatmeal. Life was grand. And it stayed that way despite what we were about to hike through.

One of the few downsides of my collecting guidebooks well in advance of actually

hiking through the areas they covered is that it sometimes came back to bite us. In general, the placement of the trail stayed the same from year to year. Sometimes there were relocations which added miles. Those were usually easy to spot — the trail suddenly showed signs of less use, then would rejoin the "thousands of people have walked here before" path again. In this instance, we discovered something far more harrowing that wasn't mentioned in our 1989 guide—a ridge top that had experienced a forest fire and was posted with EPA warnings telling people not to drink the water and urging parents not to take their kids to this area on a regular basis.

The landscape was barren and oddly beautiful, a jumble of barn gray stumps and granite slabs in a sea of blonde grasses. Due to the government warnings, we didn't want to stop. I had visions of my feet being lowered into an acid bath. We soon entered a stretch of giant boulders that gave us an impressive view of the New Jersey Zinc Company mining operation below. Dropping down off the ridge, the AT led us through the parking lot of a motorcycle dealership, over the Lehigh River and past a car rental business, where we ducked in for water. After the EPA warning, we didn't know when the trail water would be safe again.

I hit an amazing pace in the afternoon, undoubtedly because I wanted to get away from the danger zone and back into the comfort of the woods and ridges beyond. I was flying along the ridge top in the late afternoon when I heard Wayne's voice behind me.

"Hey, check this out.", he said.

I couldn't believe I blew right by one of the best spots we'd have the whole trip. The vista was spectacular, a panorama large enough to hold hundreds of farms, a handful of ridges and the entire city of Jim Thorpe, Pennsylvania. We sat with the tent door open and watched the colors turn from blue to pink to black. The streetlights, cars and barnyard spotlights provided a whole evening's worth of entertainment. A feast of vegetarian chili with eggplant, zucchini and sun dried tomatoes and the discovery of a station that played 1930s Louis Armstrong only made the night better.

October is when the largest variety of hawks moves through this area, which also brought a daily migration of people day hiking up the trail to watch them from various promontories. Hiking along the ridge top for days on end, we (and they) were seldom disappointed. The weather was perfect for sitting and watching — mid-70 degree temperatures with fair weather clouds creating a stellar backdrop for the ongoing air show.

On one late afternoon, after we had pitched the tent, I went on a reconnaissance mission and discovered an outcrop with the best views of the day. I went back and got Wayne, who filled a stuff sack with cocktail hour treats. We sat for three hours in the evening light eating cheese and crackers, sipping water and watching the hawks, some swooping within fifteen feet above our heads. That little extra motivation to explore your surroundings so often yields rewarding finds.

One more spectacular roost remained on the trip, the one purported to offer the best vista in all the Keystone State — a 1,635' granite slab known as The Pinnacle. When we arrived, we found a friendly local sitting with her dog watching a group of turkey vultures circling above. As the afternoon wore on, nine more folks ranging in age from high school to retirees arrived on the scene to take in the hawk filled view. It's a great feeling when a large group shares an unspoken, completely understood reverence for a place. Other than the welcoming nods and smiles of greetings and departures, we respected each other's solitude and reasons for being on The Pinnacle. It was a special evening in a special place. There was nothing greater to do than sit and watch.

By 7:00 p.m., the day visitors had all departed from the summit, including us. We set up camp close enough so we could scamper back to the summit after dinner. It was only fitting that the one of the last trail impressions of the trip was an unforgettable light show — heavenly above and manmade below — from a slab of Pennsylvania stone. We stayed out on the rocks until 10:15 p.m. watching it unfold.

While we sat, we reminisced about our week on the trail and began plotting our next one. Looking up at the stars with my hands behind my head, I mentally ran through the sections we'd done and the sections we had left to do. I knew Wayne was doing the same. I was leaning toward New York or another section of Virginia.

"How 'bout New York or continuing on from Port Clinton?", he asked.

"Wow. Wasn't expecting that.", I said. Up until now, we had never picked up where we left off.

"Would like to do all of PA while we're still young.", he said.

That was one solid reason for continuing. We didn't know we'd be presented with an even better one the following afternoon.

Helen

Port Clinton, Pennsylvania is a town that most folks don't stop in. It's a hamlet like so many in PA, tucked between ridges, whose main street has ironically fallen victim to the fact that it is also a state highway. The traffic moves at highway speeds past the few businesses that still survive. Drivers barely have time to take notice these establishments exist before they disappear in their side view mirror, which makes the ongoing viability of places like the Port Clinton Hotel all the more remarkable.

Wayne and I had bus tickets for the ride from Port Clinton to Harrisburg. We had already purchased them before we climbed out of East Strasburg, ten days before. The bus stop was right in front of the Port Clinton Hotel. When I say "right out front" I really mean it. The distance between the front porch of the hotel and 55 mile per hour traffic was barely a car width.

After we survived the gauntlet of sprinting across two lanes of highway with 50 pound packs on and made the porch, we set down our packs and opened the door into one of the most meaningful and poignant experiences of our 28 years on the trail.

The Port Clinton Hotel is best described as a tavern with guest rooms. The first thing we saw when we walked through the front door was an "L" shaped bar with Yuengling's and

Rolling Rock on tap. But the cold beers on tap and pub fare menu weren't the stars of the show. Not by a long shot. It was the welcoming, hard working woman that had made this place her home and her life for more than thirty years.

Helen Kubilus Carbaugh was born of Lithuanian parents in the town of Shenadoah, Pennsylvania in 1914. She married Robye Allen Carbaugh (who was also born and raised in Pennsylvania) in 1932. Thirty-three years into their marriage, after raising three daughters and a son, they became the owners and operators of the Port Clinton Hotel. At the time, Helen was 51 and Robye was 61.

Helen and Robye ran the place together for nine years until he passed

The bar at the Port Clinton Hotel in 2014.

away in 1974. And after his death, she kept the Port Clinton Hotel welcome sign lit for another twenty-four years.

You don't buy a place like the Port Clinton Hotel because you have designs on getting rich. Even though the place had hundreds of cars speeding by it every day, it wasn't easy to stop there. No, the secret to staying viable had much more to do with the woman in charge.

Helen was 81 years old when Wayne and I walked through the front door. And while it was evident that more than three decades of work had taken a physical toll, the strength of her spirit was undeniable.

"Where are you boys from?", she asked with a freshness that made it seem like she hadn't said it to hundreds (if not thousands) of hikers before.

"I'm from Maine and he's from Connecticut.", I replied. "We're finishing our trip here. We need to catch the next bus."

"Well, I imagine you need to look at menus then.", she said, as she placed them in front of us. "I'll be back to get your order."

As a New Englander, I was raised in a culture infused with suspicion, where you were taught to keep your story to yourself and guard it closely. And when it came to asking people about their story, it was generally considered to be rude. After all, their business was none of your business.

Four years of attending college in Wisconsin introduced me to a completely different world. I wasn't in the town of Ripon more than six hours when I walked into a restaurant and was greeted with a hearty, "Have a seat. Where are you from?"

My first reaction was, "Wow, these people are pushy.", but I soon realized that the reason people wanted to know your story wasn't from a place of nosiness, but of caring. It was a way of making the experience more meaningful for everyone involved.

Within the first minute of being in the Port Clinton Hotel, I knew that Helen had been raised in a culture that cared deeply about people—family, friends and strangers alike. And that even though she was stooped, losing her eyesight and moving slowly through a combination of hard work and longevity, her focus wasn't inward, but ever outward. She gained strength from the people that walked into her life no matter where they came from or how they got there.

When she walked back into the kitchen to make our burgers, I turned to Wayne and said, "What a great place to end a trip. Helen is a national treasure."

We only stayed for about an hour, but in that time we learned that Helen was the daughter of Lithuanian immigrants, that her husband had passed, that she had a lot of family still in the area and that she cared for her customers with an effervescence that could transform you from a stranger to a friend in a matter of minutes.

As we ate our delicious burgers at the bar, I asked Helen if she had any old AT hiker registers from decades ago.

"We used to have some from the 1960s and 70s.", she said with a look of disgust. "But someone stole them a while back when I was out in the kitchen."

"That's terrible.", I responded. "Who would want to steal them? What good would they be? It's not like they could publish them without getting caught."

It was clear that Helen had resolved what had happened years ago. She was ready to move on to something more pleasant.

"You guys picked a great time to hike through. I don't see many of you in the fall.", she said.

We continued making small talk and would probably have missed our bus unless Helen was on the case.

"You'd better get out front.", she said. "They may not stop unless you are pretty obvious. They certainly aren't likely to be dropping someone off."

With that, we paid our bill, left a nice tip and walked out to reacquaint ourselves with the public transportation system.

To this day, I don't understand how a bus can regularly stop in such a harrowing place without causing a pile-up. The driver was used to it, however. He tossed our packs underneath and we were seated and rolling in the fastest time I'd ever seen. We all knew the potential dangers of lollygagging and he appreciated our efforts to keep things moving.

As we pulled away from the curb, I craned my neck to look back at the Port Clinton Hotel one more time. In five seconds it disappeared into the night.

"Gone from view, but never to be forgotten.", I said to Wayne, who was sitting next to me.

"Helen.", he said. "She was quite something."

CHAPTER 9

Return to Port Clinton

The ridges of Pennsylvania hold a special place for all who venture there

Port Clinton, PA to Duncannon, PA

TRIP STATS
October 18, 1996 - October 24, 1996
67.1 miles
North to South

When it came to our Appalachian Odyssey, hiking in autumn was now entrenched as our preferred season and October our preferred month. Wayne and I would generally get out to hike a few other times during the spring and early summer. During a spring 1996 trip on the Midstate Trail in Massachusetts, we talked about our AT plans for that fall. We were still in agreement about starting our hike at the Port Clinton Hotel and again settled on a week in October.

As I looked out the tent window watching the trees around our Midstate Trail campsite slowly fade into the dark of night, I wondered if Helen was still there, tending the bar and flipping burgers for ravenous hikers.

The best way to get to the Port Clinton Hotel (and one of the few) was by taking a bus from Reading, PA. When we got to Reading, we had a more than four hour wait in store. We decided to explore the city a bit and soon found a fledgling brewery that also served pub fare. The bartender immediately looked at us and said, "You don't know anything about bottling machines do you?"

As a matter of fact, I did (due to my several youthful years as an avid brewer).

The next thing we knew, we were in the basement of the building helping calibrate a machine so that it dispensed uniform quantities of liquid into each bottle. You really never know what turns an adventure can take. (Or when someone for reasons unknown to both of you starts a question with "You don't know anything about...?" I seem to have a pretty good track record with that one.)

By the time the bus pulled away, leaving us in front of the Port Clinton Hotel, the sun was disappearing over the ridge to the west of town. If Helen was inside, we wouldn't be able to stay long.

I pulled open the door and stepped into the land of deja vu. Yes, Helen was there. Before I could say anything, she looked up and said.

"I know you. You're the two guys from New England!"

I couldn't believe it. How many scores of hikers had wandered through here between when we left and when we came back?

"That was Helen.", said her grandson, Michael, whom I tracked down and called in 2015. "She couldn't remember names too well, but she remembered where people were from."

When I mentioned what an impact she had made on us in the two brief times we met her and how clear it was to us that she enjoyed what she did, he replied, "She really poured her heart into that hotel. Other than her family, it was her whole life."

"We can't stay for dinner this time, Helen. We need to get back on the trail and set up camp before dark. We just wanted to stop in to say hello."

"Well, I'm glad you did.", she said.

As we walked through the streets of Port Clinton on our white blazed path, we realized it was probably also our goodbye.

Two years later, Helen sold the hotel to a non-family member and moved to Florida. Just three years after leaving Port Clinton, she passed away. She is buried next to her husband in nearby Hamburg, PA, only about ten miles from the place that brought her and others so much joy.

I went back to the Port Clinton Hotel in 2014. Some things have changed, but the layout is almost exactly the same. The pine paneled walls and bar lend an air of permanence to a

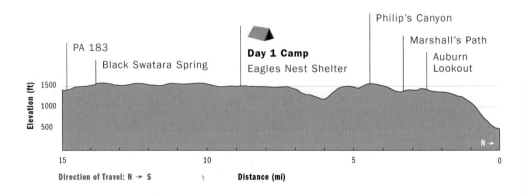

place like this. But the most important feature of my experience with the Port Clinton Hotel can never be replaced. She is gone from view, but never to be forgotten.

As we left the streets, we happened upon one more piece of history connected with Port Clinton—a railroad track. Railroads played an important role in establishing the town of Port Clinton. From the late 1820s to 1939 they carried coal here, which was in turn loaded on barges and sent to the village of Kernsville to the south. The coal crews would live at the Port Clinton Hotel (originally called the Gately Hotel) in the winter, when the canal was frozen over. The last shipment of coal to be sent via the canal left Port Clinton in 1939.

Today, the Reading Blue Mountain & Northern Railroad (a passenger excursion and freight company) is headquartered in Port Clinton, retaining a two century plus tradition of trains moving through the valley.

We looked both ways, stepped over the track and started our way up the first ridge leading out of town. It was getting dark fast. Part way up the ridge, we crossed an old woods road. It was far more likely to yield a flat campsite than our steep climb ahead. Sure enough, we found one, set up the dome and dove in just before it started raining.

The rain was brutal on our first full day out. We spent six straight hours walking in 43° weather and soaked to the bone. The thought of stopping wasn't seriously discussed. To stay moving meant to stay warm.

When we hit the Eagle's Nest Shelter at 3:30, we called it a day. It was nice to have a solid roof over our heads and some room to spread out. We hung every piece of wet gear out to drip under the eaves. Any water that dripped off would reduce our pack weight.

Despite the chance to drip dry gear, there were two major downsides of sleeping in the shelter. One, the wooden floor was predictably hard as hell. Even with the lounger inflated underneath me, it was uncomfortable. I could only stay in one of four sleeping positions for a short stint before I had to turn to another one. And two, the shelter is big and open (and therefore cold). The tent creates a confined space that traps air. Not so the shelter. I woke up with freezing cold feet and a sore throat at 4:30 a.m. and never got back to sleep again. I couldn't wait for first light so I could start the coffee making ritual.

It had rained so hard the day before that we were no longer hiking the trail so much as we were walking through a three foot wide river with leaves floating along its surface. It was no use trying to step around it. I tried it for a while, but the rocks and leaves presented a constant footing hazard. I fell twice regardless of using poles.

My feet were soaked anyway, so I just went for it — a five mile plus slog through

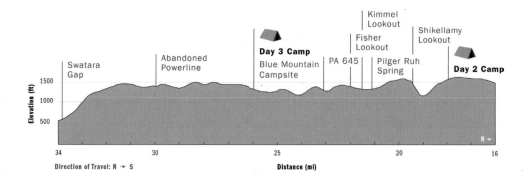

puddles and downed leaves. The rain held off all morning, but returned in early afternoon. By then, we'd had enough. Sleeping in the tent made a huge difference. My feet stayed warm and I got a solid night's sleep.

On day three the rain stopped, but the trail was still dealing with the remnants of the deluge. I joked in my journal that in places I had to detour around the trail to avoid Class I rapids. Despite the poor trail conditions, we were focused on making miles. We really needed to if we were going to make Duncannon on schedule.

I started employing my rock hopping technique, which is much as it sounds, literally hopping from rock to rock without so much as touching any dirt that might exist between (which in this part of PA was scarce or too small to place a boot in).

In order to keep a quick pace, however, you can't jump from one rock to another, stopping on every one to plot your next move. Instead, you look ahead toward your next landing spot, glancing back to your current situation only long enough to make sure your foot is planted securely and you can push off. By doing this, you can really make good time.

Of course, rock hopping is at its best in dry weather. Soaking wet rocks with leaves on them brought a new level of difficulty. Fortunately, by early afternoon the sun was finally making a play. By the time we made Fisher Lookout at 1:30, the clouds had lifted enough to treat us to views of farms below and seven hawks above.

By the time we rolled into the Blue Mountain Campsite in late afternoon, we were back on schedule and all smiles. As the lights came on in the farmhouses and over the streets below, we kicked back with heaping bowls of fettuccini and pesto.

"Man, what a life. All you have to do is take care of yourself.", said Wayne.

I wrote that quote in my journal that night. Then I added: "It is so true on so many levels — spiritually, psychologically, physically. While this trip hasn't been as physically challenging as others, it does take mental strength to keep slogging through

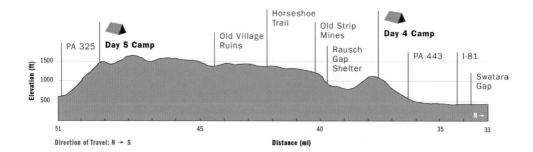

when it's wet and cold. I'm really glad we did."

As is so often the case, we were rewarded for our perseverance. The pink and steel blue sunrise was magnificent. The farms in the valley were enveloped by fog, which started lifting as the sun warmed the land.

I was overjoyed. Today would be the first day of the trip we could start out in short sleeved shirts and shorts with bare legs (as opposed to legs encased in long johns).

Getting on the trail was like merging onto a highway with a newly filled tank of gas and a ton of vacation time ahead. The ridge walk was tremendous. Mile after mile of hardwoods, grasses, granite and occasional viewpoints. Everything was clicking. The footing was solid, I had boundless energy and it was being fueled by the views and the warmth.

It wasn't just me that was happy. Pileated woodpeckers gave their jungle cries from above, perhaps gleeful that the sun had warmed the tree bark enough to make the insects underneath active and therefore easier targets.

In one place, where the trail came close to a steep drop off to my right, I passed a large doe that had bedded down between me and the cliff. I stopped and remained silent as she rose up quickly, then ran off, passing about 75 feet behind me and about the same distance in front of Wayne.

At the end of the ridge we heard the unmistakable roar of another creature, the urban commuter. The four lane superhighway I-81 was below us and the AT went underneath it all. Seeing and hearing the traffic from overhead made me feel otherworldly. After spending days moving at two to three miles per hour, it was hard for me to believe that I spent so much time in the workaday world moving at that pace. Even my forty minutes a day commuting felt like too much.

Soon the eastbound, then the westbound lanes of I-81 were towering over our heads. We couldn't see the cars or trucks, but we could sure hear them. We couldn't wait to get back into the land of views, woodpeckers, deer and relative quiet again.

The way to get there was by taking a historic walk. Not long after we left the roaring I-81 traffic behind, we came to a bridge built in 1890 that had once spanned Little Pine Creek via State Route 44 in Waterville, Pennsylvania. Built by the Berlin Iron Bridge Company, the bridge's design is attributed to William O. Douglas (who was an engineer at the East Berlin, Connecticut company and not the same William O. Douglas that was a U.S. Supreme Court Justice).

The lenticular (parabolic) design of the bridge was patented by the Berlin Iron Bridge Company and was a popular choice for short spans because it used less material than other designs and was easy to assemble in the field. But the popularity of the lenticular design lasted only a few decades. As they were slowly replaced, few examples of them remained.

When the Pennsylvania Department of Transportation determined that the Waterville Bridge was no longer adequate to serve the increasing traffic and loads on Route 44, they served notice that the bridge could be repurposed at another site. The timing was perfect for the Pennsylvania Department of Conservation, an agency faced with placing a bridge over Swatara Creek on the Appalachian Trail.

In 1985, the Waterville Bridge found a new home on the Appalachian Trail. It was listed in the National Register of Historic Places in 1988.

In 1996, we stopped next to the bridge to admire its design and take a break in the sun.

The Waterville Bridge's new home over Swatara Creek

The details on the bridge, including the finials over the arch and the nameplate of the Berlin Iron Bridge Company itself were so much more inspiring to me than the giant, utilitarian concrete pillars that supported the roadway of I-81. I was happy that the bridge had found a new home and didn't get relegated to the scrap heap of history.

Even though we had gone ten miles fueled only by a bagel and a cup of coffee, we decided to keep going. Every mile we could make today would make the last day's walk into Duncannon shorter.

Somehow on every trip we made up the mileage we needed to so that we could roll back into civilization on the appointed day and at the appointed hour. In the early years, I took advantage of Wayne's tendency to keep tabs on our overall progress. All I needed to do was listen to his morning advisories, then walk until we hit the mark. Over the years, I got more involved in that level of awareness and the ongoing conversation. It was better that way, undoubtedly for both of us. It lowered his anxiety about his having to be the cruise director and it helped get us working more as a team.

We ended the day with a pleasant climb and descent to arrive at a nice camping spot near Haystack Creek. It was nice to be back in the woods again and less than 30 miles from Duncannon.

When we awoke, the temps were in the high 40s and we were camped in a thick blanket of fog. The mist had turned the trunks of the trees a foreboding black that made them even more prominent than usual, due to the foggy white backdrop. Conditions like these always made it easy to justify staying in the tent and brewing up a second cup of coffee. Thus, we didn't get underway until after 10:00.

Once we finally got moving, my pace was horrible. Wet conditions always make my hikes take on a sense of deliberateness — something faster than a plod and slower than flying down the front stretch at Pimlico. With the visibility down to less than 1/4 mile, I also became introspective. It's always been interesting to me how much differently I feel when I have limited views versus walking along a ridge top with farms and mountains stretching as far as I can see. Those remarkable vistas fill me with a sense of positiveness, possibilities and connectedness — a citizen of the world. Conversely, days like today can bring a sense of isolation, a lone soul walking through a darkened, mystical forest with a heavy pack and heavy thoughts.

It's not that rainy days can't be filled with joy, some of them surely are. It just seems like it's a steeper climb to find it than it is when the sun is out and you can already see a fair ways through the trees.

As I walked along, I was so busy looking at my feet that the crashing of a huge doe I startled simultaneously snapped me back into the here and now and made me almost jump out of my skin. "That's what I get for taking a side trip into Downersville", I admonished myself. "You would have seen her a lot sooner if you had been in the world instead of your head."

During our last climb of the day (to the top of the 15 mile ridge that would take us to the Susquehanna River), the rain stopped and the wind kicked in.

"Hallelujah. The cold front is moving out. Should be a great walk into Duncannon.", I said to Wayne.

With the rain out of the way, the last big climb seemed a whole lot easier. The wind on the top felt glorious. After we set up the tent, we draped every piece of our wet clothing over nearby branches. Even though it would be dark soon, the wind would dry everything out in a hurry.

The dawn lit up the sky in red. I couldn't wait to get out of the tent to join the day. I took the coffee makings to a nearby outcrop, started the water boiling and looked out at the panorama. The sun lifted over the horizon, adding warmth and light to my perch. What a difference a day made!

I went back to the tent to get my journal, lounger and the rest of the breakfast makings.

"I take it it's pretty nice out there.", said Wayne.

"Spectacular is more like it."

Soon we were both on the outcrop, drinking coffee and watching the fog slowly lift from the valley below and into the sky.

We ended up staying there for an hour and a half.

"I awoke this morning knowing that only a few miles and a bridge across the Susquehanna separate me from re-emersion into society.", I wrote in my journal. "Right now, that seems too soon. One week out is just long enough to start getting into trail shape again and to put the big 'through hiker hook' into your mouth again."

I really wished we could be out hiking along the Pennsylvania ridges for more days on end. Far from being an annoyance, I felt blessed to be walking on these impressive rocks above the clouds and under hawk's wings.

I could have sat there for hours more, watching the day unfold and jotting down observations. Wayne certainly knew it. He didn't say anything, but getting up and picking his way through the rocks and brambles back to the tent was his way of urging me toward the packing ritual. He would get started without me.

I wrote for ten more minutes, took one last look back toward the 14-mile ridge we had traversed yesterday, then down into the valley, where the fog had lifted to reveal the Susquehanna River and a golden quilt of farms below.

Yes. It was time to go.

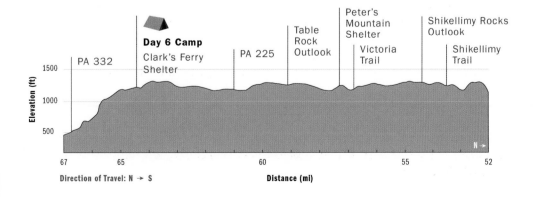

CHAPTER 10

A Time to Connect

The happy wanderers find support in unexpected places.

Daleville, VA to Bland, VA

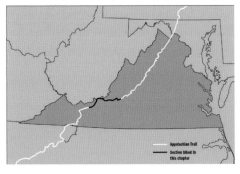

Appalachian Trail
Section biked in this chapter

TRIP STATS
October 10 - October 23, 1997
128.1 miles
North to South

In retrospect, I'm not sure why we decided to walk the 10 miles from Roanoke to the AT trailhead in Daleville. We almost always drove or got a ride to our starting point. My recollection is that the gorgeous autumn day had a lot to do with it. I am certain that my "good things happen if you just start walking" mentality also played into the decision. Whatever the reasons were, we were having a good time doing it.

A road walk is a great way to warm up for a two week trip and we were psyched to be rolling along under the VA sunshine with 70 pound packs hitting just under a three mile per hour pace. We passed the Roanoke Civic Center and our trail soon became VA Rt 11, which we would follow all the way to Daleville. The ridges in the distance created a visual finish line. When we reached them, we would turn left, downshift and merge onto the AT.

The day had taken on a celebratory feeling from the start. We didn't need to share any banter. We both felt the energy. The only words between us for the first several miles was repeating a six word phrase of affirmation back and forth, "So good to be on trail".

Halfway to Daleville, Wayne called for a break. It was lunchtime.

I spotted a sports bar up ahead, and the die was cast - wings and burgers!

One college football game, twelve wings and two burgers later, we were back on the trail with full tanks and five miles to go.

As we walked through the outskirts of suburban Roanoke, I thought of the last time we hiked our way to the trail, when Jack Davis appeared to give us a ride in his hearse. There would be no ride this time. I doubt we would have taken it anyway. We were enjoying the afternoon weather and the euphoria of two weeks of vacation still ahead.

Interestingly, the spot where the trail passed through Daleville was at the confluence of Route 11, Route 220 and our old friend, Interstate 81. There was an interchange there, complete with a gas station/convenience store.

Even though our packs were weighed down with two weeks' worth of food, the way our eyes lit up, you'd think we were about to walk across a dessert.

"Hot dogs and chips?", I asked.

"But, of course!"

Thus, our first night out was high on the edge of a meadow, eating hot dogs with a stellar view of the I-81 cloverleaf. Our tent could have been pitched in Central Park for all we cared. All that mattered is we were on the adventure again.

The ridges of Virginia, like those of Pennsylvania, stretch for miles and miles. The gaps between them were most often carved by wind or water. Generally speaking, while you are happily hiking along the ridge tops, you do so with the knowledge that at some point you are going to have to climb down to get water, then climb back up again. It's an ongoing concern, and one that dictates how your days will play out.

Sometimes you don't need to venture too far from the trail to fill your water bottles. Shelters are almost always situated near water sources. It is one of the considerations that goes into where to build them in the first place. Because of this, sometimes the shelters are close to the trail and others require a considerable side trip. We tried to keep the side trips to a minimum unless we were running close to empty.

We had cut out an aggressive schedule for a couple of 40-year-olds that would be toting

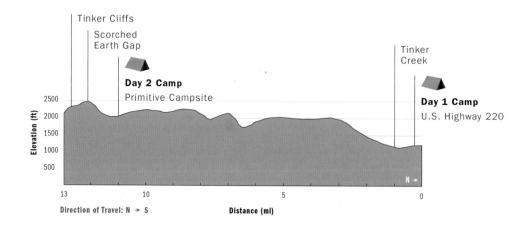

70-pound packs over the Virginia mountains. Aggressive for a couple of desk jockeys anyway — ten miles per day for twelve straight days (thirteen, if you counted our road walk). Through hikers would be averaging fifteen miles or more, but we would just be starting to hit that level of being in trail shape when it was time to scurry back behind our desks again.

When I slung my pack over my shoulder and started up the ridge, I wish we had forsaken the hot dog feast and eaten something from my food stash instead. I was sweating bullets and my hips were paying the price of the load stress test. Nonetheless, we made nine miles — enough to keep us nearly on schedule.

Day two was one of those days that stays with you forever. Cerulean blue skies, the orange hues of fall just starting to take hold and jaw dropping views from outcroppings — everything you could imagine from a day in the mountains and more.

Early in the day, as I neared the summit of Tinker Cliff and broke out onto a granite slab, four hawks flew fifteen feet from my right shoulder, then circled effortlessly on the thermals. Wayne joined me a few minutes later and we watched the first of the many air shows we would see during this peak migration time of year.

The next six miles of the ridge bent back on itself like a letter "J", such that when we got to McAffee Knob in the afternoon, we could see from Daleville to Roanoke, whose buildings were lit up by the afternoon sun. It is always satisfying to trace your progress from high vantage points. This time, we could see both starting points of our trip, the road walk from the city and the place where we jumped back on the AT.

Besides beautiful weather and inspiring views, this trip took on a third theme, one we had rarely experienced on our fall hikes — community.

On our many trips, we had benefitted from the generosity of trail stewards and shelter caretakers simply through the ample work they had performed before we ambled through (clearing blown down trees from the trail, repairing shelter roofs and so forth). But on this trip, we found "trail magic" awaiting in an unexpected place.

One of the unwritten rules of hiking the AT is that you should never leave uneaten food in your wake. Sometimes hikers realize they are carrying too much on their backs and figure the easiest way to reduce their pack weight is to purge food. We have encountered plastic bags filled with pasta hanging from trees, boxes of oatmeal left within sight of trailheads and other foodstuffs left with good intentions, but poor consequences. People rarely trust the purged food is any good and the packaging is strewn about the landscape by crows, chipmunks or whatever other animals happen upon the scene.

Shelters are another favorite purging spot. We have found partial bottles of maple syrup,

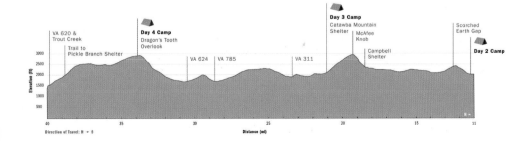

Pearisburg, VA from Angels Rest

family size cans of soup and bags of oatmeal stashed in the corners of shelters, only to serve as animal attractants unless the shelter caretakers carry them out for proper disposal.

On this warm day, we rolled into a shelter to discover treats left there quite recently and quite on purpose — two cans of soda. They had been left by the shelter caretakers who, having read the warm weather forecast, thought that a couple of cold sodas would be a pleasant discovery for a couple of people passing through. There was a note in the trail registry from the caretakers, who signed their trail names, "The Habitual Hiker" and "The Umbrella Lady". In a case of serendipity, I knew both of them.

When the Habitual Hiker first hiked the AT, he made it all the way from Springer Mountain to the Bigelow Range in Maine, where he injured his leg. While convalescing and

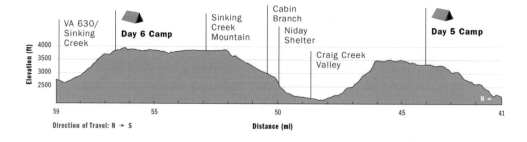

working a job in a stereo store in Georgia over the following winter, he decided it wasn't enough to pick up where he left off and that he wanted to hike the whole trail again.

The next spring, he got dropped off at Springer Mountain. Somewhere in Virginia, he met a woman on the trail who called herself "The Umbrella Lady". By the time they got to Katahdin, they had fallen in love.

One day while discussing what they should do for a honeymoon, they decided there was only one proper thing to do — hike the whole AT together.

When they returned from their honeymoon, they settled down in a cottage near the AT in Virginia. To stay connected with the trail and to give something back, they adopted Campbell Shelter as theirs to caretake. That is where we discovered the sodas.

I met Leonard and Laurie (their given names) when Leonard was giving a lecture at L.L. Bean. I was asked if I could pick them up at the airport and give them a ride to the lecture venue. Of course, a trio of veteran hikers hit it off, and I spent a few evenings getting to know them and swapping trail stories. I had lost track of them until I discovered they were shelter caretakers on this October afternoon.

The last I heard of the duo, they were planning on walking out the front door of their cabin, turning right and hiking to Katahdin. I wouldn't be the least bit surprised to learn that they had.

That late afternoon, we arrived at the Catawba Shelter at 5:00 and decided to stay there, in large part because of the nearby spring. We drank a quart each and hauled six quarts back to the empty shelter to unpack and start meal production. And unpack we did. The floor of the shelter looked like the aftermath of a hurricane hitting a yard sale — sweat drenched clothes hanging from hooks, stuff sacks full of clean clothes strewn about and food bags nearby in anticipation of dinner preparation.

In the midst of this, a southbounder hiked into the clearing and introduced himself as "Sharpshin". We made room in the shelter while he sat at the picnic table out front and made himself dinner.

During the evening, Sharpshin filled us in on his adventure. He had left Katahdin on June 8th and been hiking most of the way solo, although he asked us whether we had seen a number of other southbound hikers. The through hiking community is a loose band of travelers that change positions constantly over the half year they are out. There are reunions in towns, on mountaintops, in shelters and every place in between. Keeping tabs on people's whereabouts is part of the game.

By 8:15, I was spent. Wayne and Sharpshin stayed up talking for a while, as I slunk low in my sleeping bag and drew the hood around me to block out the glare of the moon.

The rest of the trip held some of the best extended weather we'd experience on our 28-year adventure — bright sun, daytime temperatures in the 70s and low 80s and nighttime

The Bland overpass

temps in the low 60s. The conditions were perfect for everything — views, footing, wildlife sightings (deer, hawks, wild turkeys and pileated woodpeckers among them) and making long ascents and descents from the ridge tops without enduring fog and rain.

On one of our deep descents and climbs from one ridge to the next, we crossed a significant river, one that flows more than 350 miles through North Carolina, Virginia and West Virginia.

If there was a "Things that were Curiously Named" Hall of Fame, the New River would be deserving of special consideration. The New River is in fact, one of the five oldest rivers in the world. It also has a few other interesting attributes. It is one of the few North American rivers that flows south to north. It also boasts one of the most beautiful bridges in the U.S., the New River Gorge Bridge, a single arch that spans 1700' in West Virginia.

The day we crossed the New River ended with a steep two mile climb up to a spot called Angel's Rest. There were fittingly gorgeous views there, but no place to camp. We went a while further and tucked the tent into the woods about 100 feet from the trail.

While dinner simmered on the stove, I tuned in National Public Radio. In as prescient

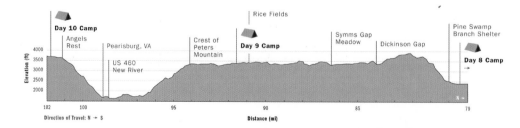

and surreal a moment as any we had on the trail, over the airwaves flowed a feature story about how one of the NPR reporters was deeply into researching and writing a book about the New River.

A few days from the end of our magnificent hike through southwestern Virginia, we experienced another piece of serendipitous trail magic.

When we were hiking north of Pearisburg, VA, we met "Yoofus", a fellow section hiker. From the beginning of the trip, we were wrangling with how to deal with a major logistical problem. We were planning to get off the trail in a place called, Bland, Virginia. We had wrongfully assumed that it would be easy to get from Bland to Roanoke, where we would be catching our bus home.

We should have researched more thoroughly. It turned out that the trail passed through Bland by way of an overpass above I-77. There was no easy way to get in or out of the place. Hitchhiking was illegal and there was no entrance or exit.

We mentioned our dilemma to "Yoofus".

"I'm getting off the trail in Pearisburg." he said. "I'll pick you up in Bland. Just tell me when you'll be there."

What a relief! All we needed to do now was reach the appointed destination at the appointed hour, something we always seemed to be able to pull off.

As we came down out of the mountains for the last time in ten days and turned up the paved road to the overpass, I looked at my watch. We were 15 minutes ahead of schedule.

I walked out to the center of the bridge and looked down at the cars and eighteen wheelers as they rushed beneath my feet and was overcome with a sense of gratitude. Slowing down and reconnecting with nature brought me the greatest joy I could imagine. The ability to do it for days on end was a pleasure I couldn't take for granted. The older I got, the more I appreciated that I could still walk among the mountains and that Wayne was here to experience it, too.

In a few minutes, we would likely be getting into a car and speeding off to be assimilated into the parade. Just another vehicle packed with folks trying to get from here to there. For a little while longer, I held tightly to where we had come from, where the pace of life slowed to three miles per hour or less.

At 12:17 p.m., a car approached with its emergency flashers on and pulled into the breakdown lane.

"Saved by Yoofus.", I said above the traffic's din. We half slid down the embankment and piled into his sedan to rejoin the high speed fray.

CHAPTER 11

Ridges, Fields, Rivers, and Byways

The trail brings a taste of all things Pennsylvania.

Duncannon, PA to Caledonia State Park, PA

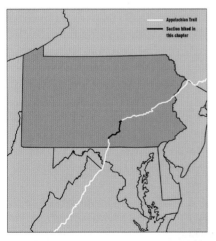

TRIP STATS
October 10 - October 17, 1998
65.9 miles
North to South

Until now, every time we had section hiked on the AT, we had either driven or taken the train. This would be the first trip that we took a plane. It would also be our last.

For this trip, we had nine days to work with, including travel time. Wayne needed to attend a wedding on the Saturday before, which meant that we wouldn't be able to be hiking until Monday at the earliest if we took the train. We hadn't discovered "shuttlers", yet, so we dismissed driving out of hand.

"Let's fly.", said Wayne. "Less transportation time and more hiking time."

I immediately agreed.

Thus, after the wedding (I attended the reception as a last minute invitee), we caught a flight out of Bradley International Airport, bound for Harrisburg with a layover in Pittsburg.

I had experienced the "taking camping gear on the plane" routine before. When boarding a plane on the first leg of a trip to New Zealand a few years before, my beloved Svea backpacking stove was confiscated because it was an incendiary device.

I had walked thousands of miles with that stove and now it was with me no more. I replaced it in New Zealand with a stove powered by propane/butane canisters. There was nothing to carry on the plane except the burner. We'd only have to find an outdoor gear store near Harrisburg, pick up a couple of canisters, and we'd be on our way.

In theory.

First camping store after asking for my specific type of fuel canister: "Yes, we've got those."

Not accurate.

Next camping store: "Yes, we've got those."

Strike two. They didn't have them. Now we were down two cab fares and half a day's worth of looking.

A place called Wildware Outfitters: "Yes. We have them."

"The blue canister, right."

"Yup. Got a whole bunch of 'em."

He was right. The cab driver waited outside, then drove us to Duncannon, where we found another kind of fuel for the trail — a couple of giant cheeseburgers. We weren't in so big a hurry as to pass those up.

The burger detour seemed like a great idea until we started the steep climb up to Hawk Rock outside of town. A full stomach and a 6-day load of gear and food made for

quite the warm up for the trip, but the views looking down on Duncannon and the Susquehanna River made it all worthwhile.

That night in the tent, we critiqued our decision to fly down. In the end, after the side trips for stove fuel, we hadn't saved any significant time. On Sunday night, we were four miles into the trip. If we had brought our own canisters, then taken the bus or a train, we would at least be this far, if not farther down the trail.

The die was cast. We declared that there would be no more flying to the trail. And we never did again.

The first three days out were much like the trail in Pennsylvania that preceded them, walking among the ridge tops with sporadic views of the farms stretched out below.

It was a thrill to be back with the hawks again. Every now and then, a steadily moving shadow would move

The farms of Cumberland Valley

through the trees and across my path. If I looked up quickly enough, I'd see the hawk before she disappeared to the other side of the mountain to ride back up on another thermal wave, perhaps making another shadowy pass — a silent, graceful and reassuring salute from above. Every time I see it, my spirit soars as well.

On day four, we dropped out of the ridges to hike through all new terrain — the farmland of southern Pennsylvania.

For the next 14 miles or so, we took a break from the rocks and walked among the horses, cows, barns and silos of the Cumberland Valley. This is beautiful country, as we had witnessed many times from the ridges above. Now we could enjoy a scenic stroll right through it. And it was gorgeous. The farms rolled on and on to the distant ridges that we would be returning to soon enough. The only thing interrupting the idyllic scene was the sound of traffic.

The same broad valley that was so attractive to farmers was also irresistible to road builders. During our hike through the farms, we would cross over three state roads, as well as I-81, U.S. Route 11 and the Pennsylvania Turnpike. We had seen the endless movement of cars and trucks moving through the Keystone State from above. Watching the 24-7 parade of commuters, shoppers, freight haulers and vacationers speeding across a canvas where progress is measured by seasons was a sight to behold.

Yet, the roads also held an unexpected gift for us.

As we were halfway across the U.S. Route 11 overpass, I looked north. There was a truck stop and hotel within range.

Wayne saw it, too.

"Lunch?", he asked.

It may have been 12:15 in the afternoon, but you wouldn't have known it at the restaurant as the shades were drawn. A TV above the bar was tuned into a soap opera.

"If you want lunch, you'll need to sit at the bar.", said the bartender.

We placed our order. At 12:30 on the nose, a truck driver walked in and sat a few seats down from us, closer to the TV. A salad instantly appeared in front of him and the bartender handed him the remote.

"I'm hooked on Santa Barbara", he said referring to the show on TV. "I time my truck routes and deliveries, so I can be here four out of five days."

Back out on the U.S. 11 overpass, I took one last look at the truck stop.

"I guess a full tank of food, gasoline and Santa Barbara can take you just about anywhere.", I said.

"Not anywhere.", said Wayne. "Just anywhere that still puts you within striking distance of a TV by 12:30."

By day's end, we were back in the woods, where our path was level and wide. Another manifestation of the arrival of automobiles was that we were walking on an abandoned railroad bed.

We were transitioning out of farmland and back into mining country. The ridges to the south of us were rich in resources that were in high demand during America's industrial age. No place is this more evident than Pine Grove Furnace State Park, our next late day stop.

The Pine Grove Furnace was built in 1830 by a man named Peter Ege to smelt iron. His operation grew to include a dam (used to power the waterwheel that powered the forge), a boarding house a coal house and other dwellings. By the 1870s, rail lines were built to haul materials to and from the forge.

As demand for iron dropped

An historical photo shows Pine Grove Furnace in operation. (Pennsylvania State Archives photo.)

off, another industry took shape at the same site. From 1890-1913, Pine Grove Furnace became a brick kiln, using locally obtained clay and soapstone (which was mined to clean the clay).

Today the state park retains many vestiges of its industrial past. Some of the rail lines have become walking and cycling trails. The quarry (now filled with water) is known as Fuller Lake. Laurel Lake (the 25-acre body of water created by building the dam to power the original Pine Grove Furnace) is now open to boaters. The most obvious feature that remains is the stunning stone structure tucked behind the park's entrance—Pine Grove Furnace itself.

We strolled down to the furnace, sat at a nearby picnic table and downed the iced teas we had purchased on our way by the park's general store.

It had been another terrific trip from the moment we procured the fuel for our stove. The weather and terrain had allowed us to cruise along the ridge tops, through the valleys and down the woods roads. In fact, as we pored over the map spread out on the picnic table, we realized we only had to average six miles per day to make our outbound flight four days from now.

"I'd like to throw an idea at you", said Wayne. "What if we do two 9-mile days and spend a day walking around the Gettysburg battlefields? Gettysburg is only about 15 miles from where we are getting off the trail."

I didn't need to be asked twice. "Let's get walking!", I said.

CHAPTER 12

Return to New York

It had been thirteen years since we stepped foot in the Empire State. It was time for our reunion.

Hoyt Road, NY to Harriman State Park, NY

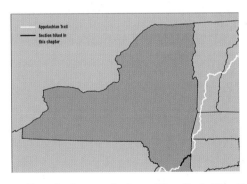

TRIP STATS
October 9, 1999 to October 16, 1999
72.2 miles
North to South

So far, as our patch-working together of AT trips progressed, we had managed to do parts or all of the New England states, Pennsylvania and Virginia. It was time to turn our attention to New York.

Despite its proximity to New York City, the trail through the Empire State offers some sweet hiking, particularly through 46,000 acre plus Harriman State Park, the second largest park in the state. It is ironic that this beautiful place where people go to escape was once earmarked to be the site of a state penitentiary.

As the story goes, railroad magnate Edward R. Harriman envisioned establishing a park in this area well before his death in 1909. However, the State of New York had other plans. In 1908, the state acquired land surrounding Bear Mountain for the purpose of building a prison. The public objected to this idea, citing the beauty of the area, as well as its historic significance. In 1910, Harriman's widow, Mary A. Harriman, offered the state 10,000 acres of land under the condition that they abandon their proposal to build the prison at Bear Mountain. The state accepted her offer, which became the impetus for the park as it exists today.

The first section of Appalachian Trail to be completed in New York (in 1923) was the section that traverses Harriman State Park. That was where we would end our hike.

But first, we needed to pick up where we left off in 1990—at a place just after the trail crossed into New York from Connecticut called Hoyt Road.

Our mission was for me to drive from Maine to Connecticut, follow Wayne to Harriman State Park (where we would leave his car for the week), drive to Hoyt Road, park my Jeep there, then find a site on the trail to end day one - 400 plus miles of driving and about 400 feet of walking, if we were lucky.

I wish I could say it went off flawlessly, but there were no real downsides to our detours other than lost time. A wrong turn somehow found us in the town of Walden, NY, where we ate a pizza at a picnic table behind a bank, then jumped back in the Jeep. By the time we finally located the trailhead just before dusk (after a few more wrong turns), I was about as sleep deprived as I could get. I was just happy I wouldn't have to drive for a week.

We got on the trail, crossed near the edge of a pasture, went up a small hill and found a flat spot for the tent. If we left anything in the car, we could get it in the morning. I fell asleep in 15 minutes and woke up ten hours later in the beautiful, peaceful state of New York.

The hardest thing for me to do on the first day out is to get the mind and body willing to hit the double digit mileage mark. It's really easy to come up with all sorts of reasons not to do it. My two favorite ones are, "The pack is at it's heaviest now" and "We've got all week to make up mileage".

Nonetheless, on this day we were able to get close with a respectable nine miler.

Day two was a soaker. The rain kept coming on hard, then backing off into a mist. We went all day on a couple of trail bars and water. We got it into our heads that we could reward ourselves with a long rest if we did the work. Along the way, I spotted a Great Horned Owl on one of the tree branches overhead and three deer crossed just in front of me.

On day three, we started playing leapfrog with two through hikers. In an ideal world, if someone comes up on my tail as I'm hiking, I let them by and that's it. We keep hiking at our own paces and there aren't any log jams. In the real world, people stop and take

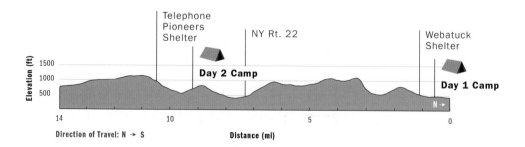

breaks, the people behind them pass, then the people that stopped get going again, only to get back on the first group's heels.

This had been happening with the four of us for miles. When we crossed Rt 52, we knew there was a store less than half a mile from the trail.

I stopped and waited for Wayne. "Let's hit the store for lunch.", I said. "That way, we can let these dudes get ahead of us for good."

We took the side trip into town and turned the corner in front of the deli to discover both of them sitting at the picnic table waiting for sandwiches.

We all had the same great idea. I laughed and so did they.

We ordered a large pizza and waited as well. It was a poor decision. The two guys got up and headed down the trail, but the pizza stayed with me all afternoon. It felt like I swallowed a bowling ball. It wasn't just the pizza. The climb up over Hosner Mountain was making my calves rebel. I shifted down to low gear until I got back in the groove. Our reward was a spot on top of the ridge with eastern and western views.

The next day's road crossing was the Taconic Parkway, which was a major construction zone. As the workers waved us through, they were shaking their heads at us, perhaps astounded by the size of our packs.

The highlight of the day was the overlook of Canopus Lake, a beautiful sliver of blue (1 1/2 miles long x 1/4-mile wide) tucked between ridges, including the one we traversed. I checked the trail guide. We had covered 10 miles and were back on double digit pace.

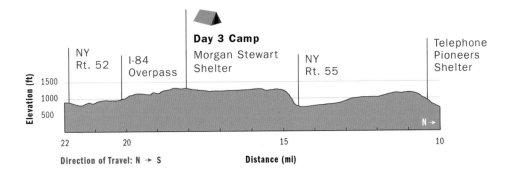

At the eleven mile mark, I started looking for camp spots. A boulder pile to my right looked like it went all the way to the top of the ridge. I started climbing. The rocks weren't as stable as they appeared for their size. Some of them shifted beneath me.

"In for a penny, in for a pound.", I said to myself. No sense in turning back.

Right then, I heard a grunt. I turned around to see Wayne seated at the base of the pile, facing the trail.

"Holy crap! Are you ok?", I yelled down.

His hand went to the back of his head.

"I think so.", he said. "I took a tumble."

I worked my way up the few more boulders I needed to make sure I didn't start a rockslide from above and waited for him to climb up.

When he got to the top, he told the tale.

"The pile gave way and I went with it. I did a double back flip, hit my head and landed on my butt facing the trail. I caught my glasses as they exploded off my face."

Under his torn bandana were two pretty nasty scratches. The bleeding didn't look too bad. We were both worried about concussion, though.

We bushwhacked up to find a suitable tent spot on the ridge. We joked that the Pleasure Dome would now double as a convalescent home—even more so than it normally did. But even though we joked about it now, we knew we were really lucky. That fall could have been much worse. It would turn out to be the only horrible fall either one of us would take in almost three decades of adventuring.

After Wayne was settled in the tent, I went up the ridge to take in the view for a few minutes. I didn't stay long, because I wanted to be close at hand in case Wayne's condition deteriorated. The fortunate thing was that we were really close to a road. If I needed to go for help, it wouldn't take me long to find it. Getting paramedics up the rock pile might not be so easy, I imagined, but I'd deal with that if the time came.

When I returned to the dome, Wayne said he still had a headache, but nothing worse than that. After dinner, I made sure we stayed up talking for a while. For my part, I wanted to make sure he was still ok. By 9:00, when it appeared he had come through the fall no worse for wear other than the scratches, I blew out the candle and went to sleep.

The next morning, as we picked our way back down the boulder pile, we found the top of Wayne's coffee cup. It reminded me of seeing pieces of a side view mirror on the side of the road after a car had been towed away from a crash scene.

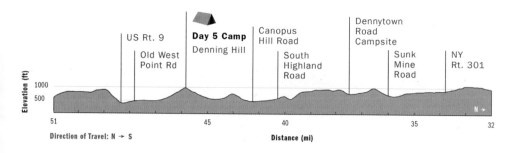

We spent a fantastic autumn day under the sun, hemlocks and maples. When we topped Denning Hill late in the afternoon, there were two gentlemen from Stockholm standing on a small outcrop looking out at the ridges.

"Which way is the Manhattan skyline?" one asked.

I took off my pack and looked with them for a while.

"I can't see it. Maybe it's in the clouds.", I finally said.

They took off and we started looking for a campsite.

In the morning, I went back to the ridge. Manhattan glowed in the morning sun. The twin towers of the World Trade Center dwarfed the city that stretched out beneath them. In less than two years, they'd be gone.

The next day was easily the best of the trip. The trail gave us sneak peeks of the Hudson River during the morning and into the afternoon, before we got to the side trail to Anthony's Nose, which offered the best view of all, looking down at the Bear Mountain Bridge. The arctic air was screaming across the summit, so we couldn't stay long.

Now came the incredible plunge down to the bridge and across the 1/2 mile span (at 124', the lowest elevation on the Appalachian Trail) to reach the far side of the Hudson.

The arctic blast blowing over Anthony's Nose was nothing compared to that blowing through the bridge. It was ice cream headache time. I only stopped long enough to glance up- and down-river from the center.

When we got to the far side, I suggested going to the Bear Mountain Inn (just off the trail) to warm up. No dice. They were filming a coffee commercial there and the public was not allowed in. We'd have to warm up in the tent.

Halfway up Bear Mountain was as far as I could get. I was on fumes. The down-climb of Anthony's Nose and the cold air knocked the energy out of me. We found a spot out of the wind and made a humongous spaghetti dinner.

The warm weather returned for our last two days out. It's so much more enjoyable when you can take long lunch breaks under the sun, and we took full advantage. After our initial climb to top of Bear Mountain (complete with observatory, restrooms and trashcans), we enjoyed two full days of ridge and woods walking as our wind-down.

The walk through Harriman State Park was as advertised—a beautiful, gentle traverse down from the ridge line through the birches with bright sun lighting the way. The same tranquility and beauty that drew us was also drawing weekend hikers. Dozens were heading in as we were making our way the final two miles to Wayne's car.

As we neared the parking lot, I thought about how these one week trips hit me with a case of though-hiking fever. I knew what it was like to be out for weeks and months at a time. And seven or eight days was entering the sweet spot that made me want to keep walking. I was getting into trail shape again, just when I had to go back to sit behind a desk.

"Well", I reasoned. "If I have to go back to the land of cubicles, at least I'll travel in comfort. Clean clothes, clean socks and, best of all, my favorite sneakers are only a quarter-mile away."

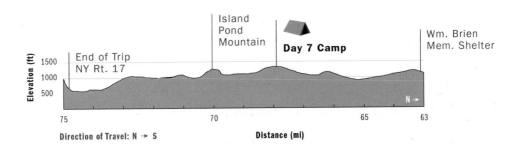

CHAPTER 13

A Truly Historical Hike

In the days following September 11, we resume our walk in a place where our nation was also mightily tested.

Caledonia State Park, PA to Harper's Ferry, VA

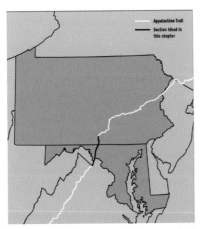

Appalachian Trail
Section hiked in this chapter

TRIP STATS
October 5, 2001 - October 12, 2001
57.77 miles (17.1 miles in PA and
40.67 miles in MD)
North to South

Everything conspired to make this one of the most emotional trips of our entire Appalachian odyssey.

Only 24 days earlier, the twin towers of the World Trade Center had been destroyed by terrorists — a scene that left a permanent scar on everyone who witnessed it, either in person or on screen.

It had only been two years since we had seen the twin towers dwarfing the rest of the Manhattan skyline from the trail. It was hard to imagine that those buildings, so imposing even from 40 miles away, were permanently gone. I could not imagine the pain that the families of the 3,000-plus people that also perished on that day were still feeling less than a month hence.

In the raw days that followed September 11th, I had several discussions with friends about the fragility of life. A common theme was that the terrorist attack was a clarion call to ensure we lived the lives we wanted to — that in a world filled with uncertainty, the best thing we could do was to ensure we stayed true to making our own visions become reality. I didn't need much encouragement. I called Wayne. It was time to get back on the trail.

It had been almost two years since we were last on the AT. In May of 2001, Wayne and I had gone hiking in the White Mountains. Right after he got home from the hike, he got into a motorcycle accident. A guy pulled out of an auto parts store parking lot into his path. Wayne T-boned the car, went up and over the roof and landed on his feet so hard that his left ankle practically disintegrated. It was a miracle that he could ever walk normally again, let alone hoist a 60 lb. plus pack and trek up and down mountains all day long. But now he was willing to try.

We pored over the guidebooks and settled on a 50 mile walk through southern Pennsylvania and across Maryland. Of all the trail we had left to do, this section was the most forgiving and closest to what Bill Bryson refers to as "a walk in the woods", complete with long ridge top sections and woodland roads. It would be the perfect place to put Wayne's reconstructed ankle to the test.

The walk through southern Pennsylvania and Maryland also presents a meaningful stroll through American history. Many of the greatest battles of the Civil War, including Antietam, Gettysburg and South Mountain, were fought near what is now the AT and the troops that fought in them moved through and over the very same mountains we would traverse.

Because I'm a history buff, I imagine I would have been affected by walking over this hallowed territory regardless of recent events. But the more I thought about being there in the throes of 9-11, the more I realized that it was exactly where I needed to be.

But first, I had to get there.

As usual, the journey to the journey was a journey unto itself.

The plan was for me to leave Maine by 4:00, which would give me plenty of time to drive to Wayne's, then catch the 10:00 p.m. bus from Hartford to New York City.

Instead, I didn't leave my driveway until 4:45, which eliminated a good part of my time cushion. I hoped for open roads and moving traffic all the way to Connecticut. That hope lasted for ten minutes. The Maine Turnpike was restricted from its normal three lanes to two, due to construction. A sea of cars, all with one person in them (including mine) constricted like a crimped garden hose. Fortunately, after several miles, the mass of us accelerated out of the other end and back toward normal flow.

All was well and good with the world again until I merged onto I-495 in Massachusetts, where my mind quickly scuttled the garden hose analogy. For the next two hours, I took my place among thousands of cars vacillating between 15 and 35 miles per hour on the interstate. Three lanes of red tail lights stretched out before me, moving ever slowly up and over hills and into the beyond. To my left and moving toward me was a faster moving stream of white headlights. I imagined myself as a red blood cell among thousands with white blood cells moving more efficiently the other way and winning the battle. Yes, our transportation system was diseased and in need of intervention. The healthy flow was constricted on a daily basis. And today, I was part of the problem.

The Red Sox game I had switched on became background noise. I never really got into the game because I needed to be on top of mine. The mostly stop and sometimes go traffic required my complete focus.

"What a way to start a vacation", I thought. "I can't wait to get on that bus so I can relax." But even that thought didn't bring as much comfort as it once did. In recent weeks we had seen public transportation used as a weapon on a massive scale. And just two days before this one, a deranged man had forcibly taken the wheel of a moving bus and flipped it over, killing six people including himself. No, I wouldn't be able to fully relax until we were walking down the path again, relying on no one but ourselves to get where we wanted to be.

There certainly wasn't time to relax when I pulled into Wayne's driveway at 8:55 p.m. He wasn't as upset at me as he should have been. He merely gave me the, "You were pushing it, man" look as I threw my pack into his car and we hurtled out of his driveway toward the Hartford Greyhound station.

By 9:40, we were standing in the bus station wondering where our bus was. It wasn't at the gate and there was confusion all around. As it turned out, it was stuck in the same highway gridlock that had engulfed me on the way down from Maine. By the time it showed up and we departed, we were 50 minutes behind schedule. Good thing our original layover time in NYC was an hour and a half.

I couldn't sleep on the bus to NYC, nor the bus to Philly, nor even the bus that took us from there to Harrisburg, arriving at 6:00 a.m. Wayne dozed off in the bus station, while I read the newspaper in a quasi-vegetative state. Today the news was like watered down

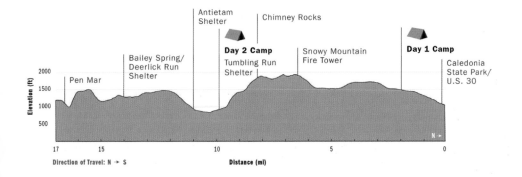

This is a piece of the dress worn by Miss Laura Keene, in the play of the American Cousin. at Fords theatre Washington & C. on the night of the assasination of President Lincoln. Friday good Friday night. April 14th 1865. and was presented to me by Miss Keene. at Woods theatre Cincinatti Ohio. where she came from Washington to fulfil an engagement, this is strictly true in my particular. Louisa Eldridge "Aunt Louisa" New York April 14th 1895

bullion. I drank it down heartily, but my system couldn't ingest any part of it.

I stayed awake all the way through our bus ride from Harrisburg to Chambersburg, PA. Thankfully, our pre-arranged shuttle dude was waiting at the station for our 12:50 arrival.

Wayne climbed into the front seat and I crawled into the back of the van to discover that the one bench seat was stowed perpendicular to its proper spot and even more disconcerting, not bolted down. On every corner, I went up on two legs and was in danger of tipping over. The floor was also awash with empty water bottles that rolled from side to side when we changed lanes.

"Sorry about that, man." said the driver, half turning around. "I didn't have time to re-install it before I left to pick you up."

Turns out the driver was a through hiker the year before and had plans to do the trail end-to-end the following year as well. "Go with the flow" seemed to serve him well in trail life. Driving, maybe not so much.

Nonetheless, he was able to deliver us to our desired destination — Caledonia State Park. The van disappeared from the clearing and we were left by the picnic table we remembered from two years ago as our last rest spot before we thumbed into Gettysburg to view the battlefield. A few hundred yards from where we stood was another notable stopover point. The Confederate cavalry, under the command of General Jubal Early, stopped here in late June of 1863 to destroy the ironworks. They were also on their way to Gettysburg.

I took one last look around the dirt parking lot, tied on my bandana, adjusted my ski poles to hiking length and slid into my pack. At 3:00 p.m., the temporarily sleep deprived 2001 Masters Tour was underway.

Even in my sleepwalk-like haze (or perhaps influenced by it), I started out with a heightened sense of euphoria. After all it took to get here, I was finally on the path again. I roared down the first half mile of trail to abruptly emerge onto the edge of PA Route 30 — four lanes of fast moving busyness.

"It would have been so ironic to have gotten flattened here." I said to Wayne while we waited for a break in the traffic.

Two miles in, we arrived at a beautiful ridge top spot on Rocky Mountain and set up the dome. We celebrated by scooping warm cheese fondue out of the cook pot with hand torn chunks of bagels.

It was still light out when I pulled my winter hat on and got low in the sleeping bag. The temps would drop into the 30s before dawn and I would sleep all the way through. I was back in the woods where I could completely relax at last.

On day two, we had a tremendous ridge top hike as our next to the last day's farewell to the Pennsylvania AT. We walked along surrounded by late fall splendor with bright red foliage above, granite outcroppings to our left and still brilliant green farmland below. My trail induced euphoria was still in play — maybe too much. As I danced along the rock strewn trail, I caught both toes at once and lurched forward. I dropped both poles, took a modified swan dive off the trail and landed hard on my right shoulder and arm. As I cleared the cobwebs, I was doubly happy that I'd had just enough presence of mind to untangle my feet so I could take the hit to my arm and shoulder rather than my knees or ankles. I knew I was lucky that it wasn't worse and vowed to keep my daydreaming to a minimum and pay closer attention to my footwork until I got to a clear section of trail again.

Our next stop was Old Forge Picnic Grounds, where a day hiking woman told us we would find a restroom with water, "right next to three guys throwing a baseball." Her description was right on. We filled up with H2O, found a camp spot in the nearby woods next to the Antietam Road and called it a day.

MASON DIXON LINE

The word "Antietam" holds a special place for me. My relative, William Harwood, a private in the 71st Regiment Pennsylvania Volunteers, was killed on September 17, 1862 in the Battle of Antietam, the single bloodiest day in the Civil War. William Harwood was an exceptional and prolific writer. He wrote seventeen letters to his sister, Louisa, describing his experiences as a soldier. One letter describes a day off in which he and some fellow officers walked to the U.S. Capitol building, where the dome was being built. On their way back to their encampment, they were met by Abraham Lincoln on horseback, who raised his stovepipe hat to them and thanked the men for their service.

William Harwood's sister, Louisa, was an accomplished actress who went by the stage name, "Aunt Louisa" Eldridge (her married name). As with most well regarded actors of the day, she knew John Wilkes Booth and his older brother, Edwin, a renowned Shakespearean actor that once gave Louisa a pair of Star Spangled stockings as a gift.

William Harwood wrote his last letter to Louisa just days before the Battle of Antietam. The last words he wrote were, "I'd write more, but I have run out of paper." A round, musket ball-like bullet found next to the body of William Harwood was wrapped in paper and sent to his family in Philadelphia. It is one of the pieces of family history that has been retained to this day. Another is a piece of fabric.

When Abraham Lincoln was assassinated at Ford's Theatre, the lead actress in the play Our American Cousin, Laura Keene, stood in shock as John Wilkes Booth jumped

onto the stage from Lincoln's private box and ran to his escape. She ran upstairs to come to Lincoln's aid, cradling his head in her lap.

In the days following the President's death, she cut pieces of her dress into squares and gave them to various acquaintances. One person she gave a piece of fabric to was Aunt Louisa when the two of them met in a theatre in Cincinnati. Louisa wrote of the gift and kept her note with the piece of the dress.

The third piece of history from that era that remains in my family is my middle name "Harwood", a nod to the great man that came before me.

As we awoke for day three on the trail and were sipping coffee in the tent, I pulled the map and guidebook out of my holster to look at the layout of the trail ahead. Today we would be walking out of Pennsylvania and into Maryland, on our way to Harpers Ferry, West Virginia.

The 40.67-mile hike through Maryland presents an incredible walk through history. And while the events of the Civil War are by far the most notable, the AT touches pieces of history from other eras that left lasting impacts.

Pen Mar County Park is appropriately situated on the Pennsylvania/Maryland border. The views westward from the ridge warrant a stop, and we took a long one, complete with crackers and chicken noodle soup at the pavilion picnic table. As usual, we drew visits from curiosity seekers. One group of four retirees were particularly amused, asking us if we wanted a ride and saying, "You guys could really use a shave" before they drove off for parts unknown.

The story of Pen Mar Park is intertwined with that of the rise of the railroad. But unlike New Hampshire's White Mountains, where tracks were laid to move a valuable commodity out of the mountains, here in Maryland, it was the other way around.

The Western Maryland railway built the park in 1878 as a destination for clubs, church groups and families for their summer outings. And arrive they did. One Lutheran gathering attracted over 15,000 people, although 5,000 was closer to the average weekend crowd. With visitors came a push to build more attractions and accommodations. There was a fun house, a rollercoaster and multiple hotels. The largest, the Blue Mountain House, accommodated 400 guests. It was destroyed in a 1913 fire.

Over time, interest in automobile excursions took hold. Train excursions were no longer popular and the railroad leased the property to an independent company. The

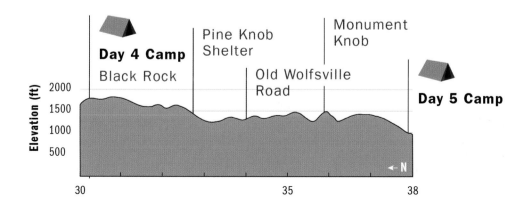

gas rationing of World War II dealt the resort a final blow. It shut down and the buildings were removed.

In 1980, Pen Mar Park reopened, thanks to citizens of Pennsylvania and Maryland, who raised the funds to build the very pavilion where we ate lunch.

Just after 3:00, we left the picnic table to cross into Maryland, stepping over one of the most famous boundaries in the world. In 1765, two British men (an astronomer named Charles Mason and a surveyor named Jeremiah Dixon) were hired by the Penn family of Pennsylvania and the Calvert family of Maryland, to settle a border dispute that had been simmering between the families and their states since 1681. The families agreed to honor the boundary that would be established by the duo and their crew to define the 233-mile border between Pennsylvania and Maryland and the 83-mile long border between Maryland and present day Delaware.

To mark the boundary, the team placed milestones at one mile intervals and crownstones every five miles. (The milestones and crownstones were both made of limestone and imported from England.) The project took nearly five years to complete and established the definitive border between the states. The Mason-Dixon line also became an important demarcation in the War Between the States and responsible for the term "Dixie" itself.

Milestone number 91 is located just off the AT on private property in Pen Mar. In the interest of time and in respect to the property owner, we crossed the Mason-Dixon Line by staying faithful to the AT and set foot in Maryland.

For the next 40 miles, until we descended from Weaverton Cliffs, we would be traversing one of the most important battlegrounds of the Civil War — South Mountain. On September 14, 1862 (only three days before the Battle of Antietam), fighting broke out in the three gaps along South Mountain. In the preceding days, General Robert E. Lee had led his troops into Maryland and sent the largest portion of them to attack Harpers Ferry. Along the way, one of his officers mislaid the general's battle plans, which fell into the hands of Union troops.

With the knowledge that Lee's troops were holding the three gaps along South Mountain — Turner's, Fox's and Crampton — General George B. McClellan ordered federal troops to go on the offensive. The battle cost each side dearly. It is estimated that the Union Army losses were: 443 killed, 1,807 wounded and 75 missing and captured. The Confederate Army losses were estimated to be: 325 killed, 1,560 wounded and 800 missing & captured.

Before daylight on September 15, 1862, Lee and his commanders decided to abandon their position and regroup. The Battle of South Mountain was over. Their next battle of significance would be two days hence at Antietam, where the one day losses would be the worst of the entire war.

My first impression of South Mountain was one of awe. Although we were among the trees, we enjoyed fine views of farms and fields spreading all the way to the horizon. As night fell, the farm and barnyard lights came on, creating a beautiful light show. The leaves on the trees fluttered in the breeze, dipping enough to cut off the view of individual lights for a few seconds at a time. The overall effect was like looking at twinkling holiday lights. A rare and mesmerizing feast.

On day four, I achieved trail euphoria. It had been a while since I felt this great out of the gate and all day long. It started with a quarter mile walk to High Point, an overlook

Highway 70

purportedly popular with hang gliders. It would appear it is far more popular with graffiti artists. Nonetheless, the view of the farmland below is plenty colorful and inspiring. We stood long enough to take in the scene, but not so long that we wanted to take our packs off.

The ridge walk along South Mountain was fantastic. After a lunchtime stop at Hemlock Hill, I really kicked it into overdrive. I didn't want to stop and kept going for nearly three hours. I gave myself a stop time of 3:00 to wait for Wayne if I didn't come to a great viewpoint first.

At 3:02, I arrived at a beautiful view, complements of a 50 foot side trail. The way we normally play out the viewpoint scenario is that the person in the lead checks it out. If the junction of the side trail and the AT is too far back from the viewpoint to maintain visual contact (as in, your hiking buddy might miss the viewpoint and proceed down the AT), then you return to the trail junction and wait.

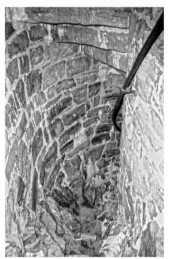

Washington Monument

I had been flying all afternoon. Even so, I imagined Wayne was doing the same and figured he'd be 20 minutes behind me, which was the norm. At 3:25, I started worrying. I grabbed a full water bottle and my first aid kit from my pack and started north, back toward where Wayne should be.

Three minutes later, I heard some leaves crunching. It was Wayne walking toward me.

"Stopped for a snack.", he said. "Want one? It's in my cup."

Inside the plastic cup hanging from his pack was a couple of cookies and a piece of chocolate.

"Brilliant", I said.

"Always fine tuning", he said. "Didn't want to take the pack off again."

The one place I wish I we had fine-tuned more was the water situation. We were running low. We climbed to the summit of Black Rock armed with one quart each and set up camp. It was another night of beautiful farmland stretched out below, this time with no trees in between. We sat at the viewpoint until the sun was long over the horizon and made our way back to the tent by headlamp.

While the water situation wasn't plentiful, we at least had enough to make dinner and have a morning cup of coffee. The good news on that front was that there was a restaurant on Route 40, less than five miles away. We could certainly make it that far, particularly as it was known to make a decent cheeseburger.

But first, we needed to drop down off the ridge and cross under U.S. Highway 70. The high speed, high volume experience made me want to scoot to the burger joint even faster, so I could take refuge with food and quiet.

We were the first customers of the day at the Dogpatch Tavern, wolfed down burgers and onion rings in record speed, topped off our water bottles, then scrambled back to the path to resume our walk through American history.

As we topped the third peak after lunch, we came to a structure that preceded the Civil War by more than three decades. In 1827, citizens of nearby Boonesboro, Maryland celebrated the Fourth of July by building the first monument in the United States dedicated to George Washington to be completed. (The Baltimore Washington Monument was started 12 years earlier, but not completed until 1829.)

The monument stands 34 feet tall today, but it was only about 15 feet tall when work was completed on July 4, 1827. A second phase of building took place later in the same year, which brought the height to over 30 feet.

Largely because it was dry laid (using no mortar to strengthen it), by the 1860s, the tower had fallen into disrepair and collapsed. Yet, even in this state, the Union Army found the view from the rubble to be sufficient for use as a signal station.

It wasn't until the 1930s that the tower would be restored to its original design, thanks to the efforts of the Civilian Conservation Corps.

The structure is pretty impressive from the outside, but climbing the stairs inside gives

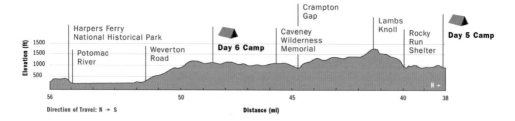

View from Washington Monument

you a complete appreciation for the skill that went into reclaiming its glory. Then there's the view from the top — another Maryland stunner. I vowed I would return again on a late fall day to soak in the sun and scenery, just as we did today.

It wasn't until 4:30 when we departed. We had two more brushes with history compelling us forward.

The first was Turner's Gap, site of heavy fighting during the aforementioned Battle of South Mountain.

The second was of historical interest to only us — a backpacker's campground with free campsites and hot showers. It was one of the few times in 28 years that we would end our trail day freshly bathed and seated at a picnic table for dinner. It was certainly the only time the amenities were free. The ability to sit outside at a real table was quite the novelty. We had the whole campground to ourselves. It was a far cry from the hubbub of Route 70. While dinner simmered, I collected my thoughts and scribbled them down in my journal.

"So much significance in such a short section of trail", I wrote. "Just the human history alone is impressive, let alone the other influences on the land. Over the years, George Washington, Daniel Webster and many other historical notables stayed at an inn just a few hundred yards from this place. Then there are the Civil War related events. South Mountain was so strategically critical to both sides that this territory was where history was made."

And we still had two days to go.

Our next to the last day on the trail was sunny and warm. We got up early, ate breakfast at the picnic table and got underway. I was looking forward to our planned lunch stop at Gathland State Park. After another fine stretch of ridge walking, we rolled in at 12:45.

Gathland was the brainchild of Civil War correspondent George Alfred Townsend, who wrote under the pen name, "Gath". Townsend wrote for the Philadelphia Inquirer

Weaverton Cliffs

and New York Herald, then became the Washington correspondent for the New York World, where his accounts of the assassination of the president and the events thereafter were published as The Life, Crime and Capture of John Wilkes Booth (which included a description of Laura Keene's efforts to comfort the President at Ford's Theatre).

Gath continued to be a prolific and nationally known writer, which earned him enough capital to build an impressive estate in Crampton Gap, which he named "Gathland". When Townsend wasn't writing, he was designing buildings for his estate. There may have been as many as twenty of them at one time. The most well-known feature of the estate is the War Correspondent's Memorial Arch. Built in 1896, it was the first memorial in the world dedicated to journalists killed in combat. The arch still stands and the AT passes right next to it.

I would have liked to have spent more time strolling the grounds of Gathland, but it would have to wait for another day. We needed to make headway toward Harpers Ferry if we were going to catch an early train two days from now. The lessons of the past were finally taking root. We were hoping that the high mileage dashes to finish sections were well behind us.

Eleven-plus miles today would give us a short 6 mile walk into Harpers Ferry and a chance to walk around town.

The last great viewpoint of the trip would be from Weaverton Cliff, over the Potomac River and toward the town of Harpers Ferry. We camped one mile short of the viewpoint with a satisfying 11.3 mile day behind us.

The last day on the trail is always an emotional tug of war for me. The greater part of me wants to stay out here on the trail indefinitely, where I can savor the greatest gifts it holds for me — serenity among them.

I experience a holistic "settling down" out here that I can't find elsewhere. Granted, I chose to be in a profession with two endless sources of pressure: the expectations for creativity on demand and adherence to deadlines. But even without those pressures, there would be plenty to take their place.

Spending days on end walking among nature is a chance for me to slowly turn off all frenetic noise. It's just me out here taking an amazing walk with a trusted companion. It may not be for everyone. But it's undoubtedly for me.

Yet, when I get the farthest away from the distractions of daily life, I start hearing a faint voice calling me back into the fold. It's amusing to me that when people say, "You can't stay out there forever", my immediate instinct is to imagine myself as the exception—the hermit that could be hiking in perpetuity and happy beyond reason.

The reality is that I need people in my life — my family, my friends and people I haven't even met (or may never formally meet at all, like those who leave jugs of water on a dry stretch of trail).

As I awoke in a tent on a Maryland ridge, I knew that as surely as we would be walking into Harpers Ferry today, we would meet someone who would extend an act of kindness or, if we were observant, allow us to extend one ourselves.

At 8:45, I finally stopped scribbling in my journal and packed up for the walk into Harpers Ferry. At Weaverton Cliff, we looked at one last Civil War stronghold, the town of Harpers Ferry. It was a fitting place to bid our goodbye to Maryland. This hike had been

filled with inspiring vistas. They had helped me take stock of the people and events that came before me. But most important for me at the moment was that they helped me reset my bearings and start healing from the events of September 11, 2001.

One week ago, when I arrived at Caledonia State Park, I was still emotionally raw, upset about the reality of what human beings are capable of doing to one another. Yet walking through this part of the world, at this particular time, helped me regain hope.

Walking through the sites of the most significant Civil War battles can't help but remind you that people and nations have emerged from horrific circumstances before. And the gestures that came out of those

events — building monuments, parks and other tributes to ensure we never forget the lessons of the past — are what I prefer to believe as gestures gratitude and optimism. That the best thing we can do to keep making things better is to keep on learning and paying it forward.

The trail into Harpers Ferry was stellar and fittingly also had historical flavor — it was a three mile walk on the C&O Canal path along the Potomac River. The 184.5 mile path stretches from Georgetown to Cumberland, Maryland and was once a primary artery for moving goods. It was sold to the federal government in 1938. An act of Congress in 1971 authorized the acquisition of additional land and establishment of the C&O Canal National Historical Park.

As we entered Harpers Ferry, we checked the time. We wanted to make one stop before we even considered food and lodging. It was at the Appalachian Trail Conservancy headquarters.

Harpers Ferry is located at the midway point on the AT. As such, it is the perfect place for the ATC to be doing their work as a confederation of the 31 local organizations with assignments to maintain the Appalachian Trail and a membership organization. In addition to working with local organizations, the ATC works closely with the National Park Service, USDS Forest Service and a variety of other agencies at all levels of government to protect the beauty and heritage of the entire Appalachian Trail. It's a daunting charge and one they do well.

The ATC headquarters in Harpers Ferry is a modest building filled with all things AT, particularly guidebooks, maps and an extensive selection of books and films about the trail. In the back of the building are a few lounge chairs where hikers can take a break, chat up the trail with other hikers or hop on a nearby computer to surf the web or send emails to family and friends. Then there are the binders.

The back and side walls are loaded with 3-ring binders that house photos taken of hikers that stopped here on their way through town. The photos serve as records

— literally snapshots in time of each person's historical journey on the AT. When we wanted to get to the ATC headquarters before they closed, we had no idea that one of the reasons would be to have our own snapshot added to the binders.

I went back to Harpers Ferry almost 13 years after we passed through. Riffling through the shots — six per page — I knew we'd be easy to find. We had each saved one clean shirt for the walk into town that day. By chance, they were both red. In 2001, the man behind the counter had asked us if we wanted to be photographed individually or together. We had chosen together.

Way back in the book, halfway down the page, I zeroed in on the prize.

On this most historical of journeys, we had left a tiny piece of our own in our wake. It is still there today.

CHAPTER 14

New York Part II

It had been thirteen years since we stepped foot in the Empire State. It was time for our reunion.

Harriman State Park, NY to High Point, NJ

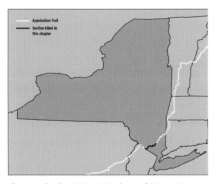

TRIP STATS
October 12, 2002 to October 19, 2002
48.0 miles
North to South

We had been eyeing this short section (that would complete our hikes through New York and New Jersey) for a while, and 2002 ended up being the right year for it. Given some of our past trail escapades, this would be quite the leisurely stroll through the New York and New Jersey. In fact, we would only climb to over 1800 feet once, at the appropriately named High Point, New Jersey on the final day.

Getting to the trail should have been easier than it was. Everything started according to plan. I had saved a seat on Amtrak train number 147 and Wayne joined me when the train made its stop in Hartford. Things figuratively started going off the rails when we got to Penn Station. We bought two tickets from Hoboken, NJ to Harriman, NY, as the train station was only two miles from where we would be getting on the trail.

We figured we had an hour to kill, so we set off to find a plate of chicken wings and cold beverages. That was our first mistake.

After we boarded our train and were underway, the conductor took our tickets, looked at us funny and gave us instructions to get off at next stop and take PATH train to Hoboken, then continue. We followed his instructions perfectly, but we arrived too late to catch the 6:38 train to Harriman, and the next train wouldn't leave until 12:35 a.m.

We were less than half a day into our trip and we were freelancing already! We figured

Canopus Lake

Pochuck Boardwalk NJ

we'd take the 7:45 train to Suffern, then wing it from there. At least we'd be closer to the trail.

It was the right call. A young conductor befriended us on the ride and lined up a cab to meet us at the station. The cabbie dropped us off at Harriman State Park at 9:15 p.m. As we walked into the park, it started raining. We walked up the park road a ways, hiked up onto a ridge and set up the dome. Home at last.

I can't look at day two as being anything but hilarious. It was raining when we woke up, so we decided to stay put until it stopped. We had a whole week to walk less than 50 miles. Why start out with wet gear?

By 11:00, the rain stopped and we decided to motivate. We climbed down out of the park, crossed Rt 17 and made the hardest climb of the week, a 700 foot ascent in 4/10ths of a mile known as "Agony Grind" on Arden Mountain. Just before we were about to head down the other side, Wayne said, "What a minute. Doesn't the Giants-Falcons game start at 1:00? We should stop for lunch."

The tent went up, the game came on and the massive feast began. Potato sticks and hot dogs were ready by the kick off. By the time the Giants-Falcons game ended and the 4:00 game kicked off, it was clear we were staying. Cheese fondue with mini-bagels was the fare. A one-mile day! We would never duplicate that feat again. At least we put the time to good use. Both of us caught up on our journaling and Wayne did some sewing, repairing his stuff sacks.

Monday was a great hiking day and we actually did some! It was glorious hiking over the low ridges of New York under sunny skies and crisp, 50 degree air. We didn't have to

make big mileage, so we set a nice 6 mile per day pace, stopping at 4:30.

While our decadent, one-mile days were a thing of the past, the rest of the trip gave us time to slow down and enjoy the scenery. The mixture of ridge walking and woods walking was superb. Then, on the next to last day, we were treated to one of the most ambitious and interesting sections of trail we would cross on the whole trip (or any trip)—the Pochuck Boardwalk.

Built at a cost of only $36,000, thanks to an incredible number of donated work hours, the mile long Pochuck Boardwalk and 110 foot suspension bridge was 24 years in the planning and seven years in the building. The hardest part of building it was reportedly hauling in and sinking the almost 900 metal piers that hold it in place. In addition to getting the trail off the busy area roads and providing a safer hiking experience, the boardwalk provides excellent wildlife viewing. Over 200 species of birds are known to frequent the marsh and it's filled with endangered and threatened plants as well.

For us, there was an added thrill to walking over the Pochuck Boardwalk and bridge. We didn't know they existed!

My 1988 guidebook description only referenced the road walk that used to be the trail. My map, on the other hand, showed a dotted line where the boardwalk and bridge were built. This is usually an indication of a planned relocation. But there was no way to know that the dotted line represented such a huge building project. Regardless, the bridge wasn't completed until seven years after the map and guide I owned were published. The net result was that we were blown away!

What an incredible walk to happen upon!

We took our time cruising across the boardwalk, admiring the view and the work that went into providing it.

At the end of the day, we started climbing the flank of High Point, found a beautiful spot with a view and called it a final full day out on the trail.

In the morning, we'd walk under a mile to reach Rt 23, then walk the seven miles down to Port Jervis to grab breakfast and a mid-morning train to New York City.

That night, as I thought back on our week on the trail, it occurred to me that the discovery of the Pochuck Boardwalk was the perfect analogy for this trip. That sometimes the best thing you can do for yourself is to get off a busy stretch of road and take a slower, more deliberate and more inspiring route through life.

CHAPTER 15

From Bland to Grand

The first days brought challenge, the last days brought joy.

Bland, VA to Damascus, VA

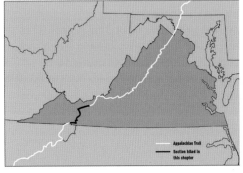

Appalachian Trail
Section hiked in
this chapter

TRIP STATS
September 24, 2003 - October xx, 2003
120.7 miles
North to South

I had just dozed off when the bus driver yelled, "Fort Chiswell". The bus came to a stop. I looked out the window long enough to see we were at a gas station/convenience store, then checked my watch. Just after 2:00 a.m. Not our stop. Ours was supposed to be Wytheville, Virginia.

"Must be the next stop.", I mused to myself, for Wayne had already gotten off the bus to stretch for a minute.

What a blessing that was! While he was standing near the bus, the driver opened the storage compartment and hauled our packs out. He was about to lock them in a shed in the corner of the lot, when Wayne intervened.

My mom used to say, "If you listen carefully, you can learn something every day." Apparently today's lesson was that Fort Chiswell and Wytheville were considered to be the same stop. It would have been nice if someone had let us know this earlier.

The bus left the lot and reentered the interstate highway system, leaving two weary souls in its wake. Wayne went into the store to ask the guy behind the counter where the Wytheville Days Inn was.

"Eight miles that way.", he said, pointing west. "You can walk the service road that parallels the highway if you want."

Burke's Garden

Wayne came back outside and delivered the news.

"Why do they call the stop Wytheville on the website, when it's eight freaking miles from town?", I asked, in the form of a complaint to the Virginia night sky.

It was closing in on 2:30 a.m. and, as usual, we weren't operating on much sleep after our trip down the east coast. (I'd been up for most of two days and Wayne not much less.) We briefly considered trying to find a camp spot nearby until we turned around and spotted the sign for the Super 8 hotel across the highway overpass.

By 3:00 a.m., I was at last lying down in a hotel bed, attempting to settle down after 48 plus hours of continuous commotion. Wayne did far better than I. He was sawing logs in under ten minutes. It took me another half hour to nod off.

Four and a half hours later, I awoke to the shower running. Wayne was motivated to get going again. We left our packs in the room and went to the truck stop next door for an epic breakfast (nothing like the double order of scrambled eggs served over two orders of cold grits our 18-wheeling neighbor at the counter bellied up to, put pretty impressive nonetheless).

On the way back to the hotel, we grabbed a piece of flattened cardboard from the recycle pile behind the gas station. Wayne went inside and bought a black marker. When he came back out, he wrote, "BLAND" in large letters on the cardboard. All we needed to do now was get our packs and check out of the hotel to be in the hitchhiking business.

Getting onto this section of trail in Bland, Virginia wasn't going to be easy, as we knew from our previous visit in 1997. It was the most difficult place to get on and off the trail we encountered, which was ironic, because an interstate highway went right underneath it. But, there was no place other than a breakdown lane next to two lanes of high speed traffic where we could get into or out of a car.

Now years later, I wondered if I would even be able to recognize the place, a nondescript overpass on the highway of life passing through a place called "Bland".

"If we get a ride, how are we going to tell them where to drop us off?", I asked Wayne as we stood with our sign on the I-77 on ramp.

"The road that crosses over is Route 612", he said. As always, the analyst had done his homework.

The on ramp was incredibly busy - so much so that when a pick up truck stopped to give us a ride, the driver almost caused a three car pile up.

Incredibly, after a few short stops (he was running errands and we were now along for the ride), he delivered us right to the base of our appointed embankment. We scrambled up and away from the traffic, reacquainted ourselves with the bridge just long enough to cross it and followed the white blazes up the road, then into the woods.

The more distance we put between us and the highway noise, the happier I got - an emotional power surge capable of overriding sleep deprivation. We were back on the trail!

Thankfully, we started out with a moderate hike along the ridge of Brushy Mountain. The late autumn sun shone down through the mostly leafless oaks, lighting up the forest floor. Life was good.

A few miles in, the trail bore right at a junction with an old woods road. Food and sleep were beckoning. We climbed away from the trail on the old road just until there was a flat-ish spot suitable for establishing camp and taking a 16 hour break.

During the night, the clouds stayed away. With no cloud cover to seal in the day's warmth, the temps dropped into the low 30s. I fell asleep without ever reaching for my winter hat. I'm not sure that's why I awoke with a savagely sore throat, but it probably contributed. It felt like I had swallowed a box of razor blades. I wasn't a happy camper.

Only once (20 years before on the Pacific Crest Trail) had I needed to change a hike due to illness. And I wasn't about to do it again unless there was no choice. One reason was the way I tended to assess the situation. If I had a personal motto, it would be something like, "Things are never as bad as they seem."

When confronted by a situation, my favored reaction is to "right size" its significance. An important distinction to make is that I don't go into out and out denial mode (as I once did, sometimes making matters worse), but more of a "this is the situation, what are my choices" mode.

When it comes to illness or injury, one thing I've always had in my favor is I'm a fast healer. This makes the likelihood of simply walking through things even greater. Even now, sitting in the tent struggling to get a bagel past the razor blade gauntlet in my throat, I was hopeful that the cold wouldn't move down into my chest - that a few days of brisk exercise would be the cure.

Nonetheless, I took a precaution I never used to take - I told Wayne about it. I used to think that my problems were for me to assess and recover from on my own. What I had come to realize was that keeping my health status to myself would be like taking the map or weather forecast away from Wayne and not letting him get updates. The only way this team could and did work well was if all the information was available for consideration.

"It's not like I broke an ankle or anything. Nothing to do but try to stay hydrated and walk through it.", I said. And with that, we buckled up our packs and continued our hike through southwestern Virginia.

We spent the day contouring Brushy Mountain, where the trail featured a fair share of minor climbs and descents. One of the morning ascents, I felt a pop in my left calf. I immediately stopped, dropped my pack and started an assessment, knowing that the rest of the hike depended on it.

When Wayne arrived on the scene, I was leaning on my left ski pole, testing my pain threshold.

"I'm falling apart. First my throat, now my leg.", I said. "I felt something pop in my calf."

I gingerly walked twenty yards down the trail and back again, leaning on my poles less and less as I went.

"It was more than a twinge and less of a pull. It still hurts, but not as much. If I downshift to first gear and keep it there for a while, I think I'll make it through." I said. "Nonetheless, I'm going to pull on my rain pants to keep the muscles warm."

Even with the slower pace, we were able to cover nine miles before arriving at a stream and a perfectly flat campsite, most conducive to sleep. If I was going to kick my ailments, this would be a good start.

But, my body had other plans. The cold moved from my throat into my chest and decided to set up camp on its own. All night long I drifted off only to awaken in a coughing fit.

The next morning, we left camp at 10:17 to begin a 3,000' climb of Garden Mountain. I was in rough shape. When I tried to take deep breaths, it initiated hacking fits. I slowed way down again and focused on steady progress. Always the optimist, I took solace in the fact that my calves were merely sore and mostly functional. But there was no escaping my breathing problem. The best I could do was take the shallowest of breaths and try to exhale through my nose - not easy to do on steep climbs.

We were able to squeeze out another nine mile day, culminating in a giant pot of lentil soup. Maybe that would help put a dent in my chest cold.

Once again, reality trumped wishful thinking. As Wayne snored in his half of the tent, I created my own symphony of chest cold sounds. Anxious to stop fixating on my illness, I reached for the radio and found a baseball game to keep me company. After a few innings, a rainstorm decided to join us, lending a background pitter patter of varying intensity. I shut off the game and tried to get some sleep, which ended up being like the storm — intermittent.

A foggy, wet climb in 48 degree temperatures wasn't the best prescription for me, but it was the one I was given. If we were going to make the town of Damascus on our scheduled day, taking a day off wasn't an option. The only solution was to walk through it.

As with most rainy days, there was little incentive to take breaks. It only meant getting colder and wetter. On the first climb, Chestnut Knob, I made it three quarters of the way to the top before I needed to stop. I took this as good news. Yesterday I would have been stopping all along the way.

At the top, we were rewarded with views of an amazing place. Burke's Garden, also known as "God's Thumbprint". When viewed from the air, it's easy to see why. Roughly 8 miles long by 4 miles wide, this idyllic cirque, heralded as the highest farming community in Virginia, is completely surrounded by mountains.

While it's easy to imagine the place's name being inspired by the Garden of Eden, the origin can actually be traced back to a joke.

In 1748, a local land owner hired a surveying party to scout the area. While preparing dinner one night, one of the surveyors named James Burke purportedly threw some potato peels on the ground.

One year later, when the surveyors returned, they discovered potatoes growing where they had camped. The place was thereby dubbed, "Burke's Garden", a name that endured.

By the end of the day, we'd covered twelve miles and were back on schedule. Even more welcome news was that my breathing was improving and I slept a solid eight hours.

The storm cleared out during the night and the forecast called for a few sunny days ahead. Today would be another chilly one - the temps stayed in the 40s - but we were treated to a great hike through woods and pastures. An eleven mile day brought us to a rhododendron thicket next to a stream, which we called home.

If ever we needed a 60 degree day, it was now. And we got it. There were two reasons we didn't want to linger at the campsite. One was we wanted to get out under the body and soul warming sun. The other was the truck stop less than an hour's walk away that would place heaping plates of eggs, sausage and home fries in front of us for the asking. I'm known to be a fast eater, but this was ridiculous. I felt like a Shop-Vac.

By early afternoon we reached a bench high on Glade Mountain overlooking the farmland below. We took off our packs and sat in the sun, simply to enjoy the moment. There hadn't been many opportunities to do that on this trip. Preoccupations with health issues and the need to make mileage can take some of the luster off of the joy if you let it. We decided that this was a fine opportunity to push back.

I pulled the stove out and we ate cheese and crackers while the soup water warmed. It seemed that I had gotten through the worst of my illness and my calves were finally making a comeback as well. And there was no place on earth I'd rather be in this moment than on this bench under the bone warming sun looking out at the beautiful world around me.

After 90 minutes of slowing down to the rhythm of Glade Mountain, we decided it was time to get moving again.

The afternoon was the best of the trip so far. I was ecstatic.

"This is the whole reason we hit the trail", I said to myself as we ambled over the top of Glade Mountain and down the other side. "Smiling, moving pain free and happy." It was a few days in the making.

Another good omen was that the last two climbs of the day went really well. No pain in the legs and no trouble breathing. Just a fabulous eleven mile day leading up to the grand finale - the climb into Virginia's highest mountains of them all — the Mount Rogers Recreational Area.

Ponies, Craisins® and Pain...oh my!

As I read the trail description in the tent on the morning of day seven, I could hardly contain my excitement. Over the years as the Appalachian Odyssey took shape, I would spend many a winter night browsing through the trail guides for regions we had yet to hike. The Southwest Virginia guide was one of my favorites. I yearned for the day I would hike the summit plateau of Mount Rogers - the highest point in Virginia and the highest point on the AT from there to Mount Washington.

The volcanic eruptions that formed Mount Rogers (and neighboring Whitetop and Pine Mountain) took place around 760 million years ago — 150 to 200 million years before the rest of the Blue Ridge Mountains were formed. The rocks of the region indicate that the eruptions that formed these mountains were more violent than those

Pine Mountain Summit

that formed other parts of the Blue Ridge (some rocks have mineral filled holes in them indicating where gas bubbles once escaped). It is also the only place in Virginia where evidence of ancient glaciation exists. The glaciers that left their mark in the Mount Rogers visited some half billion years before the last ice age.

One reason why these peaks are so high is that the density of the volcanic rock that formed them (rhyolite bedrock) is so resistant to the elements. The range towers above all else in proximity, offering amazing views from many places along the trail, including those that take in the Great Smokey Mountains to the southwest.

I was hoping that the weather would cooperate on summit day. Right now, it wasn't very promising. We were enveloped in fog and the forecast called for mist and clouds all day. As I read, Wayne did a mileage check.

"65 miles to go. Five and a half days to do it.", he said.

"Glad I'm feeling better. Should be a piece of cake. In shape and lighter packs.", I said. We'd been averaging over ten miles per day even though I was dragging. I was pretty optimistic about our ability to up the mileage closer to twelve.

As we drank our coffee, we tuned in the morning forecast on the mini radio, which in turn, called for an adjustment to our plans. The mist wasn't supposed to lift out until late in the evening. If we could do an eleven miler today, that would set us up to cover the high peaks during the two best weather days. Sometimes you can't help having to walk through areas purported to have great views without actually getting them. This time, we had a choice. We opted for the chance for great views from the Mount Rogers plateau and longer mileage days to end the trip.

The first half of the hike went really well for me, particularly day two. I was feeling the strongest I'd felt on the whole trip and was optimistic that all maladies — even the chest cold — were in my rear view mirror. We were far enough ahead of schedule to take another prolonged break, sitting in the sun in front of Old Orchard Shelter, talking with a guy who worked for Major League Baseball. Every year when the season ended, he hit the trail for a month. Sounded like a dream job to me.

The highlight of the day was popping out of the woods onto the Pine Mountain summit plateau. What a view! We were suddenly immersed in a panorama of open grassland punctuated by rock outcroppings. We dropped the packs and scrambled up the most prominent set of boulders to gain 360° views. While the entire view was impressive, our eyes were most drawn to the peaks of the distant Smokey Mountains.

"It will be pretty damn fun when we get to those.", I said as we stood with the world spread out in all directions.

"No doubt.", said Wayne. "No doubt."

The trail took us back into the woods for a while until we emerged into grassland

The Scales

again at a place called, "The Scales" — so named because it used to be a weighing station for the mountain's wild ponies. I wondered how the park service maintained the open grasslands on these high mountain ridges. In other areas, whole mountaintops are periodically burned to keep the summits open (as they were after the settlers cleared the land). The fires would keep trees from reclaiming the grasslands. Here in the Mount Rogers National Recreation Area, they didn't use flame to keep the fields open. They use cattle and wild ponies.

The wild pony herd, slightly larger than Shetland ponies and numbering about 150, spends the warm part of the year grazing on the high country undergrowth and, in turn, keeping the summit balds trimmed and open, while reducing the chance that a forest fire can get started or spread. In the winter, the herd heads down to lower elevations, where it is a bit warmer.

The herd is rounded up twice a year and checked by veterinarians to ensure the animals are in good health. But, other than that and perhaps supplemental grain feedings in harsh winters, the ponies can be considered wild. These mountains are their homes. And walking among them is one more of the unexpected privileges of hiking the AT.

We ended the day tucked into the woods near the edge of a field with tent door views of the valley and ridges beyond. The only sound other than crickets was the bleating of cows in an adjacent fenced in pasture. Tomorrow we would climb up and over Mount Rogers. The forecast called for a sunny day and highs in the 60s, followed by another one day storm. Our window would be open just long enough.

The following morning, I wrote in my journal, "I got a good night's sleep last night.

Bronchitis did not have me hacking all night. Perhaps I am turning the corner."

Little did I know that I'd be hitting the wall instead.

The day began optimistically enough. The sun was out, the leaves were putting on a fall display of color that had only gotten better during our nine days on the trail and I had a full belly, thanks to my double oatmeal packet breakfast.

I was in the lead and feeling good for most of the climb to Rhododendron Gap, but something happened just as I reached the top. It was like someone had pulled my metaphorical power chord out of the wall socket. I had had many energy deficits before, but normally I could feel them coming on. This one was sudden and severe. I felt dazed, although not disoriented. I was so exhausted though, I felt like going to sleep on the spot.

I emerged from the woods into open grassland, the scenery once again became spectacular. I could see the trail winding before me over the plateau. With the steepest climb behind me, I thought that maybe I could regain my strength. It had happened before, I reasoned.

I tried to stay ahead of Wayne, and did for the first half mile, when we caught up to a day hiking couple that had stopped to look at the ponies. They asked me if I could take a picture of them. This was Wayne's chance to boogie ahead, and he took it.

I slowed way down, struggling to get across the plateau. Normally, I fairly danced across the lands above treeline. This was my favorite type of terrain.

"What is going on? Where is my energy?", I asked myself. The day hikers and Wayne disappeared over the ridge and somewhere into the future. I was by my rubber-legged self. I wanted more than anything to take in the magnitude of the beauty around me. The only way to do that was to try to deny my energy deficit.

It wasn't working.

My footing was getting really sloppy. If it weren't for my poles, I would have fallen several times. I had to pay attention to my health, not the scenery — at least for now. I was hoping that Wayne would stop for lunch soon.

It wasn't happening.

Every potentially good rest spot I saw now became a reason to get perturbed at him. What wasn't he stopping? Of course, I could have simply stopped myself, but that brought its own issues. He'd be getting further and further ahead of me.

At 12:15, I staggered into the clearing in front of the Thomas Knob Shelter. Wayne was sitting in the shelter with two through hikers — Morning Moose and Nanowolf. He handed

Mount Rogers

me half a bag of Craisins saying, "I ate half."

I didn't even take my pack off. I poured the contents into my mouth in just three helpings. Only then did I set my pack down for a rest. I slugged down some water and handed Wayne the guidebook and map. After a few minutes, he weighed in.

"We need to make Buzzard Rock today. That will leave a 13 mile day tomorrow and a 9 miler into

Damascus.", he said, handing me the map.

"I want to bag Mount Rogers while we are here, don't you?", I asked. "It's a one mile round trip."

He nodded his approval. "If so, we'd better get going."

The Craisins seemed to make a difference. Or maybe it was the rest. Nonetheless, we climbed up to the Mount Rogers side trail, hid our packs in the woods and dashed up to the summit, which is covered with Red spruce and Fraser fir trees — it is the northernmost occurrence of such a forest in the southern Appalachians. The smell of balsam was a welcome treat for a couple of New Englanders who have spent so much time hiking through conifers. But the tree that produced the familiar fragrance is one we don't see in the northeast. The Fraser fir is only found between here and southern North Carolina at elevations above 5500 feet.

We couldn't stay on the summit for long. We had a long afternoon ahead of us, complete with a 500 foot drop and an 800 foot climb up to Buzzard Rock. With my new found energy, I thought it was a reasonable expectation. There was a shelter near Elk Garden Gap. Our plan was to stop there and make soup before the last climb.

On the way down the mountain, my energy void returned - again with startling speed. I let Wayne pass, letting him know that I was losing it again.

"Please don't get too far ahead of me.", I said.

"I'll wait for you at the shelter. Shouldn't be far.", he replied.

At just past 3:00, I entered a clearing to find Wayne, but no shelter.

"It's gone. They tore it down.", he said, adding "I got here ten minutes ago.", before I could ask. "Three miles to go. Do you want to skip the soup and go for camp?"

"Sure.", I said, without even thinking back to what a difference the Craisins made just a few hours earlier.

What a mistake.

Whitetop Gap

On the way down from the clearing of the "shelter formerly known as Elk", the clouds roared in and the temperature plummeted - a reminder of how quickly weather can change at elevation. I had experienced this many times, notably on Katahdin and in the White Mountains, where sunny days had quickly become stormy ones. I was glad we had timed our trip across Mount Rogers so well. But now, I was particularly susceptible to the changes around me. As I stepped into the open pastureland next to Virginia Route 600, I stopped to put on my fleece jacket. There was a trail kiosk there. The roof over it provided just a little relief from the rain shower that had moved in.

On the first part of the climb, we passed a spring. While we were filtering our 6 quarts of water, I started shivering like crazy. I wish we had made that soup. What a bonehead mistake!

When we started climbing up Whitetop (the second highest mountain in Virginia), I started wobbling again. My tank was empty. Fortunately, Wayne was close by and there were a few promising camp spots in our midst.

"Hey. If you want to call it a day, let's do it.", he said.

Underneath his offer, I felt a sense of disappointment that we weren't going to make Buzzard Rock. I don't know if it was true, but that was my impression. So, instead of taking him up on the offer, I insisted on going further.

Mistake number two.

Twenty minutes later, I declared myself done for the day. I simply couldn't go on. I hated to throw in the towel, but I had zero energy.

This time, there was no second guessing Wayne's feeling on the subject. His expression said, "Why the hell didn't you say that 20 minutes ago?", but his voice said, "Where do you suggest?"

He put his pack down and found a spot a few hundred feet up the trail. It wasn't as great as the ones we had passed, but it would do. I was quite sure I'd be asleep as soon as supper was complete anyway.

The next morning I wrote in my journal,

"I suspect that the day was a culmination of little sustained rest on the trip, my bronchitis, many nights of poor sleep and challenging terrain. But two things I know for certain: 1. I will NEVER hike again without a granola bar in my holster pouch. 2. I need to rebound for a 14 mile day tomorrow or we will be in danger of missing our bus on Thursday."

As predicted, I fell asleep at 8:00 p.m. When I awoke, a lot had changed. The Florida Marlins had beaten the Cubs 9-8, Arnold Schwarzenegger had been elected governor of California and the storm that had shown up so quickly yesterday afternoon had departed, leaving cloudless heavens as the backdrop to our day. Another heavenly miracle is that I felt great. I wasn't going to take it as gospel until I had a bit of a test drive, but I was hopeful.

I wasn't going to leave camp on anything less than a full tank. We went through the food bags and opted for a double serving of mac and cheese. In addition to full bellies, we had another big plus going for us in our quest for a 14 mile day - we would drop 2500 feet over the first half of it. But first, Whitecap Mountain had a treat in store. The morning light lit up the golden grasses of the immediate ridges and the distant steel blue mountains we had traversed over the last nine days. Far below, the valleys were holding onto their morning fog. Whenever I encounter a scene like this, I think of the folks that live below the fog. They will not enjoy this view for a few hours hence, when the sun has finally encouraged the clouds to leave the farms, pastures and trees behind for another day.

The view was compelling us to stay even while the reality of our challenge was urging us forward. Miles to go before we could sleep.

What a difference the day made! We covered five miles in the first two hours, as we blasted down from Buzzard Rock toward our date with Damascus. The rolling party continued all day. I felt like I had experienced an overnight health infusion. I was going nonstop up and over ridges that would have staggered me yesterday. Finally, on the next to last day of our hike, the real me was back. We just might make that bus!

We found a beautiful camp spot high on a ridge, set up the tent and dropped down a side trail to a lean-to with a nearby stream. Unlike yesterday, when I could barely form words due to my exhaustion, conversation now bubbled forth all the way to the water filling ritual, back to our camp and all the way through dinner. It was our last night on the trail and there was a lot to reminisce about.

The last morning on the trail is always bittersweet for me. I get caught in the vortex between the pull of creature comforts and the draw of being out in the mountains. As I was waiting the few minutes for Wayne to strap the tent onto his pack, I peered longingly through the trees at the distant ridges. In a few days, these mountains would be 1000 miles from my window. I did my best to savor them before I pulled my pack onto my bent knee, slid it over my shoulders and tightened the waist belt, which was snugging up a lot tighter than when I started this trip. I figured I had lost at least 10 pounds - maybe in sweat alone.

Wayne was about to put his pack on. I took one last look at the ridges, turned to Wayne and said, "I'll see you down the trail. The one with the cheeseburger at the end of it."

"And a bus", he said.

CHAPTER 16

Virginia in Winter

A December hike requires a different approach from the start.

Harpers Ferry, WV to Front Royal, VA

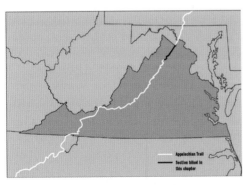

Appalachian Trail
Section hiked in
this chapter

TRIP STATS
December 16, 2004 - December 22, 2004
53.42 miles
North to South

2004 was ridiculously busy, even by my calendar filling standards and expectations. Yet, the one thing I should have made room for kept getting pushed out until there were hardly any weeks left.

Three times I had added placeholder dates for the AT only to rescind them due to incoming work. Wayne had rightfully given up on me, saying, "Maybe we can get out in the spring."

In mid November, I took another look at the calendar. The week before Christmas was a notoriously slow period for marketers — all the work that could be done to spur last minute purchases was already completed.

The 50-ish mile trip from Harpers Ferry to Front Royal would be perfect for this time of year, when the days were also at their shortest. We decided to go for it to make sure we made some headway before the dawn of 2005.

Packing for a winter trip puts a premium on preparation. In more temperate times of year, you can get away with carrying less. But in the mountains — even the Virginia mountains — you need to be ready for single digit temperatures.

The best way I've found to pack for this kind of trip is to focus on the implications cold weather has on your choices of food, clothing and water. Normally, you could add shelter to the list, but because we carry a tent built for the task, we're literally well covered.

One of the reasons we really like the design of our chosen dome is that it has 4 poles (not three), so it has more stability against wind and wind driven rain or snow. Another nice feature is that the rain fly extends nearly to the ground and can be staked out taut to do a better job of shedding water. Some tents have rain flys that are so small, I wonder why they bother. They cover the top half of the tent, so they only effectively work if rain is falling straight down (which rarely happens). Even then, the water runs off only to splash on the ground next to the tent and coming back inside through the floor seams. Visions of sitting on top of your gear in a 2 x 2' dry spot in the center of a tent while a storm rages outside doesn't cut it. And the fact that we've sat out dozens of rain- and snowstorms in this tent while staying completely dry is one huge reason we dubbed it "The Pleasure Dome" in the first place.

With the choice of shelter out of the way, I turned my attention to other gear and clothing. As you may imagine, I have accumulated quite a collection of winter gear. Northern New England is a great winter camping playground. I was lucky to have spent my formative years and decades thereafter with friends and colleagues that loved putting on skis or snowshoes and exploring the woods and mountains. The alternative (spending entire winters indoors) can do a real number on you mentally. By the time late March rolls around, you are going stir crazy.

Before I even started packing for this trip to Northern Virginia, I looked at historic weather data for the region and, as our departure date neared, the local forecast. Simply put, the temps could range anywhere from single digits to above 50°F. We had to pack for the coldest, while being prepared for the warmest.

I hauled my giant plastic tub full of winter hats, gloves and other cold weather gear down from the attic and set it on the living room floor. For this trip I'd need a lightweight winter hat for sleeping, a heavyweight one for being outdoors, a balaclava (a polypro "helmet" that covered my entire head except my eyes and nose), two pairs of gloves (one lightweight set for use in the tent and heavier weight ones for the coldest

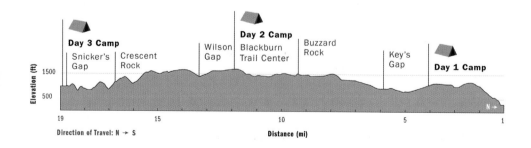

temperatures). The lightweight gloves could also be used while hiking. I liked to wear them in the mornings until I warmed up. Then I'd stuff them in my guidebook holster to keep them handy.

For clothing, I choose two sets of long johns, two sets of "short johns" (for warmer weather walking), nylon shorts and both short- and long-sleeved shirts. I also brought a fleece jacket with "pit zips" that could be zipped open from mid-upper arm to mid torso to vent perspiration. I'd wear it more than anything I brought with me on the trip. Finally, there was my storm layer — a Gore-Tex anorak (a pullover with a hood that also has pit zips) and Gore-Tex rain pants. It takes a raging storm to make me hike with both pieces on. I detest hiking with rain pants or any kind of traditional pants for that matter. The fabric is so restrictive to the kind of leg bending required to climb hills. My preferred cold weather set up is long johns and nylon shorts. If it's really pouring or snowing hard, I will reach for the rain pants — most often accompanied with a sigh of resignation and mutterings of, "this sucks".

My choice of socks never changes with the seasons. Plenty of wool/polyester hiking socks and a fresh set of liner socks for every day out on the trail.

I stuffed my hats and gloves into one nylon sack, my shorts, shirts and underwear into a second one and my socks into a third. I'd wear the fleece jacket on the trip to the trail along with my rain pants. When I was almost done packing, I'd stuff the anorak into the pack, so I could get to it on short notice.

Next choice: sleeping bag. I went back up to the attic and looked at my stack of sleeping bags. This is akin to Goldilocks weighing her porridge options. I own six sleeping bags, which I suppose sounds excessive, but most of them get regular use.

I looked at the manila tag hanging from the cotton storage sack on top of the pile.

"-30°F. Too hot.", I said aloud.

I dug down and tossed the 40° and 20° bags to the side. They'd be too cold.

I looked at the tag on one of the three remaining choices. "Aha! My zero-degree bag. Just what I was looking for." Even if the temperatures dipped into the teens, I'd be plenty comfortable in that. The tent adds about ten degrees of warmth just by creating a confined space with two people in it. If we lit a candle, it would even be a tad warmer. I pulled the bag out of its large cotton long-term storage stack and stuffed it into my favorite nylon compression stuff sack (to shrink the bag down to its smallest size for carrying). That took care of shelter and clothing. Now for the food.

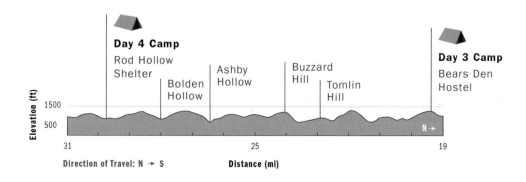

Leading up to trips, the two things Wayne and I banter most about are the transportation and food choices. For this trip, the traveling would be as easy as it gets — one train to Washington, D.C., then another to Harpers Ferry.

The food planning for this winter trip took a little more discussion that usual. We decided to skew more toward warming meals (more oatmeal/fewer bagels for breakfast and more soups to eat as a preambles to dinner). Adding already warmed fuel to the furnace is always a good idea.

The one place it may seem most logical to eat warm foods — on a blustery day's lunch break — is the least likely place for us to do it, even if it's only heating water to make instant soup. There are two reasons for this. The first is that we need to stand or sit idly while the water warms up. In the meantime, we cool down. If the wind is a factor, it takes the stove even longer to do its job (even though we employ a wind screen) and the wind will chill us down even faster.

The second is that something as easy as boiling water takes valuable set up and packing time. This is of no concern when they days are long and we can make up miles in late afternoon or early evening. But when it gets dark closer to 4:00, every minute counts.

As always, we go with what the conditions have to offer. A lean-to is often a great place to duck out of the wind, if we happen upon one at lunch time. Or, if we are ahead of schedule, we may decide to stop for soup regardless. But, we carried plenty of granola bars, crackers and cheese for the days we didn't want to linger.

For dinners, we added more pasta to the menu. With only five of them to prepare on the trail, I went over the top, buying cheese tortellini with black olive pesto and Parmesan cheese as the coup de gras. No all broth/no noodles soup for me, thank you.

As the trip approached, I'd begin each day lying in bed going over my mental food and gear list. Batteries for my headlamp and candles were at the top of my list. When you are in the tent for up to 16 hours a day, you want to know you can read the guidebook, write in your journal or whatever without doing it under a failing and fading bulb. Candles reduce the need for using batteries and also add a few degrees of warmth to the tent. We created and perfected a candle lantern design that weighs almost nothing and hangs from the roof of the tent at the right height for warmth, illumination and safety.

I was 99% there with the gear list, when one morning I sat upright in bed. I had forgotten two critical pieces of safety gear — hunter orange fabric vests and reflective wrist bands. I ran across the hall to my office and typed "Virginia hunting season" into

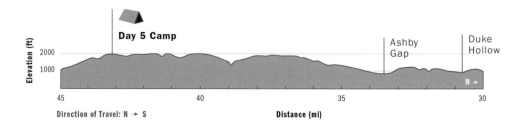

the search engine. Just as I suspected, deer season was still underway. We'd need to drape hunter orange over our packs to ensure we'd be seen.

Some people believe that hunting is not allowed on the Appalachian Trail and surrounding lands. This is seldom the case. Even if there was no hunting allowed on the trail, it would be difficult for hunters to know either when they were on the trail or shooting toward it. The trail corridor is narrow (1000 feet wide on average). It is easy for people to happen upon the trail from other directions without knowing it is even there.

The reflective wrist bands were for safety off the trail. If we needed or wanted to leave the trail to say, eat a cheeseburger at a restaurant and we were racing the light to get back to the trail, we wanted to be sure to be seen. Drivers aren't used to seeing hikers out in the cold weather months and road shoulders can be awfully narrow. In one case, in Tennessee, we were thankful that we'd brought the wrist bands along. It was obvious that the drivers were seeing us well in advance of approaching us and giving us wide berth as a result.

With a few days to go, there was only one detail left. Where were we going to stay when we got to Harpers Ferry? Because the town is a three-season tourist destination, we knew the lodging options in December would be sparse. Most places would be boarded up for the winter. But we didn't want to arrive at 6:15 p.m. and be walking out to the trail in the darkness either. Luckily I found a campground willing to rent us an unheated cabin for the night for $40. The owners sent me an email the day before the trip confirming the reservation and letting us know that the key would be waiting for us in an envelope in a predetermined spot.

It was the right decision. When we arrived in Harpers Ferry, it was in the high 20s and headed to an overnight low of 15°F. Man, was it cold in that cabin. I wasn't complaining (much), but I couldn't wait to dive into my sleeping bag.

On December 17th, we experienced a new first from the trail — writing Christmas cards from a table in a cafe as we awaited delivery of omelets, home fries and bottomless cups of coffee.

Only two more stops before we would climb out of town. The first was at a 7-11, where I bought two gallons of water. The second was at ATC Headquarters, where we found our picture in the black binder marked "2001".

When we got underway, I didn't put my anorak on, thinking I'd warm up quickly. What a mistake. The bridge across the Shenandoah River was long and an arctic blast was blowing through the gap. By the time I got halfway across, I was in no man's land. Should I stop and put my wind shell on, all the while exposed to the piercing wind or keep on walking? I decided to gut it out.

On the other side, we hiked steeply up the ridge and thankfully, escaped the wind. I was having a really hard time finding my groove. Wayne passed me half way up and led the way to the top. Once there, we took a quick break. Thankfully, there was little wind just shy of the ridge top, and with the leaves down, bright sun above and temps in the 40s, it actually felt warm. After a pleasant four mile walk along the ridge, we found a flat spot with a view and hunkered down for cheese fondue with pieces of fresh baguette (the first of the over the top dinners).

The next four days featured a rollercoaster of temperature swings, just as the weather data had foretold. On day one, the temps climbed to the mid 30s and we enjoyed some spectacular December hiking. It was a real treat to be feeling good and trekking over gently rolling terrain all day. The landscape was a giant canvas of brown ground cover. All the leaves had come down, letting us enjoy views through the trees you can only get in early spring, late fall and winter. Eight miles in, we set up camp with a western view and watched the sun go down from our loungers, albeit also in our sleeping bags.

On day three, the temps climbed back into the 40s and the wind held off again. It was cool enough to keep us moving along, but not so bone chilling that we couldn't comfortably stop for breaks. After seven miles and five sustained climbs, we made Snickers Gap, where it was only 3/10ths of a mile between us and burgers, fries and wings at the Horseshoe Curve restaurant. We went for it, then finished the day by climbing one mile back to the ridge top.

Day four was the crux day. As I wrote in my journal, "Leave it to us to do the hardest ten miles in Northern Virginia on one of the shortest days of the year."

While the day before had its share of undulations, they didn't warrant an official nickname. That changed when we turned the page to December 19th. The rises and falls on the section we hiked today earned it the name "The Rollercoaster". It earned that name and a few more new ones from me as I couldn't get close to establishing a rhythm.

Our goal was to reach Rod Hollow Shelter, ten miles out. By 11:30, we were less than one-third of the way there. Nonetheless, we stopped to make soup and snarf down a few handfuls of dried cranberries and almonds. If we were going to make a go of it, we needed fuel.

It was the right call. The temperature started dropping and kept right on going. By the time I reached the top of the next to last ridge of the day, I was greeted by snow showers and a brutal northwest wind. Now the footing joined the lateness of day as threats to our making Rod Hollow before dark. I was so glad I had poles to help me stay upright as I picked my way down into Bolden Hollow.

One more climb and descent to go. When we arrived in Rod Hollow Shelter, we were absolutely gassed. By the time we got the tent set up, I was shivering like crazy. We still needed to get water and it was almost dark. Neither one of us had to say anything. We grabbed our water bottles and the filter, threw our packs in the tent and bolted down the side trail to the stream.

Once we started filling up the bottles, there was no way I was going back to the tent without all of them topped off. In theory, we could grab enough only for dinner and come back in the morning for more, but I didn't want to wake up and leave the warmth

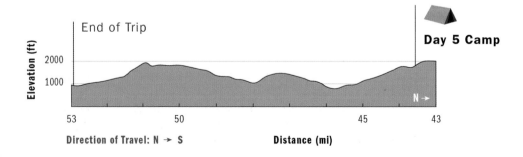

The view from the ridge above the Blackburn Trail Center in northern Virginia on a much warmer September day.

of my sleeping bag to go pump water, when I could be drinking hot coffee instead. I was sure Wayne agreed.

Back in the tent, we made a big pot of soup. The temps dropped all night until it got down to the low teens. Again, we made the right call. We could stay warm and hydrate.

Now our greatest challenge would be keeping our water bottles from freezing overnight. I put my two full quarts into my sleeping bag with me. My body heat would help keep them from freezing, but it was annoying to have them there. Waking up at 2:00 a.m. in 13°F weather with the equivalent of an ice pack against your leg or the small of your back comes with the territory, even when you carry insulated water bottle carriers. Yet, it was still better than having to make a colder walk to the stream to fetch morning coffee water.

Saturday, December 20, 2004 was the coldest day of our 28-year adventure. I woke up when the sun was high enough to illuminate the tent. The walls and roof were frosted from our overnight respiration. I sat up and lit the stove to get the water going for making coffee and instant oatmeal (in that order). Some may question the sanity of cooking in a tent. But another reason we carry the dome is that it provides enough floor and overhead space to make operating a stove quite a bit safer. In addition to open flame, another concern with tent cooking is that it may attract animals. On a twelve degree morning in late December, we were willing to take the chance that any animals that would normally be interested were also hunkered down somewhere.

Man, it was cold. As soon as the stove sputtered forth, I got my arms right back into the bag. The high temp for the day was only predicted to hit the low 20s. I'm glad I brought the right cold weather regalia. Even so, once we left the campsite, I knew we'd have to keep moving until we found our next camp spot.

When I put my pack on to get started, it was one-third smaller. I was wearing almost every piece of cold weather clothing I had — fleece jacket, rain pants, anorak, even the balaclava and neck gaiter. Even so, the wind was literally mind numbingly cold. On some ridge tops, we were greeted by ice cream headache inducing blasts. It was invigorating to say the least.

At exactly noon, we hit Ashby Gap, marked by a paved road.

"There's a barbecue joint less than a mile from here. Just sayin.", I said to Wayne, who had just ambled into the gap.

"Works for me.", he said.

That less than one mile walk was the toughest of the day. The wind was screaming through the gap in skull splitting fashion. At times, I turned around and walked backwards just to find relief.

We found even greater relief in the sunny front window of Doc's Barbecue. It was the next best thing to a tropical beach. We set up an impromptu drying rack in the blazing sun as we waited for pulled pork sandwiches followed by German Chocolate Cake to emerge from the kitchen.

The one-hour infusion of food and warmth was nirvana. With full bellies, full water bottles and the wind at our backs, we set sail for the ridge tops with new found enthusiasm. Even though the temperatures would drop down again, we had weathered the worst of it.

The next morning we stopped at the first stream to get water. The filter was frozen and inoperable. I stuck it inside my jacket until it thawed enough to use. It was the last cold related hiccup we'd have on the trip.

As we crossed through the G. Richard Thompson Wildlife Management Area, we met a father and son team of bird hunters who told us they were glad to see we were wearing blaze orange.

"You should have seen this place last Saturday.", they said. "It was mobbed with deer hunters. We've never seen it so packed."

During the afternoon, the temperatures climbed into the high 40s. No more need for winter clothing. The walking was free and easy again. At the end of the day, we found the best site of the whole trip, tucked high in the corner of an open field with farms and mountains stretched out before us. The late afternoon sun spread long, Monet-like shadows across the fields, with the ridge we had traversed all afternoon rising behind them.

I sat outside on my lounger to watch the show, scribbling in my journal between viewings.

"I am really glad we got this great day and very nice weather overall — at least no rain all week. Just a bit of snow. What a treat to only have a short winter of non-hiking ahead of me. I am usually taking a trail break from October until some time in April. This time, it will only be three plus months until I get back on the path, wherever it may be."

The last day it was hard to get motivated, this time not because it was so cold, but because it was so beautiful. No need to keep the arms in the bag today.

I sat up and unzipped the tent door to view the sunrise unencumbered while sipping my French Roast. The forecast called for sunny skies and 50 degree temperatures. The idea to have a second cup of coffee was tempting, but we opted for having it somewhere down the trail instead.

The hike out had a festive mood to it from beginning to end. We stopped and chatted a few times, notably at the newly constructed Molly Denton Shelter, which had a huge porch facing the sun. Sitting trailside at noon in short sleeve shirt and shorts, it was hard to believe we were recently dealing with arctic temperatures and a frozen water filter. It was one of the best late season days on the trail I could remember.

And if I hadn't finally made it a priority, I would have missed it.

CHAPTER 17

The Test

I had hiked thousands of miles in my career leading up to this trip. Several of them had been grueling. Yet, I wasn't prepared for the lingering bouts with self-destructive thoughts that accompanied me through the mountains of Tennessee.

Damascus, VA to Erwin, TN

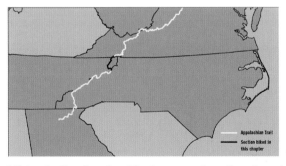

TRIP STATS
November 24 - December 8, 2005
128 miles
North to South

One thing for sure, we'd be among the last section hikers on the Appalachian Trail in 2005. We would have liked to have been hiking in October, but I had mountains of work assignments I needed to climb first.

It looked like the first window of opportunity I was going to have to get back on the trail was just after Thanksgiving. Things were shaping up nicely for me to ease into the trip until a number of projects that were looking like "someday possibilities" at once became here and now realities with "by Thanksgiving" due dates - radio scripts, newspaper and magazine ads, articles, product descriptions for catalogs, you name it. My orderly plan for hike preparations went out the window and was suddenly thrown in with all my other assignments - 18 hours stretches of writing like a short order cook trying to keep the patrons happy became my routine. This, of course, has all the makings of a recipe for disaster. Something had to give and it was my health.

I made the final edits to the final piece late Thanksgiving morning and hit the "send" button. Now to pack. Late November in the mountains can be cold anywhere in the northern hemisphere. I wasn't going to underestimate the real chance for single digit temps in Tennessee. This meant carrying a heavier load - zero degree sleeping bag, long underwear, heavy socks, extra hat and gloves, etc.

As usual, I collected all the "must have" and "maybe take along" gear and clothing and threw them in quasi-organized piles on the living room floor. Damn, I own a lot of gear! Sitting with legs akimbo, I swiveled around and made pre-emptive strikes. "How many wool socks and liners do I really need?", etc. Amidst this orderly inventory, I periodically leapt to my feet and dashed off in search of something I'd just thought of... AA batteries for my headlamp, topping off my vial of olive oil for cooking pasta and the like. Anyone who knows me knows not to disrupt my train of thought during an intense packing session.

Once I determined what clothing made the cut, I placed "like items" in nylon stuff sacks (e.g., shirts, underwear and bandanas in one, socks in another). Then I repackaged every bit of food. All extraneous packaging had to go. It's too heavy. Most everything went into zip-seal bags. Then I threw all the food into its own giant stuff sack, which felt like it could double as a canoe anchor.

I placed everything in my pack, hoisted it on and staggered under the load. I wasn't too concerned. I would have another chance to weed out gear at Wayne's house. For now, I was due at Thanksgiving dinner with the family in 15 minutes.

After the pumpkin pie, it was time for planes, trains and automobiles, Master's Tour style. First I drove to Wayne's house in Tolland, CT, then stayed up until 1:30 a.m. repacking (weeding out more gear, finalizing menus, double checking fuel canister choices, etc.). This was the last chance to get everything nailed down.

The next morning, we were off to catch a train from Hartford to Philadelphia, another one from Philly to Lynchburg, VA, a bus from Lynchburg to Bristol, Tennessee, then a ride from Bristol to Damascus, VA. We worked in a quest for a Philly cheesesteak and a few hours at karaoke night at the Lynchburg Holiday Inn to spice things up. Karaoke night was the best. We were certainly a sight walking in with our ginormous packs!

By the time we were dropped off in Damascus, I was on fumes. I didn't sleep much on the train ride down the east coast nor the ensuing bus rides across Virginia to Knoxville or from Knoxville to Bristol - a combination of being jostled around and not wanting to miss the adventure in front of me.

The hardest trip of all

Of all the journeys we took on the AT, I remember this one as being at once one of the most beautiful and mentally excruciating.

I have noted many times over the years that the most beautiful sights on the trail are often preceded by difficult climbs. That was true on this trip, but there were also feelings that were new to me - there were times I struggled when there were no climbs and even more frightening - there were times I struggled to find joy.

In thousands of miles of hiking, this was a completely foreign and terrifying concept. In the past, I never had any difficulty finding enjoyment on the trail. It was my access to fun and adventure. The whole time I was on or near the path, I was either in or near a blissful state. Sure there were times when I got frustrated or felt off of my game, but the episodes were merely little bumps in the road. This trip was different, with longer, more intense detours into negative thoughts that threatened to color my experience like a winter gray sky.

In retrospect, I can see that the whole lead up to this trip was setting me up for exhaustion and frustration. But at the time, I was too deep into the woods to have a healthy perspective. All I knew is my body and mind weren't performing in ways I was used to.

On day one, we climbed out of Damascus in 60-degree weather to arrive at a side trail to water a few miles in. We pitched the tent and fell asleep outdoors on our ground pad/loungers. At 4:30, we went into the tent, made dinner, then crashed for a solid 14 hours.

Day two was another glorious day. The temperature reached 67 degrees, It would be the last of the delightfully warm days and the first I would feel exhausted by mid afternoon. We called it a day when we arrived at Abingdon Gap Shelter at 3:30. I was hoping another good night's rest would do the trick for me. The wind had other plans. It gusted 20 mph all night, making prolonged sleep impossible.

Day three was a full day of rolling hills. The ups and downs were kicking my ass. My journal said it all. "We began a sustained climb through the oaks until we reached the summit of Locust Knob. I was really dragging. Each uphill was an endless struggle. Reduced to psyching myself up by saying "one, two, one, two" as I slowly placed one foot in front of the other all the way up. What the hell is the matter with me?" I had almost nothing in the tank and was emotionally and physically exhausted.

For 48 years, I had learned to trust - even lean on - my ability to draw strength from my reserves. But today, for the first time, on a mountainside trail in Tennessee, the tank was almost empty. Doubting my physical and mental ability to continue was a scary new territory to explore, and my mind took off and ran to a place that scared the hell out of me. I began hearing an unfamiliar inner voice chastising me for

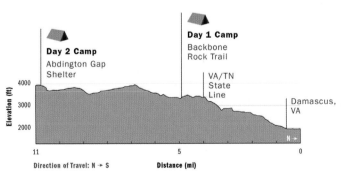

being weak, for not being in shape, for carrying too much gear and for not being able to scamper up mountains like I could 30 years ago.

For a time, I bought into this thinking, yelling at myself like a drill sergeant, exhorting myself to climb up and over the peak.

"Come on, don't be a wuss. Get your ass up and over this frigging mountain."

It was effective, but even in the moment, I recognized that my joy killing inner drill sergeant wasn't someone I wanted to be with again.

Thankfully, I was able to leave the berating voice and negative self talk on the mountain's summit. A nice downhill trail helped, I'm sure. We set up camp under oaks and rhododendrons next to a trailside spring and staked the tent fly out so it was extra taut. Rain was on the way and we wanted to keep the inside of the tent as dry as possible.

It poured all night. The tent stayed remarkably dry inside, despite 12 hours of incessant 20 mph wind driven rains - except the corner where I had stuffed my rain jacket. It was soaked.

Day four was perfect hypothermia weather - 42 degrees and steady precipitation. A wet day dampens the body and the spirit. A cold, wet day can do even more damage. As

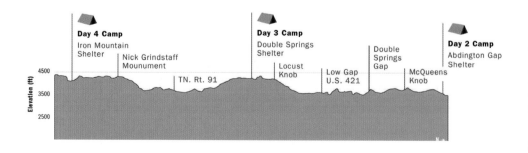

uncomfortable as it is to walk in this kind of weather, stopping in it can be dangerous - even deadly. The first signs of hypothermia are uncontrollable shivering and slurred speech. After that, your brain functions get increasingly unreliable, Then, you just want to go to sleep and die.

There are a number of ways to fend off hypothermia. Among them are making sure you have enough fuel (food) in your system, staying on the move to keep your body warm and staying as dry as possible. We covered the food part with double servings of oatmeal served with handfuls of dried apples.

We loaded our packs inside the tent, then stepped out into the rain to take it down. Carrying a soaking wet and heavy tent fly all day is part of the rainy day hiking bargain. The first glimpse of the sun always brings hopes of a tent drying celebration.

On cue, one mile into the day, just as we crossed a pasture, the rain stopped and sun came through. We were psyched! It looked like the storm was lifting. Big smiles. But they were short lived. The wind switched to the northwest again and the rain came back with added purpose. Soaked to the bone, we had two choices: pitch the tent and dive in or keep walking to generate our own warmth. We had too many miles to go and we were already behind schedule. We kept walking.

At the 8 mile mark, we came to the Iron Mountain Shelter, a good place to duck out of the rain for a few minutes. While we waited for the ramen water to heat, we wolfed down a bagel with cream cheese. Man, was that needed.

The rain made its last stand in the afternoon. By the time we dove into the tent at 6:10, the rain and wind were gone. The clouds disappeared to reveal wall to wall stars and the bare trees let us to get a panoramic view of the show - one nice benefit of winter hiking. The temps plunged to the low 30s. So glad to be warm, dry and full of piping hot soup and after dinner tea in the comfort of the tent.

Day five arrived with bright sun. We were so happy to see it after yesterday's psychological slog. Early on, we stopped for a half hour to soak in the heat while looking down on Watuga Lake. For the first time on the trip, I was able to cruise along over the ups and downs for miles without the latent uphill drag. Could I be overcoming my rant inducing affliction and getting into trail shape? Late in the day, we crossed Watuga Dam Road, then climbed to a ridge top camp spot. We ate a heaping plate of pepperoni, cheese and crackers, then promptly fell asleep.

Day six was sunny and cold. The trail dropped us down to the paved dam road, where we rejoiced in our ability to crank some miles while barely lifting our feet. We walked over the impressive concrete dam, gaining a neat perspective on the giant intake turbines above, then climbing a ridge next to the lake for an aerobic morning jaunt.

We stopped at the boat launch area to make an early lunch. The real test of the day was coming—a 3-mile uphill climb of Pond Mountain that would begin 200 yards after lunch. I did the first 2.5 miles nonstop and was still feeling pretty good. Even the last half mile, while slow, was steady enough to make me think that maybe the run down feeling was gone, and the drill sergeant was safely out of my existence.

In the afternoon, we plunged down off Pond Mountain. The first 1.8 miles was dramatic and knee jarring. The deep leaves on the trail added another element of danger. You couldn't see what was underneath. The sun went behind the clouds, making me want to keep my speed to stay warm, but my cooler head prevailed. Better to stay slow, cold and upright.

Finally, the trail settled down a bit. We stopped for a sip of water and could hear the rushing water of Laurel Fork below. This gorgeous deep pooled stream, lined by banks of rhododendron was one of the highlights of the trip. The trail followed the stream faithfully and offered a few choice camp spots nearby. We snagged one and tanked up with water. Tonight there was no falling asleep after appetizers. Alfredo and hot tea ruled the roost.

The morning of day seven was an amazing walk in Laurel Fork Gorge under nearly cloudless skies. The trail contoured along the stream, going up to a small ridge with an overlook, dropping down to the stream's edge for a time, then climbing steeply by rock steps while providing views back to Laurel Creek Falls. Simply a beautiful and beautifully designed stretch. Having climbed out of the gorge, we now faced a 1500' climb of White Rocks Mountain. Fortunately, the trail was kind. Long switchbacks (zig zags) made it so. We descended the mountain and found a flat spot near the convergence of three streams. It had been a most satisfying 9.7 mile day. The forecast was calling for really nasty weather starting the day after next. We went to sleep knowing that we needed to make miles tomorrow.

Day eight - So much for that plan. We almost immediately came to a trail relocation (a "re-lo" as we call it), that unexpectedly added 3.8 miles to the trail. This meant we were now 18 miles from a potential food resupply at Tennessee Route 19E, not the 14 or so we anticipated. Fortunately, much of the relocation followed an old logging road, so the extra miles were pretty easy. I was glad to have a day of relief from big climbs and especially happy to be walking under full sun. This would be the last sunny day for a while. It was nice to put in a relatively effortless 10 mile day for a change.

That night in the tent, we did a food assessment and decided that luncheon meat and

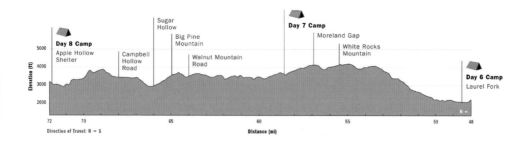

ramen should be the grocery priorities tomorrow. I also suggested getting Pop-Tarts. It sounded like the weather was going to be awful for our upcoming hike over the wide open mountain tops (called "balds" in this part of the world). If so, it would be nice to have something that didn't require cooking available for a quick snack. You don't want to be dealing with a sputtering stove on an exposed mountain summit as your body is rapidly chilling and when every minute of daylight counts.

Day nine - This is the day that things really started going south. On the positive side, we got an early start and it wasn't raining yet. I was hoping that the wind and clouds would be all we'd have to deal with until we walked 8 miles, got to the store, got back on the trail and hiked 1/2 mile to the Apple House Shelter.

Things didn't even go remotely according to plan. First off, I took a wrong a turn on the trail and walked a few hundred yards down an old road by mistake. Because I had my head down, I missed seeing a double white blaze on a tree, which indicated an upcoming change in the trail. Thus, I went straight ahead when the AT actually turned left and down a hill. In the short time it took me to get back to the spot where I took the wrong turn, Wayne slipped past me and continued on the AT. I was convinced he was still behind me and waited for 20 minutes for him to show up. When he didn't, I suspected he had gone past me.

I shouldered my pack and started south again. Soon, I saw his footprints in a muddy section of trail. He was speeding up to try to catch up with me and I was speeding up trying to catch up with him. We started climbing up and over small ridges, he always out of sight, so I couldn't yell to any effect. Every ascent was pissing me off. And the drill sergeant took the opportunity to reenter the conversation. This time, he turned his wrath against Wayne.

"I can't believe he's not stopping. He must realize you're not ahead of him. He can see that there aren't any boot prints in the mud." On and on it went. Again, I was being driven by anger. What the hell was going on? I could write off the earlier episode in this trip as an oddity. But now it was becoming habitual. Was I actually trading finding strength in beauty and joy for finding strength in anger? I didn't even want to think about the implications of having anger as my default setting.

Finally, I popped out onto Route 19E. Wayne had only been waiting 10 minutes. "I told him about my wrong turn back in the trees. He hadn't figured that I was behind him until he got all the way to the highway. He was just glad to see me. I didn't tell him that I had spent the last few miles either screaming obscenities at him or cursing him under my breath. It didn't matter. I wasn't mad at him anyway. I was mad at myself for missing the turn in the first place.

Now that we were reunited, we could focus on the 1/2 mile road walk that would end with big, juicy hamburgers and food bags restocked with the grocery items of our dreams. A future this bright held no place for anger. And my inner drill sergeant again receded to his far away barracks.

The burgers and groceries happened, but not as imagined. The store that was 1/2 mile from the trail had gone out of business. And the bar next door didn't serve food. Fortunately, the nearest supermarket was only 1.5 miles away in Elizabethton. It was 2:30. We put our packs on and walked as fast as we could down the paved and busy Route 19E into town.

The supermarket was incredibly sparse, but had what we needed: ramen, salami, ham, pecan pies, Pop-Tarts and stuffed oatmeal cookies. It's amazing what food groups are important to you when you are hiking. Next stop, the Snack Shack for burgers and fries. There wasn't any indoor seating, so we ate and ran. We were racing against the fading light to get back up to the trail. The cars were flying by and there wasn't much of a shoulder. I was really glad I had brought high visibility wrist bands along in case we were stuck on a late night road walk.

It was dark when we snagged a trailside flat spot just below Route 19E and over the first bridge on the AT. The rain started less than 15 minutes after we settled in. We had planned on an 8.5 mile day and ended up doing twelve. That extra 3.5 miles would take its toll on me.

Day nine - As I awoke, my mind immediately sprang into action. No loitering allowed today. A big climb in the rain was waiting outside the door. That was really the theme this whole trip, including the days leading up to it - always needing to keep moving and make mileage.

The time of year definitely had an effect on keeping us from recharging our batteries. We were carrying heavier winter gear, the temperatures didn't invite long rests and the amount of daylight was approaching its shortest length. Then we had a couple of curve balls thrown in - the 3.8 mile addition to the trail and an unplanned side trip into town for resupply. The cumulative impact was days of a "you're either walking or you're sleeping" existence, that kept us constantly on the move and only enjoying the surroundings on the fly.

What a difference it would have made if we were doing this same section in early October, when the temps and daylight would allow for lengthier stops along the way. But we couldn't set the time machine for two months ago. We needed to join the 38° rainy day and climb 3,000 feet in the next five miles instead.

Again I felt really strong out of the gate. The climb up through rhododendron, granite and oaks was quite pretty, even in the rain. I was doubly pleased that my waterproof baseball hat was keeping me comfortable - no need for the restrictive rain hood.

After two plus hours of steady climbing, we emerged onto a plateau called Doll Flats. Even though the terrain was more forgiving, we couldn't stop. The cool down would be swift. The only way to stay warm was to keep walking until we were ready to set up camp at the end of the day.

We walked through an open pasture, then began a 1.3 mile traverse of a ridge under the oaks and over granite, roots and occasionally loose rocks, all made slicker by the rain. Even with hiking poles, it was slow going and treacherous. I was getting frustrated, but the drill sergeant stayed away for the moment.

Finally, the trail turned right and began a steeper climb up out of the woods and onto the windy, wet, open ridge of Hump Mountain at 5500'. The blonde and rust grasses of the bald summit were really pretty. I wish we could have had an even better view, but the fog kept our visibility to under a mile in all directions. What we could clearly see was the path ahead - one giant rut filled with standing water.

It was fun to be above tree line for miles on end, even with diminished views. I always enjoy being in a place that makes me feel honored to be on the scene. There's nothing like a great expanse to remind you that there are greater forces at work.

We made a number of 500 foot drops and climbs during the afternoon, fueled only by a 5 minute stop for Pop-Tarts and the need to keep moving. It was still raining and in the low 40s when we climbed the last 500 feet to arrive at Stan Murray Shelter. It was 5:00 p.m. and getting dark fast.

We dumped the packs, grabbed the water filter and bottles and scrambled down to the stream to fill 4 quarts. We pitched the tent, then ducked into the lean-to, where we could easily stand upright and change clothes. We hung our gaiters, stuff sacks, rain pants and other gear in the shelter to drip dry. Pretty sure there wouldn't be any late arrivals to claim the space.

Back in the tent—and the luxurious comfort of dry clothes and zero degree rated sleeping bags—we gobbled down steaming mac and cheese with ham and celebrated the hard earned and beautiful 10.4 mile day.

Day ten - During the night, the rain switched over to snow. We got just over an inch of accumulation. The trees were beautifully frosted and looked spectacular against the now cloudless bright blue sky.

Because it had dropped into the 20s, everything we had left in the shelter was frozen and stiff as a board. My boots, which were stowed inside by the tent door, were so frozen that I couldn't tighten the laces. Even more inconveniently, the tent poles were frozen. We needed to unthaw the pole sections with our bare hands to disassemble them. All this added up to a late start, but we didn't much care. Standing outside drinking coffee and packing in the sun was so much better than doing it in the wind driven rain - even though we were hopping around in frozen boots trying to keep our circulations going.

We had a steady climb from the shelter to Grassy Ridge, above tree line at over 6,000'. I was throwing off enough heat to warm my feet, even though it was cold enough to see my breath. When I broke out of the frosted trees and looked over my shoulder, I yelped with joy. The views of the mountains we had traversed in the rain and fog yesterday were simply awe inspiring. The payoff was once again worth the effort. What a glorious winter morning! I stopped to marvel at the scenery and tighten my boot laces, which required removing my gaiters first. It only took about 3 minutes per boot, but that was enough to get nudged along by winter's chill.

The trail through the snow covered grasses of Grassy Ridge and Jane Bald was sensational. I just love hiking above tree line, and these wide open, grass covered peaks were a real treat, offering views in all directions.

We soon dropped down to cross a parking area in Carver Gap, enter the shade and woods again and begin the big climb of Roan Mountain - the highest point of the trip at 6285'. We bypassed the summit shelter and walked 1/2 mile further to emerge into the sun again, crossed a paved road and discovered a large cement box (presumably a water pumping station) that made a warm seat for lunch. We laid out the tent and rain fly under the midday sun to see if we could get some of the ice to melt and evaporate from them while we each ate a package of Pop Tarts ®.

After our snack, we started a 2,000' drop off of Roan Mountain. My knees were screaming. I slowed down and Wayne took the lead. Once again, I was uncharacteristically cold, weak and dispirited. When we bottomed out at Hughes Gap, Wayne was nowhere to be seen. He had continued up the trail. I wasn't upset at that at all. We all need to hike at our own pace. I was upset at me. I defaulted to, "What is wrong with me?" language and the drill sergeant arrived right on queue. The sun had disappeared behind a ridge and the cool air hit the sweat on the back of my neck, sending a shiver through me. A nearby farmer started yelling to his hunting dogs.

"Oh, shut the f*** up.", I muttered under my breath, as if I had more of a right to be here than he.

I started the last climb of the day in this crappy mood and it didn't improve all the way up. Everything I owned was wet or damp, including my boots and feet. I was barely moving fast enough to keep warm in the 30 degree temps and snow covered trail. The "one, two, one, two" mantra kicked in. This wasn't fun. It was work.

I fought my way to the top of the ridge and discovered Wayne with a new found friend – a hunting dog with a radio collar. The dog had been lying and shivering in wet oak leaves beside the trail. We coaxed him to follow us down from the summit toward the next shelter, where we hoped to camp. The poor thing was colder than we were. Part way to the shelter, the dog trotted back up to the summit, bayed toward the valley, then disappeared - perhaps back to the farmer in the dell.

At 5:15, we hit a blue blazed side trail that we incorrectly thought led to the shelter. Instead it led to a dry spring. Double bummer. It was too dark to continue. A 9.7 mile day would have to be enough. We melted snow water to make dinner and both passed out from exhaustion by 7:00 p.m.

Day eleven - Two days left and no choice but to make a dozen miles today. Due to lack of water, we had to melt snow to make oatmeal. It would have taken way too much effort and time to make coffee, so we skipped it.

The trail battled me all day - or was it the other way around? Lots of ups and downs

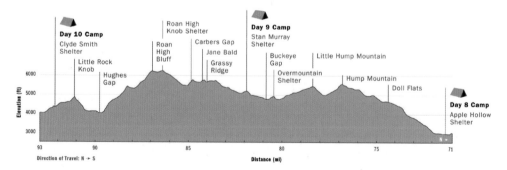

between 3800' and 4500' all day long. Unlike prior days, there weren't many switchbacks. The trail was more in the New England fashion of straight up and straight down again. Fewer opportunities to "rest while walking" added to my exhaustion.

I started hitting the wall by late morning. I began obsessing about the need to have a full day off somewhere in a two week trip. The fact that we had been working hard for most of the past 12 days really beat down hard against my normally indefatigable demeanor. My reserves to fight the downdrafts were incredibly low. An overcast sky and freezing temperatures didn't help either.

Up and down. Up and down. Even the little climbs were zapping me. I couldn't believe I was this weak. I actually spiraled down to a point of resenting the trail and cursing its designers. Before today, I didn't even think that reaction was in my repertoire. As I shuffled along feeling emotionally and physically vulnerable, guess who showed up? The drill sergeant.

He was ready to start chastising me and I was ready to listen to what he had to say. It was a pitiful pairing - one I would like to say will never happen again. Working together, we created mountains of misery for a whole 8 mile stretch. The negative self talk was beyond intense and incredibly unhealthy. This was my reward for pushing myself to the brink both before and during this journey.

I reached the emotional low point of my entire hiking career at a place called Cherry Gap Shelter at 3:00 p.m. on December 7, 2005. Wayne had arrived 15 minutes before me - one more indication that I was laboring. I am usually the one out front by 15-20 minutes. I had hiked with him enough to know that taking the lead was his way of trying to encourage me through.

I sat in the front of the shelter with my legs dangling over the edge of the floorboards, unbuckled my waist belt, slipped out of the shoulder straps and let the pack fall to the shelter floor behind me. I was spent. I stared at the fire ring in front of the shelter. I didn't want Wayne to see that I was tearing up, but it didn't matter. He heard the frustration in my voice.

"What do you think about staying here and walking out by the nearby dirt road tomorrow?", I asked. "I'm toasted."

"I'd rather climb up Unaka Mountain and call it a day.", he said.

I pulled the guidebook and map out of my waist belt holster. "2.4 miles away and 1200' up.", I said.

"If we're going to go for it, we'd better get going.", Wayne said.

I thought about it for a few seconds, for I didn't have minutes. If we went for the summit, every one of them would count. If we stayed here, near the shelter, I wondered if I would start having regrets about it as soon as I got warm again. It's easier to start or end a trip at a well defined place (say a paved road crossing) than an obscure dirt road, And it sure would be nice to walk right into the campground hostel we had reserved at the end of the section, rather than trying to walk or thumb our way in from the outskirts of town.

Given all that and the benefit of a 10 minute rest without my pack on, I decided that the climb was worth a try. "OK. I'm game. I may be a bit behind you, but I can do it."

Wayne took the lead and we began the ascent via long switchbacks - just when I needed them most. We passed a piped spring and the climb got steeper. We were racing the dark yet again and there weren't any good camping spots. We scoped out one, but it wasn't nearly flat enough. That cost us at least 10 minutes.

Miraculously, I now found a hidden reserve - enough to drive me to the summit anyway. I took the lead up through the rhododendrons and into evergreen stands. When I really needed that final boost, it was there after all. I'm not sure where that energy boost was hiding out earlier, but I was sure happy to feel my body kicking into gear and powering me toward the top. We might beat the darkness yet.

At 5:15, we topped a flat plateau just short of the summit and above 5,000', complete with a perfectly flat campsite below the pines. My mind hadn't been willing, but my body carried me there.

This was one of those times that setting up a tent hundreds of times together really paid off. We have the routine down so well, that it only takes 2 minutes. We dove inside and into the warmth of dry clothes and our zero degree bags. We were so exhausted that we just piled up the last of the crackers, pepperoni and cheese in a humungous heap and

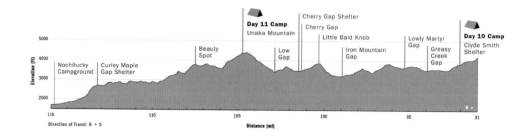

ate them for dinner. Even though we had soup and noodle dinners, we didn't have the will to stay awake long enough to cook and eat them. But I did stay awake long enough to think about the decision I made in the shelter a few hours ago. It was the right one. And a defining moment in this 12 day lesson in attitude and perseverance.

Day twelve - 12/8/05 was another cold day in the Tennessee mountains. There was snow on the ground and, thankfully, bright skies above. We weren't sure how long that would last. We were hoping to win the 12.7 mile race between us and the predicted late day storm. At the finish line was our reserved space at a campground hostel.

Powered by oatmeal, I took the lead up and over the nearby true summit of Unaka Mountain (the last time we would top 5,000'), then 1.5 miles down the other side. I stopped to grab a giant icicle from a rock formation. The conventional wisdom is not to eat ice or snow, because it takes too much work for your body to gain any benefit. I didn't care. I was so damned thirsty. Water had been a real challenge on this trip. Wayne scampered down the path, made sure I was ok, and continued on.

Three miles into the day, I caught up to Wayne, who was waiting for me at a side trail to a spring. We filtered and guzzled one quart each and carried a few more. It felt so good to have plenty of liquid in my system and set me up for a much more enjoyable afternoon.

The highlight of the day (other than the turkey dinner at the end of it) was Beauty Spot - a wide open field of spectacular views of the huge mountains around us and the towns of Erwin and Johnson City nestled in the valley below.

Now I took the lead. For the first time in days, I felt like my trail worthy self again. Even uphill sections weren't getting me down. And the drill sergeant was gone - hopefully forever.

With 5.5 miles to go, we stopped in a gap with a view of Erwin, Tennessee below and ate the last of the Pop-Tarts - the perfect tribute to this ever moving forward, on-the-go trip. No cooking required!

The trail now began a series of amazingly long switchbacks (could one have really been about 2 miles long?) that seemingly kept Erwin, and the campground hostel, at arm's length. It reminded me of the times when my high school cross country coach would drop us off at one end of a curved, sandy beach and ask us to run the 6 miles to the pier at the other end. For the first few miles, the pier didn't seem to get any closer. Finally, halfway there, you could begin to see real progress.

"There's a pizza out there somewhere with my name on it", I said to myself, glancing longingly at the town below. "And a shower and a roaring wood stove to dry my gear and warm my bones." This time, my self-talking sentiments were backed by hope and possibilities. Yes, after a 13 day journey that tested me so hard on so many levels, I really was back to my trail loving self.

CHAPTER 18

Joyful Spring

Four months since we hopped off the blessed path in Erwin, Tennessee, we rejoined the AT to complete the New Jersey section. The budding trees mirrored my attitude — or was it the other way around?

High Point State Park, NJ to Fox Gap, PA

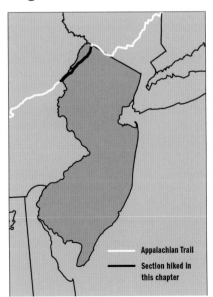

Appalachian Trail

Section hiked in this chapter

TRIP STATS
April 22 – April 28, 2006
NJ Rt 23 - Delaware Water Gap, PA
42.5 miles
North to South

PA Rt 191 - (Fox Gap) to Delaware Water Gap
7.2 miles
South to North

When spring arrives in Maine, which I loosely define as, "when the snow is either gone to stay or the remnants of a rogue spring storm can no longer last more than 2 days", I really start yearning for a long stretch of trail.

I love getting out into the snow, but putting my winter boots in the attic for an eight month rest borders on a spiritual event. Long, sunny days and budding trees are the life for me, and I can't wait to be among them for a while.

I sent Wayne an e-mail about grabbing some trail, thinking he would be on the same wavelength and recommend a 3-day jaunt somewhere in southern New England (where the trail would be snow free. We both knew that if we went anywhere north between now and late May, we'd likely be trouncing around in the white stuff at least part of the time).

So, when he suggested a week on the trail to finish the NJ and PA sections of the AT, I was overjoyed. "Hell, yeah!" Just what I needed to hear after last fall's trying adventure in Tennessee.

From the start, almost everything about this trip was the opposite of the last one, and set me up for a phenomenal time. First off, there was the planning. Work wise, I wasn't in a pillar to post frenzy right up until my departure. Gear wise, I did a thorough inventory. Along with making necessary small repairs, I fixed the broken tent door zipper and bought a new pair of hiking boots (the first in over two decades).

You see, in one of the most fortunate outcomes possible, I was destined to own and operate a matching set of size 9 Medium feet (this just happens to be the size that most footwear companies produce as test samples). When I worked as a writer for a well known outdoor gear company, I was often asked to field test hiking boots. I was hiking nearly every weekend, so they got nearly immediate feedback, which helped them decide which models to sell, and I got over 20 years' worth of all weather treads.

Now the cupboard was bare. I had squeezed the last miles out of the last pair of test boots and tossed them in the rubbish last November. I bought a new pair and treated them to a several week break in period.

The new gear stash didn't stop there. The other big new pieces of equipment I bought were:

1. A new pack - one with carbon fiber stays (supports) inside. (This shaved a few pounds off the weight vs. conventional aluminum stays.) I had coveted a carbon fiber pack for years and could finally justify the expense when I found one on sale for half price.

2. Two "bear proof" food canisters (one for Wayne and one for me). Delaware Water Gap, and the surrounding area on both the New Jersey and Pennsylvania sides, is loaded with black bears. The age old way to discourage them from foraging through your food (and likely your tent), is to suspend your food in bags hoisted 10 feet off the ground and a good distance between trees. The newfangled way was to use bear proof plastic canisters with lids that worked like tamper proof drug containers. The theory is that bears can't open the canisters and give up in frustration (a reaction similar to many humans trying to open their prescription bottles, I suppose). If the canisters worked, they would sure eliminate the hassle of hoisting bags at night and retrieving them each morning as part of our campsite routine. The weight of the canister would more than negate

the weight savings gained by carrying my new carbon fiber pack, but I'd rather deal with that then risk losing our food…or worse.

On April 20, I barely caught the 11:15 a.m. bus out of Portland, Maine, bound for Boston. As soon as I sat down, I realized I'd need to employ the "radio self defense" strategy against the din behind me. I plugged in the headset and the first song that came on was, "Midnight Train to Georgia", by Gladys Knight and the Pips. One of my favorites and a sure omen.

That evening at Wayne's house, we packed and repacked the bear canisters. He had better luck. I tried every combination possible and was still left with two days' worth of food outside the cylinder. We'd take our chances. The fact that we seldom stayed near shelters made me rationalize that we'd be safer.

As it turned out, we wouldn't be reducing our food stash or pack weight the first night on the trail. After we got off the Metro North train from NYC to Port Jervis, NY, we were ravenous. We found a pub willing to stuff us with chicken wings and salads, then took a $12 cab ride up and out of town to the trail. It was raining steadily at 7:00 p.m., when we shouldered our packs and headed up the ridge.

"First flat spot.", I said.

Wayne nodded in agreement.

"Half a mile in, just short of the ridge top, we set up shop. Less than a minute after we climbed into the tent, the rain switched from merely steady to absolute deluge. Timing is everything. We were damp, not soaked. And there was no need to cook tonight (we were still full of pub fare), so we wouldn't be sending any aromas bear-ward. I took a look at the jammed full bear canister sitting next to me. It was supposed to be water resistant, but I questioned its ability to shed this kind of downpour.

"Maybe bears don't like to venture out in the rain either.", I said.

"I'll take my chances.", said Wayne.

Meanwhile, my attention turned to my right knee. I had done something to it on the trip down. I wondered if it was hyperextended. Not something I looked forward to walking through in this wet, granite filled, knee knocking stretch of trail. I popped a few aspirin and conked out for the night.

At first light, I unzipped the tent door flap to look out. Steady mist and fog. Pretty to look at, but not great for footing. My knee was still throbbing. The first full day on the trail is great for rationalizing. The "we'll make up mileage later when we are in trail shape and have lighter packs" mentality can really set in. Add a bit of unpleasant weather, and you have all the makings of an extended stay under the dome.

We sat and drank another cup of coffee and looked at the maps and guide book. We were in good shape. We only needed to cover 50 miles in seven days. We did a leisurely packing job, stepped out into the drizzle, got underway by 10:00 a.m., then quickly got ourselves into some self-induced trouble.

About 1.5 miles into the day, I came to a viewpoint, which would undoubtedly be more of one on a higher visibility day. Wayne joined me about 10 minutes later. We chatted briefly and had a quick slug of water. I was cooling down, so I continued on through the mist. Based on what was then a 1500 plus mile history, I assumed that Wayne wouldn't be far behind.

I followed the AT down off the ridge and immediately into a confusing section of

double blazes. The trail zig zagged once, then headed to my right. It took some doing not to continue left, because enough people had taken the wrong turn that they had blazed a new trail in that direction. Once I sorted things out, I crossed the valley floor, steeply climbed the boulder pile/trail to top the next ridge, leaned against a tree and waited for Wayne.

Ten minutes passed. I wasn't that far ahead of him. I should have heard or seen him by now. I still hadn't taken my pack off, reasoning that if something had happened to Wayne and I needed to backtrack, I would regret leaving it behind. I ran through the scenarios. 1. He went the wrong way when he left the viewpoint where we had the water. 2. He fell off the viewpoint (or elsewhere) and needed medical attention. 3. He took the wrong turn at the double blazes.

I backtracked down the ridge and across the valley to the double blazes, yelling and whistling when I got there. Nothing.

I went back up the small ridge to the viewpoint where we drank the water and looked over the edge. Nothing.

I returned to the double blazed section. I started wondering if he had gotten back on trail and was actually ahead of me, as had happened before. Amidst all this uncertainty, one thing was absolute. We had planned on eating lunch at the Mashipacong Shelter, 5 miles into the day. I would head there.

I speed hiked up and over the ridge and on toward the shelter. About 1/3 mile from it, I spotted a northbounder coming my way.

"Say, did you see a guy headed south?" I asked.

"You mean a couple? They're in the shelter."

That was all I needed to know. He was behind me. But, I decided to go to the shelter to double check. The couple was indeed there. It started drizzling heavily and they invited me to join them under the roof.

"No thanks."

I still had to find my friend. I walked behind the shelter and sat on a boulder to wait. Now it started pouring. time to backtrack again. This time, I was approached by a southbounder.

"Did you see another southbounder?"

"Guy with white hair? He's on his way."

I perched on a flat topped boulder and waited. Sure enough, the telltale yellow jacket soon appeared. Wayne had gotten turned around and gone all the way back to High Point.

By now, it was past 2:00. We had both done enough back and forthing for the day. We climbed up to a nice flat spot, pitched the tent and watched the weather change. By 3:30, the sun began burning through the remaining fog. By 4:00, it was full sun and blue skies. This, in turn, had us leaping out of the tent to create a massive nylon yard sale — everything must dry! We draped every piece of wet gear over branches — gaiters, rain jackets, rain pants, stuff sacks, you name it — creating a field of blooming nylon.

We propped our ground pad/loungers against nearby trees and soaked up the sun for the first time in 6 months. The heat felt spectacular after our soggy walk. Even though we had only made a net 5 miles of progress today, we weren't behind schedule. A series of 8-10 mile days would keep us on track, and the terrain and temps would be much more forgiving than those of Tennessee last fall. We just needed to stay on trail!

We had so much food for this trip, it was hysterical. No wonder it all didn't fit in the canister! We started with a first course of crackers and cheese, followed by corn chowder, mac and cheese, chocolate cookies imported from Scandinavia and licorice. By the time we

were done, I could fit all my food stores in my bear canister. I hobbled outside and stowed it a good distance uphill from the tent behind some small boulders.

Back in the tent, I popped two aspirin and willed my knee to improve.

Day two - The clouds rolled back in during the night, and an intense thunderstorm served as our alarm clock. I checked my phone for the time — 6:30 a.m.

We brewed up some coffee as the worst of the heavy rain subsided and the theme of the day turned to mist.

Despite the moisture, we enjoyed an excellent day long stroll along Kittatinny Mountain, which actually is a 40-plus mile ridge with several distinct summits, stretching from High Point (1803') just north of where we started this trip and Wind Gap, some 15 miles into Pennsylvania.

Not surprisingly, the name "Kittatinny" derives from a Lenape Native American word meaning "endless hill" or "great mountain". The range was formed during three geologic episodes. The first, 1,000 million years ago, formed peaks as high as today's Rocky Mountains and trapped sedimentary Paleozoic rocks (including sandstone, shale and limestone) between large blocks of Precambrian rocks (mostly granite), formed by intense heat and compression.

The resulting erosion by streams, wind and glaciers left the nearly continuous and remarkably consistent in elevation mountain range that we see today. The only major breaks in the range occur at Culvers Gap and Delaware Water Gap. Both of these breaks showcase the power of water. While the range rose, the water continued to cut its way through. In the case of Delaware Water Gap, the Delaware River won. It still cuts through the gap to this day. Culver Gap tells a different story. Here the river successfully cut through the gap for a time, but was then "captured" by the Flat Brook system on the west side of

the range. The water stopped flowing through the gap and this break in the range became known as a "wind gap".

Little change in elevation meant we could make steady mileage, even in the drizzle. About 3 1/2 miles into the day, we emerged onto the summit of Sunrise Mountain. At 1653', it was the second highest peak on the range. We sat next to the stone shelter on the summit, cooked soup and watched the clouds start lifting out to the west.

With a feeling that we had futzed around enough on this trip so far, we kicked it into another gear after our rest stop. I ripped off a good seven miles, pausing only to watch two sparring male woodpeckers and for getting an up close view of a red crested warbler.

My knee was feeling so much better. Whatever it was that I did to it had worked its way out. "Sometimes just putting the head down and walking through the discomfort is the right way to go", I mused as I cruised along the ridge.

By the time I climbed the Culver Fire Tower for a gorgeous 360° view, I was in full blown trail euphoria. It was spring, I was outdoors and feeling fantastic. Looking down the range toward our afternoon route, I picked out Lake Owassa to the left, the smaller Lake

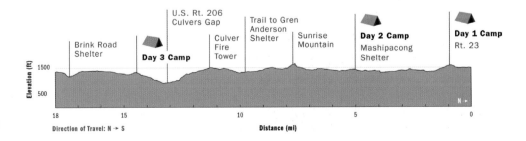

Kittatinny to the right. Most impressive of all was the snaking form of Kittatinny Mountain itself, stretching all the way to Delaware Water Gap.

I turned around and took a photo looking back toward High Point (I could pick out it's observation tower), just on the other side of Route 23 from where we started this trip. It's so much fun to see your progress laid out in this perspective. I took a deep breath filled with fresh mountain air and satisfaction, then waited for Wayne to climb up and enjoy the same.

By 2:00 p.m., we were cruising along once again when my euphoria ended in an instant. I stepped awkwardly off the end of a log bridge and completely folded over my right ankle. The pain shot right to my brain and my eyes filled with tears as it throbbed and throbbed inside my boot. There was no walking off this one. At least not yet. "Damn. Damn. Damn!", I yelled, progressively louder. I was pretty sure that if the sparring woodpeckers and red crested warbler had been nearby, they would be somewhere back in Maine by now, perhaps riding the crest of my screams.

After a bit of hobbling, I was able to put some weight on it. My hiking poles certainly helped. The trail ascended the ridge again (another plus — it would have sucked more to be down-climbing). When I got to the top, I found a nice flat spot to camp with great views of the farms below. I popped two aspirin and hoped for the best.

Day three - Today's alarm clock was my throbbing ankle. The first test was crawling out of the tent to check the weather. That was enough to convince me that I needed to wrap my foot for the day. I took out my first aid kit, ever thankful that the ace bandage inside was not one of the items I sacrificed in my gear purging sessions. I popped two aspirin and pinned my hopes on a tight bandage, gentle rolling terrain, hiking poles and very deliberate foot placement. I wouldn't try to sneak in views while I walked today. I needed to keep 100% of my focus on every step.

The sun was out, which definitely helped my attitude. So did our newly hatched plan for the rest of the trip.

We were scheduled to take a bus from Delaware Water Gap to NYC on Saturday. But we needed to hike 8.8 miles beyond DWG to get to Fox Gap, where we had jumped on the trail in 1995. We thought about hiking to Fox Gap and thumbing back down to catch the bus, but I proposed an alternate plan. What if we hiked into Delaware Water Gap (which the trail passed through anyway), took a cab to Fox Gap, then hiked back into town on Saturday to catch the bus?

"We could even grab a meal in "The Gap" before we call the cab.", said Wayne.

"Brilliant!", I replied.

The trail stayed faithful to the ridge crest most of the day and we enjoyed "great to be alive and on the trial" inspiring views of lush, spring green farms and steel gray glacially

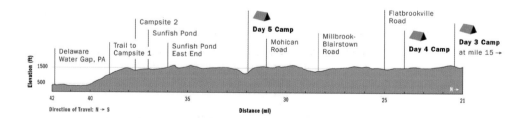

Sunfish Pond - the southernmost glacial tarn on the Appalachian Trail.

formed lakes below and frequent hawk sightings above. It was perfect terrain for nursing a bashed up ankle. No serious down climbs certainly helped.

I was able to place more and more confidence and weight on my ankle as the day progressed. "I may be able to whistle past the graveyard yet again.", I thought. "As long as I stay concentrated on my footwork."

By 3:15 we had done our day's walk along the ridge and grabbed a camp spot on a grassy stretch of old road near the overview of Crater Lake.

Day four - I have a really bad habit of forgetting to pack sunscreen on the first spring hike. My arms and nose were paying for it. The arms I could do something about. I pulled on a long sleeve polypro shirt.

That little annoyance taken care of, the rest of this day played out as fantastic. My ankle didn't even bark once.

It was simply a perfect day for hiking. And unlike last November's trip, we had the seasonal warmth and daylight to truly enjoy it. The weather attracted other hikers as well—30 kids and their chaperones, all from California, were out to experience some of the best trail in New Jersey. We worked our way patiently past the first dozen or so, until one of the adults yelled ahead to let us through.

After a gorgeous day of traversing jut below Kittatinny's summit, we did a bit of a steep down climb to cross Flatbrookville Road, then scrambled back up to the ridge top to pitch camp and enjoy tent window views of the sun setting over the farms and lakes below. We celebrated with a huge helping of appetizers, followed by mac and cheese.

Day five - Sometimes it amazes me how quickly my body can recover from a nearly debilitating injury. My ankle was still tender, but I felt really good about my improvement. I marked the occasion by moving my ace bandage from the top pocket in my pack to back inside my first aid kit.

The day had two additional highlights. The first was dropping slightly off the edge of the ridge to hike along Sunfish Pond, another glacial gift left for us by the Laurentian Ice Sheet.

Before the last glacier (the Wisconsin Glacier), left the area, it carved out a 44 acre bowl just below the summit of the Kittatinny ridge. This bowl, also known as a glacial tarn, filled with the melting water of the glacier itself. It is the southernmost glacial tarn on the AT and a simply beautiful sight—so much so that it was named a National Natural Landmark (a designation bestowed by the National Park Service) in 1970.

The scene at the pond was all ours and worth lingering over. Those who had lingered

How do you cook?

Because of the time it takes to gather wood (not to mention the smoke, the mess, the fire hazard and the time it takes to heat food), fires are out of the question for daily life on the trail.

Our cook stove of choice is a butane/propane camp stove that burns cleanly, brings water to a boil quickly and has a finely adjustable simmer setting. Two fuel canisters per week and we're good to go.

before us had built an impressive array of rock and driftwood sculptures along the shore. There must have been hundreds of them. A brown weasel sunning among one grouping was bothered enough by my arrival that he scampered away, leaving me alone in the gallery.

The trail now began its descent into Delaware Water Gap. We were so far ahead of schedule that we could afford to slow down the pace and enjoy the ride. We stopped at an "official" trailside campsite (meaning there were established campsites and an apparatus for hanging food away from the bears) to fire up some ramen for lunch. As the water began heating on the stove, I walked downhill to inspect the aerial food cache system. It was a log crossbar with metal hooks suspended between two huge oaks. Using a nearby long aluminum pole with its own hook, you could hoist your food bags to the hooks above. The lower several feet of the trunks were encased in sheets of aluminum to help keep the bears from climbing up. Instead of their native silver, they had been liberally slathered in forest service brown paint.

"Better than leaving them unpainted.", I thought. "They blend in better." I supposed that this spot got a lot of use in the summer, a fact that was quickly confirmed when I spotted two cheap-o cotton sleeping bags left in the bushes.

"C'mon people. Carry-in, carry-out.", I said out loud. I would have done it myself, if I had been carrying a garbage bag or two.

Back at the stove, the canister had burned out of fuel before it got the water to a full simmer. "Close enough", said Wayne, after dunking his finger in the pot. Translation - I don't want to dig for the full canister in the bottom of my pack, and besides, we'll be eating chicken wings and burgers later this afternoon. I obliged, but wished I hadn't.

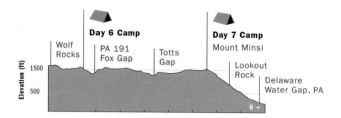

Delaware Water Gap

I'm not a big fan of ramen anyway. I carry it mostly because it is light and compact. But lukewarm ramen has as much appeal to me as drinking dishwater. This was the watershed moment for me. For the second time in my hiking career, I declared the "Fall of the Ramen Empire." Next trip, I'd be carrying soup instead.

A few more miles down, we encountered the side trail to Campsite 1. A big downed log offered seating for two. What a joy to take the packs off, down a few quarts of water and just sit in the woods for a while, appreciating our ability to do so. Times like these are my happiest moments in life. Nothing but the opportunity to enjoy this moment in the world and all the natural wonder around me. These are the snapshots I can often retain, think about years later and experience all over again.

It was also a nice experience to have once more before plunging down off the mountain into the embrace of a civilization that was on a much different wavelength.

Wow. I don't know which was more disconcerting—the speed or the noise. We ambled across the Delaware River next to 4 lanes of highway speed traffic. Whoosh. Whoosh. Whoosh. Whoosh. It was dizzying and quite the contrast to the river below and the calming influence of nature we had just experienced on the ridge above.

We exited into the town of Delaware Water Gap. It would seem that most people don't. It was a charming and quiet town. So quiet that the Trails End Cafe and Deer Head Inn were closed and the Europa Cafe had gone out of business.

One thing about us though, if there's a restaurant within miles, we'll find it. Sure enough, we found one that opened at 4:00 p.m. We took advantage of the one hour wait by emptying the trash from our packs in a nearby dumpster and reading a newspaper in

the sun. After our oh, so predictable burger and wings infusion, we called a cab for the second time on the trip.

It had been so many years since we had climbed the long hill out of East Stroudsburg, PA on Route 191, that we didn't recognize where the AT crossed the road. We asked the driver to let us out near the height of land. We had to be close. He let us off, then continued up the hill to turn around at the top.

On his way back down, he stopped and rolled down his window. "It's right up there.", he said. "100 yards."

"Thanks, man."

We walked uphill, turned onto the trail and walked northbound until we found a nice flat spot. No need to cook tonight. What a pleasure. We sat in the tent, read the rest of the newspapers and caught up on our trail journaling. Tomorrow, we would continue north the mile or so to Wolf "Rocks—a view we both remembered from many years ago, and a quick walk without packs—then head back to hike south toward Delaware Water Gap on the AT by way of Mount Minsi, another spot with impressive views.

In all of our trips to complete the AT — there would be 28 in all — this would be only the second one where we were both northbounders and southbounders.

Day six - Another stellar spring day! We awoke to azure blue skies and the head of a big, white dog plunging into our tent! Good thing the door was partially open. He was quite anxious to say hello and went bounding off when the owner yelled out. Apparently we were a new addition to the morning exercise route.

We finished our coffee and oatmeal, packed our gear in our packs and left them inside the tent while we scrambled to Wolf Rocks. The removable hood on my pack doubles as a hip pack, so I stuck my phone, wallet and wind shell inside for the trip.

The view from Wolf Rocks was as I remembered. A vast view of the farmland broken only by the interstate and the suburban hamlet of East Stroudsburg.

We didn't stay long. Our gear was unattended. Even though we trusted any passing trail hikers to leave well enough alone, the seeds of doubt were enough to make us want to make tracks back to the site.

Our glorious southbound day culminated with a tremendous view of Delaware Water Gap from Mount Minsi (1460'). We sat in the afternoon sun, watching the daylight fade, the hawks riding the thermals above and the lights going on in the valley below. I pulled out my journal and scribbled down a recap of the day.

"The older I get, the more I appreciate days like the last several.", I wrote. "What a special part of the world. I've really enjoyed this part of the Trail."

At dusk, we moved to the nearby wooded summit and found a level camp spot in the corner of a seldom used grassy woods road turnaround. After dinner, we walked out to the ledge to sit for a few minutes and bid goodbye to Delaware Water Gap.

"It was a great trip.", said Wayne.

"One of the classics.", I replied. "Can't wait to get out and back on it again."

"Thinking about getting back to Virginia."

"Sounds like a plan."

CHAPTER 19

Worlds Between

The timing is right for exploring the days between seasons and why the trail is such a strong influence in my life.

Davenport Gap, TN to Erwin, TN

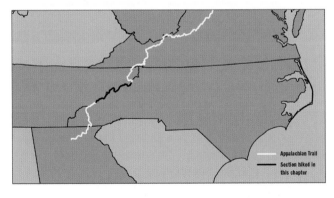

TRIP STATS
November 26, 2006 -
December 8, 2006
102.5 miles
South to North

A beautifully designed map of the Appalachian Trail hangs on my office wall. On the 20th anniversary of the start of our adventure, September 21, 2006, I poured a large cup of French Roast and gazed at the map — a tangible display of how many miles we had walked and how many were left to go.

Because I had already done the Maine section of trail several times, the pieces that would be new to both of us were all on the southern end. And because flying introduced a host of hassles (finding fuel for our backpacking stove among them), this meant cobbling together train, bus and car rides to get to and from the trail. We had come to enjoy this part of the odyssey — so much so that we shared a philosophy that the journey didn't start when we stepped onto the trail, but rather, when we walked out the doors of our respective homes on departure day.

But my greatest challenge in getting to the trail wasn't the travel, it was carving out the two week chunk of time I would need to make the trip happen. The first opening in my schedule wasn't until after Thanksgiving.

"I'm game if we can leave that weekend and take two solid weeks off.", said Wayne. "We'll need four days just to get there and back."

And so it was.

After taking the 5:00 a.m. train from Portland, ME to Boston, I boarded Amtrak's 93 regional, bound for points south. I saved a seat for Wayne, who joined me in New Haven, and the 2006 Master's Tour was underway.

After train rides to Washington, D.C. and Lynchburg, VA and bus rides from Lynchburg to Roanoke to Knoxville to Waynesville, North Carolina, we stepped out of the bus and into the bright mid-morning light to find Curtis of Standing Bear Farm waiting for us, just as he said he would be.

Curtis was an organic farmer that doubled as an AT shuttle driver/youth hostel operator. His farm was close to the trail and he had found a nice source of extra income tending to hiker's needs.

"I built a couple of his and her bunkhouses, added coin-op washers, dryers and showers and also shuttle kids to town to buy pizza, beer or whatever.", he explained as we wound through the mountains on the way to the trail. "It's getting so I scarcely have time to tend to my farming.", he said. "Not that I'm complaining."

I asked him a few questions to keep the conversation going, but I was too sleep deprived to be much of a conversationalist.

Soon we turned onto a road that crossed over the Pigeon River, filled with Thanksgiving weekend whitewater rafters, passed a power plant, turned to dirt and climbed up into the ridges. Curtis stopped at a pullout, popped the trunk and announced, "Here we are."

Sure enough, there was an AT blaze on a tree to our right. We were home.

We handed Curtis our fare and he bid us a great hike before he disappeared back down the dirt road. The only sounds we could hear were the high whir of traffic on Route

40 and the white noise like rushing of the Pigeon River rising from the gorge below.

After 31 straight hours of leaving the driving to someone else, it was time to become our own modes of transportation.

A few weeks ago, I had been wondering if I would even get to the AT this year. Now I was standing in the glorious North Carolina mountains on a sun-filled 60 degree late November day. The punch drunkenness of my sleep deprivation was overcome by the joy of simply being back in the hills — at least for a while.

We went up and over a little ridge, then began crossing the Pigeon River on the same bridge we had recently ridden over in Curtis's car. Rafters were still coming down the river in clusters. Halfway across, we met a older guy (as in, older than us) walking toward us who called himself "Chip off the old trail".

"How long have you been on the trail?", he asked.

"Twenty-five years.", I said.

"NO WAY!!!!", he exclaimed. He extended his hand and wished us continued good fortune.

"The trail community runs like the mighty Pigeon River", I thought as I continued on. "Continuous, unpredictable and deep."

The climb out of the gorge was enough to give my sleep deprivation the edge. Every time we hit the top of a ridge, we couldn't find a level, tent-worthy site. There was no choice but to continue our zombie-like stroll.

It was almost dusk when we found our camp spot, high above the valley. The views were a bonus. We were so tired that flat ground became the only important factor.

I sat in my lounger, finally looking through a window without the world whizzing by at 65 miles per hour behind it. As the sun dipped behind the ridge to our right, we made a hasty meal of turkey sandwiches using the last of the Thanksgiving leftovers I had packed for the trip. Anything more fancy would just get in the way of sleep.

During the night, I awoke and stepped outside. The stars were spectacular and it was mild enough that I could sit outside and watch the setting quarter moon. I smiled a smile of deep gratitude. It was great to be back on the trail. Joy was in control and would be for the rest of the trip.

Giants of the east

The mountains in this part of North Carolina, near the Tennessee border, are big as mountains in the eastern U.S. go. The trail through these foothills of the Smokeys

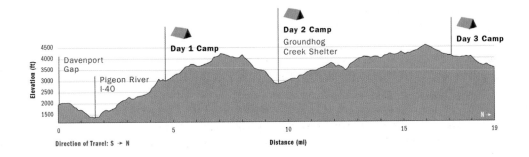

would take us to summits over 5,000 feet several times — not the 14,000' peaks of Colorado to be sure, but significant enough to make ferrying a 70 lb. load up and over them a worthy endeavor.

What amazed me as this trip played out was that this same kind of terrain that kicked my ass and brought tears of frustration one year before was now the backdrop for sustained happiness.

Why the difference? One important thing was that I hadn't worked myself to a frazzle before I boarded the train. This time, I was merely tired from the marathon it took to get here, not doubly exhausted. It only took one good night's sleep to recover. As a result, I was able to rip off several mile stretches without taking breaks — not stopping and starting to the point of never gaining momentum. I started out feeling strong and vital, and it just kept getting better.

The other thing that kept my spirits up was our walks above the trees.

The origin of the often grassy, open summits known in the southern Appalachians as "balds" are an enigma. What is known is that they were here before Europeans arrived to settle in the area. What is unknown is how the balds formed in the first place — whether it was by the hand of nature or of humankind. Regardless, the balds of today are endangered. Climate change, pollution, changes in soil and the invasion of trees

are constant threats to these special places that host the highest concentration of rare species on the entire AT.

One way the National Park Service works to keep the balds open and healthy is by conducting controlled burns. Another is by allowing grazing by animals such as angora goats. Both of these efforts help keep invasive species at bay.

Walking among the balds is an incredible experience. The mountains that surround you ripple forever outward as far as your eyes allow, those closest to you taking on a purple hue, those in the farthest distance painted black against the sky. To paraphrase Thoreau, the open summits compel you to stay among them, but at some point you know you must hike down.

When we reached the summit plateau of Max Patch Bald on day three, we stayed deep into the afternoon. Mount Mitchell rose above all the peaks in the Smokeys to the east of us. When we turned to our south, we could trace this trip's route all the way back to the FAA tower on Snowbird Mountain we had passed the first full day out.

The signal that it was time to go was the sky itself. Powder pink was our cue. I stood up and started moving toward my pack.

"First flat spot.", said Wayne.

We camped under a big oak tree with the shoulder of the mountain as our backdrop. As the pasta water came to a boil, I went outside and looked up at the ridge. There wasn't a cloud in the whole sky. That meant a cold night ahead.

"Better to be down here than on the summit.", I thought.

Like us, I imagined Thoreau would have headed down from the heights of Max Patch Bald at the end of the day. But I'm pretty sure he wouldn't have had pasta Alfredo with crab as his reward.

The next few days stayed mild, although high, thin cirrus clouds indicated that a change in weather would be coming our way soon. The woodpeckers were tuned into a much longer forecast than the clouds could provide. They'd been getting ready for winter for weeks. I saw three oaks that had been so ravaged by woodpeckers looking for bugs that the wood chips they left behind looked like a first snowfall.

I was enjoying this section of trail in every way, a sentiment captured in my journal with entries like, "Haven't felt this great on the trail in years. Simply beautiful trail switchbacking through oaks, rhododendrons and occasional pines. Round and round the ridges we went, my legs powering me up and over each one, scarcely stopping to rest."

Then came winter.

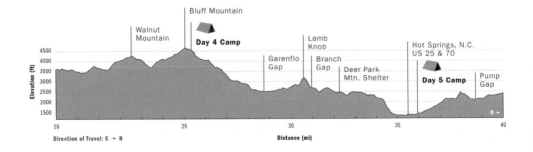

Appropriately enough, the falling temperatures arrived with the month of December. I awoke first and unzipped the tent door flap enough to take in the dull gray sky surroundings.

"Oy", I announced to Wayne. "Looks bleak out there."

The forecast on the radio called for rain with occasional thunderstorms with temperatures in the mid to low 40s. We both knew we wouldn't be stopping much today.

We had passed through the town of Hot Springs at the end of the day before, which meant we had also passed a diner.

"How far back to that diner?", I asked Wayne.

"About a mile", he said.

That bleak weather wasn't much of a motivator, but pancakes, omelettes and coffee sure did the trick! We broke down camp, stashed our packs in the woods and were seated at the counter in under 45 minutes.

While we ate, it started pouring. We looked out the window at the rain and ordered another round of coffee.

The rain let up on our way back to our packs to begin the thousand foot climb out of the French Broad River valley. If I had "temporarily unlocked the fountain of youth" as I had claimed in my journal earlier in the trip, I had at least temporarily misplaced the key. I looked at my feet and repeated my, "one, two" mantra until I got up and over the ridge.

I thought maybe I'd find my pace once the trail leveled out some, but it just wasn't there, despite (or because of) having a full belly of fuel. After five trail miles (plus an additional two diner-related miles) we called it a short day and pitched the dome to rest and regroup.

That was the best call we could have made. The clouds blew out as we broke camp the following morning and would not return until the afternoon we stepped off the trail. Sunny skies improve your footing and your attitude. They also helped me relocate my "fountain of youth keys."

Instead of plodding up thousand foot climbs, I was doing four and five mile stretches nonstop and feeling fantastic. High temperatures in the 40s were certainly part of the motivation to keep moving, but it was much more than that. The mountain topography was beautiful. I couldn't wait to see what was beyond the next bend or ridge top.

"As always, perseverance is the strongest motivator of all", I thought as I ambled along. "If I folded my tent and went home, I wouldn't know this contentment."

One of the greatest rewards was the view from the Camp Creek Bald (4844') fire

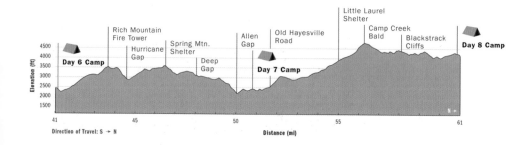

Big Bald summit

tower, with stupendous views of the Smoky Mountains, including Mount Mitchell, the highest peak in the east. The lateness of day and the chill down we experienced from our sweaty bodies being hit by a steady 40 degree breeze urged us down.

Less than a mile from the tower, we found a sweet camp site. We should have taken it, but the trail guide spoke of amazing views from the White Rocks ridge over the next several miles. Because of our short mileage "diner day" a few days before, we decided to hike a ways further.

It was the worst decision of the trip.

The views were as promised. The only problem is we couldn't stop to enjoy them. There were no good campsites and we were in a race against daylight.

"The big dilemma", I wrote in my journal. "Trail ascended around bare knobs of rock

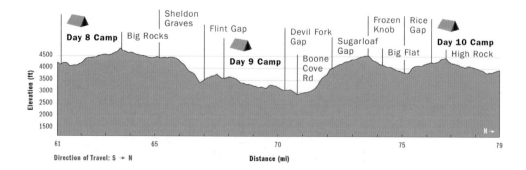

Smokies from Big Bald

and up onto the narrow ridge crest with no camping spots to be found. Ridge just kept going and going. Beautiful rock climbing up and over knolls. Stunning views of setting sun from every one, but had to get off ridge and find campsite before darkness fell."

At 4:20, we found a yellow blazed side trail and scoped out possible sites. There was only one — wedged tightly between two rhododendron thickets. It didn't look promising, so Wayne stayed to try setting up the dome while I left to look for something better.

I found a divergence of trials — the white blazed AT climbed up and over rocks and a blue blazed "bad weather route" that bypassed the open ridge. I went a little ways on both of them, finding nothing but steep terrain, then returned to Wayne, who pronounced the first option "unusable".

Now things were really tight. We needed to find a spot pronto.

When we hit the divergent trails, we went up. I was convinced that the ridge walk

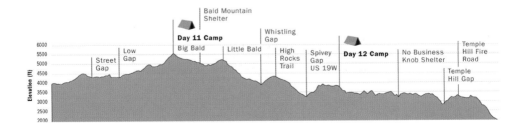

would end soon and reward us for our efforts.

Just after 5:00, we found it — a heaven sent flat spot beneath giant oaks and next to a large thicket of rhododendrons. By 5:20, we were devouring appetizers from the protective environment of dry clothes, five degree rated sleeping bags and the protection of the Pleasure Dome. The trail gods were smiling down upon us to be sure.

Our good fortune extended into beautiful sun filled days — woods walks punctuated by high mountain views. Besides the sun, our other source of constant companionship was pileated woodpeckers, their unmistakable jungle cries and loud knockings in the quest for bugs always brought a smile, and I'd stop to watch their high swoops between the leafless oaks.

It was great to be out this time of year, just us and the woodpeckers. If this were April or May, we'd be two among hundreds attempting the walk to Katahdin. We were being treated to a completely different experience. Granted, 22 degree nights and 40 degree days aren't for everyone, but we were having a blast.

The final highlight of the trip was the view from the summit of Big Bald (5518'). We arrived on the top of the golden grassed mountain at just after 4:00 and sat to watch the sky and mountains around us change color by degrees. As we watched the simple, glorious miracle of time passing in complete silence, I felt a familiar surge of gratitude flowing through me. The one that makes me feel so blessed to be out here witnessing something so grand and indescribable. The one that keeps me coming back to feel it again and again. Yes, this is why, at almost fifty years old, I was still hoisting a pack and climbing up for the views. I couldn't begin to imagine a time when I would ever want to stop. But soon I would have to — for this trip anyway.

The first day of a hiking trip is the toughest physically. The last is the toughest mentally. You are finally in great shape, attuned to your surroundings and able to enjoy them to the utmost, yet it's time to fold up the tent until the next adventure beckons — place and time TBD.

Predictably, I awoke on the last morning of our trip with my emotions playing the Tug-o-War between not wanting to get off the trail and the need to hike the nine miles to Uncle Johnny's Hostel, drop our gear then make an additional three mile round trip walk to reach Nochilucky Campground, where we got off the trail the year before. We didn't want to have to come back to walk a three mile gap in some future year. The time was now.

Making the hostel with plenty of daylight left turned out to be much less of an issue than we imagined. Our light packs were no doubt part of the reason, as was the trail layout, but we quickly hit the "miles flying by" mode.

Yet, the faster we went, the more I wanted to stay out among the oaks, ferns, moss, ridges and woodpeckers. Deep down, I knew that Thoreau was right, that I'd have to come down off the mountaintops to face the obligations of life. But the pull of the trail is almost strong enough to make you want to keep them forever at bay. It's amazing how this daily ritual of walking over mountains can make me so complete. Out here, it's just me, my companion, my gear and the situation changing by the day and the minute. It's a life skill that's good for the soul — even necessary.

Our only lingering of the day was on a mid-afternoon stop on Cliff Ridge, above the Nochilucky Gorge. The sky was steel gray, as was the river, but the views were still terrific. We watched an exceptionally long freight train filled with coal negotiating through the gorge on a single track. The cars, orange and red, provided some color against the pale backdrop. The river's rapids literally provided a splash of white as well.

We took a few last looks from the ridge, where we tried to guess the location of our hotel (wrong) and pinpoint the location of the campground where we spent a windy December night in a cabin nearly a year ago (right on the money).

On Big Bald, the landmarks had been expansive and humbling — the Smoky Mountains and the heavens among them. Now we were recalibrating our view to encompass trains and campgrounds. The transition back to life's obligations was in sight and they would soon be back in control for a while.

CHAPTER 20

The Smoky Mountains

One of the most beautiful and accessible landscapes in the United States also held something much less accessible than we'd imagined.

Nantahala Gorge, NC to Davenport Gap, TN

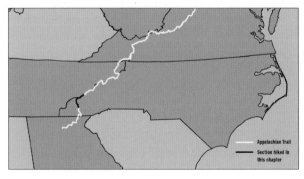

Appalachian Trail
Section hiked in this chapter

TRIP STATS
November 13 - November 25, 2007
101 miles
South to North

I spent most of my summer behind a desk. This wouldn't be a good thing for most people, I imagine, but for me, it was sanity threatening. At age 50, I still hadn't learned the important concept of moderation. It wasn't because others hadn't been warning me. It's that I wasn't yet willing to listen. Moderation was for others. The only way you accomplished anything was to get busy and stay busy.

Thus, I produced 350 hours of billable client work in the 5 1/2 weeks from the end of June through the first week of August. Even by my workaholic standards, I was way out of balance.

By mid September, the paychecks associated with my word binging began pouring in and I felt I could finally ease off the throttle and get outside. Wayne and I met in the

White Mountains for a 3-day hike in mid-September, which served as a nice preamble for our November hike through Great Smoky Mountains National Park.

The first time I visited the Smokies was during a college break. Four of us borrowed a classmate's father's Buick and drove from Champaign, Illinois to the park. To give you an idea of how green an outdoorsman I was, I suggested the shortest trail into the Mount LeConte shelter. What I didn't figure out until we were underway was that the shortest trail also meant the steepest. The other dumb thing we did was prepare pork chops in the shelter. My buddy, Charlie, wrapped the bones in foil and tossed them in the corner of the shelter as we had advised.

In the middle of the night, he announced from the bottom bunk that there was an animal inside the shelter.

I shined my light down onto the most enormous skunk I'd ever seen.

"That isn't an animal. It's a skunk. Don't move until she gets out of here.", I said. "If she sprays, we're all screwed. Especially you."

When the skunk decided she'd had her fill, she wandered off, leaving an indelible life lesson in her wake. I never knowingly left a scrap of food in a shelter again.

Besides the skunk episode, my most vivid memories of that 1977 trip were of the spectacular vistas in the park and the trip we made to Clingmans Dome, the highest peak in Tennessee. We drove to the parking lot and walked up a concrete ramp to reach the observation deck, which I remembered as being rather Frisbee® like.

For my encore, I'd be traveling on foot. I wanted to find out how the National Park Service accommodated thru-hikers — specifically, whether there were any things we'd need to keep in mind regarding camping. Were the lean-tos first come, first served? Were there any general restrictions regarding where you camped (distance from trail, for example)? I'd rather find out beforehand than at some point during our traverse.

When I heard back from the NPS, I was pleased to learn that we would not have to submit a lean-to camping itinerary, as long as we started well outside the park boundary. If we did that, we'd be considered thru-hikers and would not have to hike on a tight schedule.

The Park Service warned us of something we were also thankful to know about — drought. There were going to be places, including a 23-mile stretch after Fontana Dam, where usually reliable water supplies would be non-existent.

I packed a collapsible water bottle just for that event and was doubly thankful when it came time to use it.

Even before the NPS contacted me, I had an inkling that we'd need to be more prepared for this trip than the ones that preceded it. There wouldn't be any resupply points on the trip and we'd be traversing the highest summits on the east coast in November. That was enough for me to make sure my gear was still up for the test.

I treated my boots with waterproofing spray, bought new insoles, applied waterproofing goop to the floor and rain fly seams in the tent and sprayed my rain jacket and pants with a waterproofing solution, so that rain would bead up and run off.

I also went on food foraging missions. I am always on the lookout for new and better food solutions. For this trip, I found maple sugar (which I couldn't wait to add to oatmeal). I also dried vegetables that I bought at the farmer's market to add to soups and stews and made two batches of homemade beef jerky. I repackaged all the food and

stuffed it all in the plastic bear canister we'd been warned we should have.

When I completed packing, I couldn't believe my good fortune. This was the most prepared for a trip with three days to go that I could remember. Even my work was complete!

My euphoria lasted until I checked my email. A client gave the "go" signal on a project and suddenly I needed to write a 36-page catalog in three days.

Once again, the night before a trip was a wild frenzy of writing that had me rolling into bed at 12:20 a.m. and back out of it four hours later to catch a 6:00 a.m. bus to Boston, followed by a train to Lynchburg, VA, another bus to Roanoke, then yet another one to Knoxville, TN. The final leg was a car ride with a trail shuttle driver from Knoxville to the Nantahala Outdoor Center, (a major hiking and whitewater rafting mecca) where the AT awaited.

At 10:00 a.m., I slung my 70 lb. pack onto my back and started climbing out of the valley, with Wayne right behind me. I felt surprisingly good, given that I'd been awake for 29 hours and had so little sleep before that. Even though my mind was foggy, I couldn't help but notice the effect of the drought. The trail was deep in dry leaves that made it sound like we were walking through a bag of potato chips. Some trailside shrubs still had leaves on them, but they were shriveled and desperate hangers on. We crunched our way through a 3,000' ascent over the first five miles and called it good. By 6:45, I was starting a 12-hour crash in the comfort of the refurbished Pleasure Dome. The only time I awoke was to hear a barred owl repeat the refrain "Who cooks for youuuuuuuu?" into the deep night.

When we awoke, we immediately started the water conversation. It would be the ongoing dialogue of the trip. Our well being hinged on the answer to two questions: How

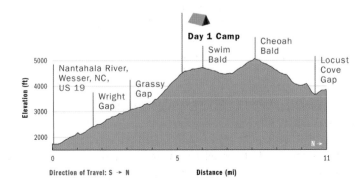

much water did we have? and where was the next likely source?

Fortunately, on the way to the trail, we had asked Bill (the shuttle driver) to stop at a convenience store, where we bought two gallons. We still had two quarts each when we woke up. Coffee and oatmeal wouldn't take much, but the rest of the day would be a crap shoot.

Early in the day, we met a group of six hikers on the summit of Swim Bald (4720'), who told us there was water at Locust Cove, 4.5 miles away. When we got there, the spring was dry. This was particularly vexing, because we were now down to one quart between us. We kept going, hoping to find a fresh source soon. At Stecoah Gap, we hit pay dirt. A trail angel had left several jugs of water for hikers under a picnic table there. We grabbed one gallon and left a gallon for the next folks through.

On the climb out of the gap, we met a band of southbound through-hikers that told us the water situation up ahead wasn't as bad as we'd been told. "There are water updates posted in the shelters.", they said.

That was enough to put a little extra spring in my step for a few miles anyway.

The next day, I hit the wall. It was a combination of rain drifting in and out,

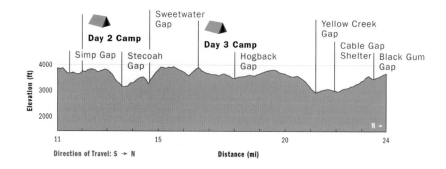

carrying nine days of food on my back, incessant climbing and much cooler temperatures that made me want to keep walking slowly instead of taking breaks and cooling down even further.

As always, the drizzle cast a pall over the day. We plodded along into the late afternoon, passing one nice flat spot by rationalizing that we had enough energy and light to cover some more ground. Big mistake. We walked deep into "the land of no flat spots" and it started pouring. I didn't want to stop to put my pack cover on. I just wanted to find the elusive camp spot. I vowed that the next time I took my pack off would be the last for the day. Ten minutes into our complete drenching, we found a reasonable spot, threw the tent up and dove in. I was really happy I had sealed the tent seams now! We stayed warm and dry all night. No doubt the massive pot of soup, filled with farmer's market veggies, helped.

By morning, the worst of the rain had moved on, to be replaced by fog and drizzle. The irony was that although water had poured all around us, it did nothing for the general lack of drinking or cooking water. The ground was so dry that it instantly soaked it up. The aquifer was so low it would take dozens more storms for it to get the springs flowing again.

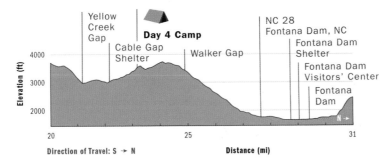

I looked out at the mist realizing that I would be lashing a wet rain fly to my pack — even more weight to carry. I was glad the first five miles of the day would be downhill, where we would load up with water at Fontana Dam, then start our 23-mile walk through the drought stricken mountains beyond. I took a brief look at the profile map to see what the climb would be like after we filled the water bottles, then tossed it aside. I'd deal with it when I got there.

Over the next 76 miles, we would be hiking through an area greatly affected by the pull and draw of history. Two projects that came to fruition in the 1940s forever changed the landscape here — one initiative brought citizens together to stem the tide of progress and the other one to fuel it.

Fontana Dam was built by the Tennessee Valley Authority in the early 1940s to generate power in support of the war effort. When you look at this incredibly imposing structure it is hard to believe that it only took three years to build. Standing 480' tall and 2,365' long, the dam is the largest concrete dam east of the Rockies.

While there had been plans to dam the Little Tennessee River to provide the energy needed to power nearby aluminum plants for decades, it was the advent of WWII that jumpstarted the project. And jumpstart it did! Over 5,000 workers, working in three shifts, completed the project in remarkable time — the project started on January 1, 1942 and the dam was producing power by January 20, 1945.

The first impact of the dam was felt by the locals. More than 1,300 families were relocated and four towns were evacuated and subsequently inundated by the rising waters. The most visible lasting impacts are the 26-mile long lake that formed behind the dam that is a popular recreational boating and fishing destination (the village that once housed the workers that built the dam is now a summer resort).

The resort had long closed for the season when we arrived on November 15, 2007, but the Visitor Center's outdoor soda machine was gloriously stocked and working. Even more important, was the ability to stock up with potable water. The 23-mile waterless stretch was ahead. We stayed just long enough to fill every water container we had, empty our trash and make the one mile walk to the dam.

My pack weighed a ton, due in part to the 6 plus quarts of water I was carrying and my shoulders and legs barked their disapproval. I stopped at the half-mile mark and convinced Wayne to split my smallest bottle of water, the 24 oz. one. At least that got rid of a little more than one pound.

Walking over the dam was astounding. The views from the trail/road delivered the full sense of what a large scale undertaking this project was, particularly in the time it was achieved. It was and is an incredible engineering feat.

As I approached the opposite side of the valley, I took a deep breath, stepped onto the wooded trail that signaled we had entered Great Smoky Mountains National Park and began to climb. My calves wanted no part of it.

"This is what you get for spending the whole summer chained to a desk. A problem of your own making.", I said aloud. But maybe it was more than the inactivity. I turned 50 years old in July. Could it be that my age was a factor? That I was no longer the indefatigable mountaineer? That I was getting too old for this?

"Shut that voice off right now", I also said aloud. Somehow hearing my own voice seemed to provide extra conviction when my mind started stirring up doubts. Besides,

Wayne was far enough behind me that he couldn't hear me, so he wouldn't think he was walking behind a crazy person — at least any more than he normally would.

"Preposterous. It's only the lack of conditioning", I said between breaths. "I know how to get up and over these hills."

It was true. I did know a few tricks that would power me to the top and beyond. They wouldn't make me any younger, but they kept me in the game. One of them was breathing.

Early on, I learned that I got a lot less fatigued if I could pull air deep into my diaphragm instead of doing shallow breathing, which made me gasp and stop more frequently. When I opened my mouth and let the air go seemingly all the way to my stomach, I could generally make it to the top of any hill in question. In bug season, deep breathing often has you pulling in more than air. The feeling of a black fly lodging on the back of your throat is pretty high on the wretchedness scale — one more reason early spring and fall are my favorite hiking seasons.

My other ascending trick is "rolling stops". While I'm still getting in shape, I pick out a spot on the climb — a trailside tree or rock for example — and promise myself I won't stop till I get there. Just before I arrive, I pick out another spot and so on, until I reach the top of the hill. When I reach the top, I can feel my calf muscles switch from being the primary drivers to sharing the burden. It is enough of a change that I can often convince myself to keep going, especially if I'm finally in trail condition. In this way, I can often go miles without taking the pack off. I keep the guidebook, map and compass in a belt holster, so checking my progress is convenient.

To be sure, my tricks of the trade helped me continue to move forward. But my greatest source of strength was the reason I was out here in the first place. From the beginning, I have felt that it is a privilege to walk through some of the most fascinating

Snowy Smokies

and inspiring places on earth. It is something that makes me feel more complete and connected to nature than any activity I can imagine. Trying to do it for as long as I can is the greatest gift I can give myself. Yes, there are tough days. There are also many more glorious ones — just like life in general. And experiencing them out here helps keep things in perspective when I return to the man made universe of projects, deadlines and the like.

I employed both tricks on the 2,300' climb to the summit of Shuckstack Mountain, where we planned to camp. I was sweating like crazy when I got to the fire tower on the summit. I dropped my pack to the ground, pulled on a wind shell and climbed up for the view. Wayne was right behind me. The cloud ceiling was high enough to allow stunning views of the Smoky Mountains and Fontana Dam far below. It was hard to believe we were just there.

It was too windy to stay on top of the tower for long. We were chilling down fast. Time to set up the tent. Rain was in the forecast, so we staked out the rain fly extra taut. Good thing, because in the early evening, it really started pouring. For 12 solid hours, wind and rain buffeted the Pleasure Dome. The key to staying dry was the great job we'd done of staking out the rain fly. If the fly were to touch the tent underneath, the water drops would inevitably start falling on us. But, that wasn't the case this time. Every once in a while during the night, I'd unzip the front window and look down at the lights of Fontana Dam below through the storm. The scene was surreal.

The temperatures dropped through the night and although the rain had stopped, the tent fly was now soaked and frozen. Somehow I seemed to be gaining pack weight every day instead of the other way around. I took some comfort in knowing that this morning would finally be the high water mark for pack weight. I took even greater comfort in knowing we were on a National Park Service trail.

The trails in the national park system are generally better conceived and maintained than other parts of the Appalachian Trail. There are more switchbacks to reduce erosion and make climbs less dramatic and the trails also tend to get more regular maintenance. "Blow downs" (trees that fall across the trail) don't stay there long as a rule. Other sections of trail rely on the generous efforts of volunteers to stay in good shape. There the quality of maintenance depends on the strength and capabilities of the organization itself. If, for example, the maintaining organization is a college outing club, the trail may see some years of loving maintenance followed by a few lean years, during which hikers may cut new paths around fallen trees.

We needed to make consistent 12-mile days from here until the end of the trip and I was confident the trail itself would make our task easier. In looking at the stats, we'd need the help. Over the next 71 miles, our cumulative ascent would be about 18,000 feet (an average of over 260 feet per mile). As always, the privilege of experiencing the mountain highs required the willingness to work for them.

By 10:00 a.m., we were hiking under spitting snow. Just two days ago, we had to move into the shade to eat lunch. The November weather we expected had finally arrived in the Smoky Mountains. Twelve miles into the gray, largely uphill day, we found a nice spot to camp near Spence Field Shelter, where a sign warned of bear activity in the area. As soon as we got the tent up, the snowstorm picked up. It snowed all night, but because the ground was saturated, only the last two inches blanketed the ground and shrubs when we awoke.

It would be a temporary frosting. The forecast called for 60° temperatures and ample sun. Even so, it was hard getting motivated. We drank coffee for the first time in three days, due to the water situation, then packed up and hit the trail at 9:00. In 1.2 miles, we reached Rockytop (5441'), where we could look back on the ridge we traversed yesterday, the day before and the day before that!

The place demanded a stop to look around. Yet, at the same time, we needed to be making forward progress. It was closing in on 10:30 and we had a long way to go today to make it past Silers Bald Shelter, which would keep us on schedule.

I stopped once more on top of Thunderhead (5527') to perch on a boulder pile and grab a photo looking north to the highest part of the range, including Clingmans Dome (at 6643', it was the highest point on the entire AT). If all went well, we'd be there tomorrow.

But it didn't go well.

After dropping off Thunderhead, we started a series of ups and downs that really zapped my energy. I thought I was doing pretty well until I got to the last two climbs. Twice I was convinced that the Derrick Knob Shelter (where we planned to stop for lunch), was in the gap I was entering, only to find

a steep, no switchback climb ahead of me. The only solution was to keep walking.

Just after 1:00, I passed a tree with a sign on it pronouncing my arrival at Sugartree Gap (4435'). I began to wonder if I had actually passed the shelter. It didn't seem possible that we hadn't yet covered 6.4 miles. I took out the guidebook. Damn. Another mile to go.

I cursed the trail builders all the way up and out of the gap. Easier to blame them than my heavy water load, my game or my conditioning. At 1:30, I rolled into the shelter, dropped my pack on the food preparation bench and worshipped the sun while I waited for Wayne. He arrived at 1:40. He had also stopped at Sugartree Gap to check his trail guide.

"No soup today", I said.

Wayne nodded in agreement. "Don't have the time", he said.

We were in a race with the sun. We still needed to make 6 miles to keep us remotely in range of making Davenport Gap.

First things first. We dashed down to the nearby spring, where water was flowing out of a pipe suspended 2' above the run out. We filtered six quarts, drank two on the spot, then ran back to the shelter to eat Pop-Tarts® and beef jerky for lunch.

Twenty-five minutes after we arrived, we were back underway. We desperately needed the trail gods to be kind. And they were! The trail began a series of long traverses between the knobs and even switchbacking to their summits. If the trail had been the way it was before lunch, I'm sure we would not make a 12 mile day. Now it was back in the realm of the possible.

Siler's Bald Shelter was at the 11.5 mile mark. We wanted to get there by 5:30, then find a camp spot beyond. As I made my way up the snowy ridge, I encountered what looked like large coyote or wolf prints in the snow. I thought back to a note a hiker named, "Little John" left in the Derrick Knob Shelter two nights before. An animal had chewed through the steel cables designed for hanging food near the shelter to keep it from being marauded by bears. At dusk, he saw what he described as "a dog like animal"

View from Clingmans Dome

trotting away. I wondered if I was following the same creature up the mountain.

At 2.7 miles from Siler's Bald Shelter, the Miry Ridge Trail merged with ours. Now human footprints joined the AT creature cavalcade. I walked a while further and checked the time. It was 5:00. I figured we were close to the shelter. When Wayne showed up a few minutes later, I suggested camping nearby, figuring we were close enough to our goal to call it a day. We were gassed.

It was a good thing we stopped. The tent's front door zipper broke. More precisely, it got untracked. Unlike say, a jacket, the tent doesn't have a doohickey for lining up the teeth. We had to get it started by hand, then put a strip of duct tape on each side to keep it from breaking again. The immediate objective was to keep the cold air from getting in so we could get a good night's sleep. We would be climbing the highest mountain on the Appalachian Trail tomorrow.

The 7:50 start was just what we needed, especially since we were more than a mile from the shelter. Little John was there and so was a flowing spring. No sign of the wolf, though.

The 4.8 mile climb to Clingmans Dome began with my now familiar morning lack of energy. Lots of climbing this week. Even so, not a good time to be lagging.

1.9 miles into the climb, we hit Double Spring Gap Shelter. No need to tank up here, but we each drank half a quart to lessen our loads for the climb.

I was getting mentally prepared for a steep climb with no switchbacks. Thankfully, I entered a glorious stretch of switchbacks. In just a few minutes I went from dragging ass to entertaining the thought of climbing nonstop to the summit of Clingmans Dome. It's crazy how a day or a mentality can turn on a dime.

"No stopping" became my mantra and I rode it all the way to the top — even though there were three other peaks between. The footing was tricky on the summit plateau. One inch of snow over patches of ice. Just as I arrived at the observation tower, I hit an ice patch and went ass over tea kettle. So glad I had a large pack on to take the brunt of the fall.

The wind was screaming up on the observation deck. But that didn't stop a handful of

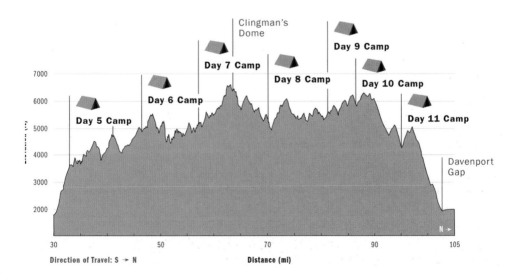

people from walking up there from the nearby parking lot, then quickly departing. I did a quick walk around the "Frisbee" for the 360° view, and scooted back down to ground level to find Wayne and get out of the wind.

I got it half right. I found Wayne coming into the summit tower clearing and went back up onto the observation deck with him. On one side we see Fontana Dam and the brilliant red foliage on the ridges beyond. To our north, we could see the smokey blue mountains that awaited our arrival, including Mt. Collins, the next summit on our itinerary.

The wind and the time both urged us on our way. We hadn't even taken our packs off, nor would we until we got down in the trees and out of the arctic blast. The good news was that we had our first prolonged descent of the whole trip. The not so good was that we were descending the north side of the mountain, where the snow and ice made footing treacherous, even with our hallowed ski poles to assist us. The four miles down to the Mount Collins Shelter trail seemed to take forever and included a 300' climb up and over the mountain itself. I was pretty wobbly on the climb. I had used most of my energy to get up and over Clingmans Dome. At 2:00, I hit the junction and sat on some ice covered stumps. Again, I kept my pack on. When Wayne arrived, we downed some snacks and stayed on the move.

Along the continuum, we passed a spring. Another omen to drink up. We grabbed two and drank one.

Now to find a camp spot. It wasn't easy. Finally, about a mile from Newfound Gap, we found the perfect one (maybe the only one). Despite being careful, the duct tape had peeled off the zipper. This time, we fixed it by sewing a "dam" of thread behind the toggle, so it wouldn't come undone again. I was sure glad I carried dental floss and thread.

We celebrated the long, yet exhilarating day with a double batch of mac and cheese. It was fantastic to be out among the big peaks. "The country here is awesome", I wrote in my journal that night. "Sometimes I had to play the mental toughness card to get up and over the peaks, but I'm damn glad I did it. I am still hopeful we can get out of the snow for the last night or two. It would be nice to have boots that aren't frozen and wet when I put them on or to have a completely dry sleeping bag and ground pad. Now 32.5 miles from Davenport Gap. We just might make it!"

We awoke to discover that a thick fog had settled over us like a giant down comforter. The temperature rose during the night, signaling the end of our early winter festivities. From here on, the trail would be snow free—another plus for a couple of guys trying to make miles for three more days.

As we made our way to Indian Gap, we realized how fortunate we were to grab the spot we did last night. There were no places to camp along the way. By the time we got to Newfound Gap, the fog had completely burned off, such that we were greeted with a splendid panorama of the northern part of the park.

The view here was so inspiring and accessible that it was on this spot that Franklin Delano Roosevelt dedicated the Great Smoky Mountain National Park in September of 1940 with hundreds of fellow Americans looking on. His speech included the following paragraph:

"There are trees here that stood before our forefathers ever came to this continent; there are brooks that still run as clear as on the day the first pioneer cupped his hand and drank from them. In this Park, we shall conserve these trees, the pine, the red-bud,

the dogwood, the azalea, the rhododendron, the trout and the thrush for the happiness of the American people."

As I looked around for a water spigot, I passed the place from which FDR made his remarks, an impressive two-tiered monument honoring the $5 million donation by the Rockefeller foundation that was the catalyst for making the park a reality. It reads:

"For the permanent enjoyment of the people. This park was given one-half by the peoples and states of North Carolina and Tennessee and by the United States of America, and one-half in memory of Laura Spelman Rockefeller by the Laura Spelman Rockefeller Memorial, founded by her husband John D. Rockefeller."

FDR at dedication of Great Smoky Mountains National Park. (Courtesy and copyright, Calvin M. McClung Historical Collection, Knox County Public Library).

On my way to find water, I ran into a Park Ranger who verified there was running water in the rest room. He then nodded toward my pack, which was propped against a stone wall half way across the parking lot where Wayne also stood. The sun made something glint on my pack.

"Is that a solar panel on your pack?", he asked.

"Yes. I have a small one to power my phone as an emergency precaution", I said.

Boy, did he like that idea.

"That's really neat. I've never seen one out here."

"Yeah, we're sure cutting edge.", I said with a laugh. "I'm sure you'll be seeing more of them."

It was like old home day where Wayne awaited. There were about 20 cars worth of people milling about and taking pictures of the view. Some rolled up to roll down their windows and ask us about our adventures. We were some kind of curiosities.

"Maybe they should put us in cages.", I said under my breath to Wayne.

"You love it.", he replied. "I'm going to tank up, so we can get going."

After we left the gap, we came into the best hiking of the trip. We still had some major ups and downs ahead of us, but our pack loads were a week's worth of food lighter and we were getting into trail shape.

The first stop was a big trailside sunny spot, where we draped all our wet gear over trees and ground to dry while we made soup for lunch. What a treat after our recent arctic days!

*Citation: Franklin D. Roosevelt: "Address at Dedication of Great Smoky Mountains National Park.,"
September 2, 1940. Online by Gerhard Peters and John T. Woolley, The American Presidency Project.
http://www.presidency.ucsb.edu/ws/?pid=1600*

While we ate, a group of college aged kids went by. We'd end up playing leapfrog with them all afternoon.

It can be really frustrating to catch up to a large group on the trail. The fact you caught up with them at all means you are hiking faster than them. But getting past them is another story. Most folks don't want to let you by. Their inclination is to try to speed up, which only works for a while. Fortunately, that is usually enough for them to let you pass.

In this case, the group was making pretty good time. They were almost 30 years younger and were carrying weekend packs after all. But, there was one young man that was definitely showing signs of trouble.

The oft cited rule of hiking is that one of the leaders should stay back and hike with the slowest member of the group. But that wasn't happening here.

Instead, I came around a bend on the trail to find the disconsolate guy sitting on a rock. "Are you ok?", I asked.

"Yup. Just taking a break.", he said.

"Are you with the group that went by?"

"Yup."

'Well, at least he isn't hiking alone.', I thought. I eased on ahead and told him I'd see him down the trail.

What I didn't expect was for him to get back on his feet and try to keep up with me. He kept it up for about a half mile, then we started a steep climb. I could hear him dropping further and further back, until I couldn't hear him any more.

As I topped the ridge, I felt a moral dilemma. Should I wait for the kid? I knew Wayne was behind him, so I shifted my focus to the group ahead. Maybe I could catch them and warn them that their friend was in trouble. I opted for that answer and picked up speed.

I kept up a good pace for a few miles and still wasn't catching the group. You would think they would have stopped by now to wait for their friend. Finally, I caught them taking a break. I turned around and saw Wayne approaching from behind me. There was no kid in sight.

I walked back to Wayne first.

"Hey. Did you see a kid really dragging back there?"

"Yes.", he replied. "When I first saw him, he was sitting on the side of the trail with his head in his hands. When I went by him, he jumped up and tried to keep up with me. He's really making slow progress."

The rest of his group was standing up and getting ready to keep going.

"Hey. You guys.", I said. "You're friend back there is really hurting."

"Yeah. We know.", one said. A few of the others laughed.

"I mean he's in serious trouble.", I said. "Somebody needs to go back to give him encouragement and assess the situation. You don't want to be looking for him out here after dark."

Once upon a time, it would have been much harder for me to say this. But I'd had three experiences on the trail that could have gone really badly if I hadn't spoken up.

One time was in the Cascade Mountain Range, where a college orientation group was staying in a shelter. It was raining at 6500' and they were going up a trail that would take them into snowfields above 8000'. When we awoke in our tent, the weather was so poor that we decided to stay put. There was no way we were going up in the snow in zero visibility conditions — and we had the gear for it!

Those college kids were wearing cheap rain ponchos and whatever gear they could borrow. When we went to the shelter to chat with them, they were gone! We couldn't believe they were headed up the trail.

We ran up the trail with just the rain gear we had on (the other three in our group were back at the tents with the gear). We caught them just before they were about to walk out onto the snowfields.

"You can't go up there.", I said to the chaperone (a guy at least 20 years older than me) with a waver in my voice that I hoped he didn't hear.

"It's crazy.", said my hiking companion, Mick. "You can't see anything up there."

"We need to meet the other half of our group.", the man said. "They started from the north and we're supposed to exchange car keys at the half way mark."

"Do you think they went ahead?", I asked. "They probably stayed put, too. It's better to stay down in the shelter and wait for good weather than take the chance of someone getting lost or hurt."

The guy looked down at the ground for a bit, going through his decision, no doubt. He yelled up ahead.

"Hey Chuck.", he waited for a response. "Hey Chuck. We're heading back down."

Thank god.

We went back down to the shelter, got a big fire going in the stove to warm up with and spent the day popping the popcorn my mom had thrown in the last food drop box and yucking it up.

I thought back to that day as I tried to convince the group to send someone back for their friend. At last, two of them got up to go find him.

I shot a glance over to Wayne and we set off again.

When we got out of earshot, I said, "Our work is done in this town."

"Right.", he said.

There was no need to say more, we both knew we had done the right thing.

We figured the group would be staying at Pecks Shelter. When we got there, the sun was getting really low. We started looking in vain for a flat spot just beyond the shelter trail junction. There appeared to be only one, at a sharp bend in the trail.

The only problem for me is that it was almost on the trail. Wayne protested going further.

"I'm done.", he said, tossing his pack at his feet.

"Give me one second.", I said. "I'll be right back."

I set my pack down and ambled up the trail a few hundred yards. There on the left was a site just large enough for the tent. The land dropped off steeply beyond what would be the back window.

I went back and got Wayne. I think he was a bit skeptical, but when he saw the spot, he declared it a winner.

We were still close enough to the shelter to hear the group of college kids arriving at dusk. With just barely enough light left to see the trail, we heard the last three people arrive to applause.

Yes, we had done the right thing.

CHAPTER 21

Back to Maine

Where mountains, lakes and streams are most inspirational companions.

SECTION 1

Caratunk, ME to Monson, ME

TRIP STATS
June 1, 2008 - June 5, 2008
37.0 miles
South to North

During the winter of 2007, Wayne shot me an email regarding our AT hiking plans for the following year.

"I'd like to finish up Maine" he wrote, "before heading back down south. You're way ahead of me. I can do it solo, but it would be great if you would join me for it."

It was true. I had hiked the 250 miles of Maine closer to four times to Wayne's less than one. Together, we had hiked the western edge of the state, but Wayne was still a little over 140 miles behind me.

I don't need much encouragement to hit the trail, especially in Maine, so I quickly agreed.

Like neighboring New Hampshire, Maine is chock full of granite rock formations. As soon as the trail crosses into Maine, it drops down off the Mahoosuc Range and enters a one mile stretch hailed as "the toughest mile on the AT".

This is ridiculously inaccurate as far as I'm concerned, but makes for a good story. From my perspective, there are some vertical climbs on the AT that are much more difficult than the relatively flat traverse across the base of Mahoosuc Notch. The feature that raises the level of difficulty is the giant boulders that were deposited there after the last glaciers retreated and the sheer cliffs above - left entirely exposed to the elements - collapsed. Negotiating over, under and around the boulders that filled the valley below is challenging, especially with a large pack on, but I wouldn't elevate it to the status of "The AT's most difficult mile".

Leaving the notch, the trail ascends Maine's second highest peak, Old Speck (4180'), drops down to Grafton Notch, then climbs up and over one of my favorite mountains in Maine, West Baldpate (3662'), where the above tree line stretch makes for some of the best viewing and lingering available. I have spent many afternoons on the granite slabs of Baldpate and always take leave of the panorama with a tinge of regret.

Wayne and I had already covered the trail from the New Hampshire border to Sugarloaf. Now, we set our sights on the remaining 140 or so from there to the base of Katahdin, where we had climbed the Hunt Trail an astounding 22 years before.

We decided that the section from the village of Caratunk (just east of the Kennebec River) to the town of Monson (on the southern edge of the trail's famed "Hundred Mile Wilderness") was the trip for us.

For this section, we decided to employ a shuttle. Instead of spotting a car at one end, then driving to the other, we could drive one car to Caratunk, hike north, then have one

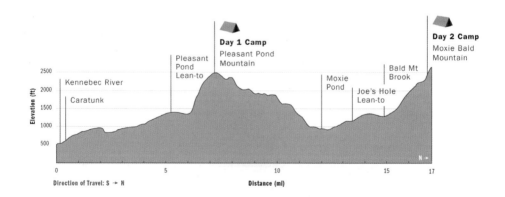

of the many people that make a little extra cash each year shuttling hikers to and from the trail take us from our end point in Monson back to Wayne's car. This way, we could spend a few hours less driving cars around and a few more on the trail.

Although Caratunk is called a "village", that word paints a larger picture than what you find when you get there. It's really a single country store with a few homes and summer cottages (known in Maine as "camps") scattered in proximity. Still, for a hiker coming through, a cold drink and other goodies can be a real psychological boost.

I was looking forward to the two summits we would visit early in the trip, Pleasant Pond Mountain and Moxie Bald. Both promised sweeping views of spruce forests, lakes and ponds framed by mountain ridges. I loved standing on top of Maine mountains surrounded by peaks I knew so well. Each one had its own character making them easy to identify — the broad swayback between East and West Baldpate, the cat ears of The Horns on the Bigelow Range, the flat, mesa-like profile of Katahdin. If I sat and looked long enough, I could often spot a peak on the distant horizon that I hadn't expected to see. The prospect of getting above tree line again on a picture perfect day was enough to get me fairly running up the trail. I knew that Wayne would join me on the summit in due time.

Sure enough, our campsites on both mountains brought the views and solitude we both craved, as well as the chance to take a morning side trip over to Moxie Bald's North Peak for another aerial perspective.

What I hadn't anticipated is how much I would be moved by the spectacle that I experienced below the mountaintops.

I had hiked the trail between Moxie Bald and Monson three times before. Each time I had been in the position of trying to make up ground over the relatively flat terrain.

The Horns on the Bigelow Range stand out on the horizon.

Moxie Bald from North Peak

This trip was markedly different. Maybe it was the time of year, the chance to slow down and really take in my surroundings — probably both. But as I hiked along the banks of the Pisacatiquis River, my senses breathed in an abundance of color, light and sound — trillium (both red and white) in full bloom suspended over wall to wall carpets of moss, delicate white foam flowers, purple violets, cinnamon ferns at their lushest green. All the while, the normal steady sound of my boots finding their way through roots and rocks was held at bay by the sound of water, a reassuring, steady stream of white noise.

At times, the trail crossed the stream, which meant removing boots and socks, unbuckling our waist belts and wading across. Unbuckling the waist belt is a safety precaution. The idea is that you can jettison your pack easier if you start getting washed downstream, so the pack weight won't drag you under. But having your waist buckle unclipped makes your pack sway to and fro in ways you aren't used to. It can catch you off guard if say, your foot plunges into an underwater hole. It's one more reason I love carrying poles. Those extra two points of contact really make a difference when you are trying to pick your way across a frigid, fast-moving stream and you can't see exactly where your feet are going.

The trail faithfully followed the river for miles. There wasn't always enough room next to the river for the trail to stay at its level however. Instead, we took little detours up on its banks, then back down again. On one high spot, something caught my attention in the river below. It was white, but it wasn't one of the many riffles. I stopped and looked again. There in the center of the river was a boulder that had been stained white by bird droppings. And on top of that sat a large white bird with a black back and a red beak. I had never seen a bird like it.

His mate was sitting on another boulder about six feet toward the opposite shore. Between the pair, the swift water of the Piscatiquis moved past them before cascading over a 5 foot waterfall about ten yards downstream.

What happened next was another first for me. They both jumped into the water and rode down over the falls! I watched in jaw dropping amazement as they rode the white water down the river and eddied out in a calm pool below.

Birds running whitewater! Are you kidding me? A sense of joy and gratitude washed over me. I couldn't believe my fortunate timing. It was all because we made the effort to get out here in the first place.

That evening, we fittingly set up camp on a spot overlooking the river. We didn't see more waterfowl running rapids, but we were treated to the songs of ovenbirds, white throated sparrows, woodpeckers and warblers, who were are at least as happy to be out in the Maine woods as we were.

Before I nodded off, I pulled out my journal for a writing session. "Only three miles from Route 15 and the end of our trip.", I wrote. "This has been one of our shortest trips, but at the same time, has also been one of the most uplifting. And some of the most inspiring moments came not on the summits as I had anticipated, but down in the wooded valleys along the river's edge. Another lesson from the trail: If we focus only on the path and where it leads, we miss the beauty and joy all around us."

SECTION 2

Baxter State Park, ME to Monson, ME

TRIP STATS
October 21, 2008 - October 31, 2008
113.7 miles (95 trail miles, plus 18.7 of road walking)
North to South

The words "Hundred Mile Wilderness" will enter every AT hiker's consciousness at some point. These last hundred plus miles between the last meaningful resupply point in the town of Monson, Maine and the summit of Katahdin are the closest the trail comes to offering a sustained wilderness experience.

Signs posted on either end of the section warn hikers that there is precious little access to food or rescue once

they head out. A few logging roads cross or come close to the trail, but depending on someone magically riding by to help you out of a bind would not be a situation you'd want to be in.

The most compelling draw to those hiking through is the beauty of the place. In many ways, it looks much like it did when Thoreau looked across the landscape from Katahdin and declared that the effect of the sun reflecting off the many lakes reminded him of so many pieces of a broken mirror scattered between him and the horizon.

This is a land of spruce trees that grow so tightly together they are nearly impenetrable, where lush, seemingly fluorescent mosses can blanket everything in sight—dead trees, live trees, granite boulders—and where rivers and lakes of all sizes thrive in the spaces in between. The mountains in this remote stretch, while not nearly the scale of those in say, Virginia and the Smokies, are undeniably rugged and offer above tree line vistas of the remarkably undeveloped landscape as their rewards.

It was partly the beauty of the area and partly my desire to complete the entire AT with Wayne that made me want to hike the Hundred Mile Wilderness for a fourth time. One thing that would make the trip a little different for me was that it would be the first time I would be hiking it from north to south, with Katahdin in my rear view mirror, instead of having it as my very prominent goal.

We decided to employ a shuttler to drive us from Monson to Baxter State Park. That way, we could simply walk south to Wayne's car. It was a beautiful late October day. The woods were tinted yellow and brown, the hues of late fall. We remarked that there appeared to be several seasonable days left before winter arrived.

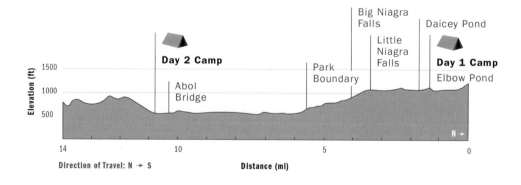

The shuttler was certainly talkative. I was trying to transition into being in the woods again. But before I could, I needed to go through my metal gear list one last time (especially important given that there were no easy places to purchase anything I might have forgotten once we got on the trail). For that, as you well know by now, I needed a moment of silence. Our driver, on the other hand, was relentless in trying to engage us in conversation. Chipping in enough to keep the conversation going while simultaneously taking gear inventory was like being the chef, the waiter and the maître de on a restaurant's opening night with waves of guests and critics pouring in. I couldn't wait to be standing in the solitude of the forest.

At 3:00 p.m., the car pulled away on the unpaved perimeter road. We stood and listened as the sound of the vehicle disappeared. The only sound now was that of our feet on the gravel as we walked over to the AT trail sign that marked our arrival. It was 23 years since we had climbed from this spot to the summit of Katahdin to begin our adventure. Now we would be walking in the other direction to get 100 miles closer to our goal. We shook hands and started toward Monson, filled with the euphoria of being back

In the Hundred Mile

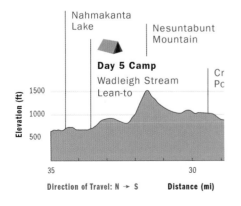

and the promise of great late autumn weather ahead.

We walked until we found an inspiring spot overlooking a pond and set up camp.

The high pressure system blessed us for another full day, and what a day it was! The walk next to Nesoudnehunk Stream is one of my favorite hikes. It's really a microcosm of what makes the Hundred Mile Wilderness so spectacular. At places, you can walk out next to the waterfalls on huge granite slabs, where you can get a true sense of the power of the water that formed this beautiful place. The granite has been sculpted—worn smooth—by thousands of years of water, ice and snow. Here and there, giant boulders remain, moved here by glaciers and left as souvenirs. We stopped many times along the way to enjoy the day to its fullest, sitting in the sun and taking in the views that changed with almost every bend in the trail.

At the nine mile mark, Nesoudnehunk Stream flowed into its much larger neighbor, the West Branch of the Penobscot. It was also the confluence of the trail, a bridge designed to accommodate logging trucks and the last and only store between us and Monson. "Store" is probably a bit generous. It's really a cabin at the edge of the wilderness stocked with beer, chips and ice. As with any successful business, you need to cater to your customer and the Abol Store certainly does that. They did, however, carry lip balm, which was the one thing Wayne forgot and was especially glad to find.

We paused on Abol Bridge to take one last look at Katahdin, rising up from the landscape beyond the river. We'd only be saying "so long" for now. I knew from experience that while the mountain that Native Americans called "The Great One" would get progressively smaller as we moved south, it would retain its magnificence from wherever it could be seen.

The first of those places was on Rainbow Ledges the following afternoon. The ledges

were classic topography for the area, large granite slabs overgrown with moss with granite boulders sprinkled on top. The views back into Baxter State Park made us wish we could have stayed more than a half hour, but the lateness of the day and the long-term forecast, which called for rain, made us want to make miles now while the footing was more certain.

In the Hundred Mile Wilderness, "more certain footing" is a relative term. Because the trail frequents the edges of lakes and streams, the trail often consists of nothing but roots, rocks and mud. In dry weather, this makes for slow, deliberate walking. In wet weather, it's slippery, annoying and potentially dangerous. I had already fallen twice under sunny skies, folding over my ankle the first time and taking a chest first forward plunge on the second (nothing like face planting with a full pack on your back).

On day three, we rolled into Rainbow Stream Lean-to just as the drizzle turned into steady rain. We piled in to take a break and decided to call it a day. Even though we were certain we'd have the place to ourselves if we wanted it, we opted to set up the tent. The forgiving ground underneath would be so much more comfortable than hard boards.

The cold front brought more than rain to Maine's north woods. It also brought winter's first calling card. When we awoke, the rain had slackened back to drizzle, but now there were snowflakes mixed in. I imagined that Katahdin probably got more snow than rain and I was right. When we topped Nesunabunt Mountain in the afternoon, the view revealed the mountain covered in white.

On day six, the sun came out early and stayed all day. Less than one mile down the trail, I came to the side trail to Sand Beach on Namakanta Lake. There was no way I was going to skip the chance to warm my bones under the unencumbered sun. I took two steps toward the beach and heard a big "ker-SPLOOSH", like someone had dropped a giant stone into the water from several feet above. I knew what it was.

I moved slowly toward the lake and saw the beaver now swimming away from the shore, forming a "V" wake behind. Her head was above water and lit up by the low morning sun. It was a beautiful sight.

I heard Wayne coming up the trail and stuck my right arm out to the side—our signal for "wildlife sighting ahead". He was also welcomed by a "ker-SPLOOSH". This time, I saw the beaver twist up and out of the water to generate the incredible tail speed required to make the sound. Another unexpected thrill complements of the trail.

We spent the morning walking along Namakanta Stream. For hours, the stream and far bank to my left were in blazing sunlight, while the thick spruce forest to my right remained dark and impenetrable. I had the sensation of sitting in a darkened movie theatre watching the show go on. When we stopped for lunch, we took turns walking out onto the boulders of the stream to warm up.

We would have one more beach day. On day seven, we sat on the sunny sands of Lower Jo Mary Lake while the soup water came to a boil. It would be the last leisurely lunch for a while.

When we listened to the forecast on the radio that night in the tent, we knew we were in for some really wet walking. The rain was supposed to hold off until the late evening of the day ahead. It was overcast, but not raining yet when we got to the saddle between Little Boardman and Big Boardman Mountains late in the day. There were a few nice

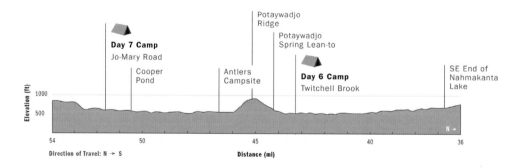

spots below the ridge, but if the rain came on like it was supposed to, I was concerned they would fill with run-off water. So, we moved to the top of the ridge and set up there instead.

The rain didn't arrive until 3:00 a.m. But when it did, it was hellacious. It reminded me of the storm we had weathered above Fontana Dam. By dawn, it was still pouring. We drank coffee and looked out the window with glum faces. There was no way to put a happy spin on walking through a 50-degree soaker.

We were up and out by 9:40. The first thing I did was pass by the spot where we would have camped. There was 6 inches of standing water where the tent would have been. We would have been even more miserable had we camped there.

I was soaked to the bone in the first mile. The trail was so jammed with puddles, that I gave up trying to walk around them. I stopped and waited for Wayne at the bottom of a rocky section. The rain was interminable.

"With all this water draining off the mountains, we could be screwed when we get to the East Branch.", I said, referring to the Pleasant River crossing coming up.

It didn't take long to find out. The river was absolutely raging—a loud, angry, churning river that looked like chocolate milk foaming in a blender. There was no way we could safely cross.

We backtracked and bushwhacked our way west to see if we could work our way around the pond just upstream.

That didn't work out too well.

We got turned around in a maze of ancient, partly grown in logging roads, game paths and other dead end detours, all the while, dealing with the incessant rain which would have brought frustration on its own.

We crashed through spruce trees for about a mile, only to find ourselves back on the banks of the raging East Branch.

We decided to change our approach and try to get onto one of the more well established logging roads in the area. We took a compass bearing and headed toward the only one on our map. In under an hour, we found it. The good news: we could hike on open road. The bad news: open road meant zero rain protection. It didn't really matter. We were drenched.

As the miles went by, I wondered how sound our plan was. If we were correct, the road would eventually turn left, cross the East Branch on a bridge, then curve back down the other side to eventually pass the place where the AT crossed. The further away we got from the trail, the more I doubted we were even on the right road.

The trail maps we had only have you a thin strip of perspective on the world. And GPS was out of the question. My phone battery had died in the cold days ago.

At 3:30, we arrived at a gate across the road that appeared to be the same one shown on our map. If we were right, we'd hit the trail soon.

I soon saw a brown sign with white letters up ahead. Could it be the AT?

YES!

A two mile climb up the side of White Cap Mountain brought us to the Logan Brook Lean-to. Hard boards be damned. We were sleeping under the roof tonight. We were exhausted, cold, wet and absolutely ready for dry clothes, warm sleeping bags, hot food and glorious sleep (which was only interrupted by the resident mouse looking for an easy meal).

The front moved through during the night. During the mouse escapade, I looked out at the stars filling our part of the universe. "It would be really nice if we could have some sun to dry out the gear tomorrow", I thought, before I shifted onto my side and went back to sleep.

I got my wish. We were up and out of the site early. I wanted to get up above the trees and into the sun as soon as possible. My body wasn't as keen to get there as my brain after yesterday's epic slog. When we arrived at the summit, we threw our packs down and began a thorough drying session. We could only stay long enough to do the job. Yesterday's detour put us behind schedule.

Dry clothes, lighter packs and sun are always a great combination. We spent the day "saw toothing" over the summits of Gulf Hagas. It was nice to have another warm day

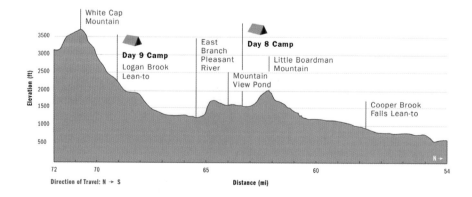

after the deluge and every view seemed to reward our perseverance.

Then came the West Branch Pleasant River. We had been optimistic, but when we got to the river (the second major stream crossing of the trip) the effects of the past storm were still in evidence. There was no way we could cross the raging beast. This time, however, the way around the problem was well defined. We cobbled together a 6.5 mile detour by following sections of three existing trails and a logging road to gain our reunion with the AT.

On the way up Chairback Mountain, it started raining again—a mist that turned to steady as I climbed. Including our detour, we were almost eleven miles into the day and had made only 4.5 miles of forward progress.

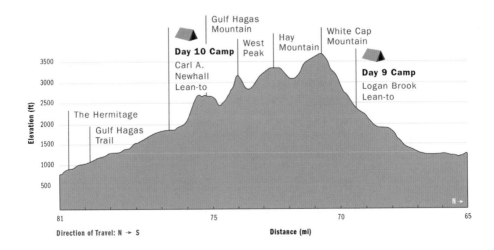

I stopped and waited. Wayne was only ten minutes behind me.

"Twenty-eight miles between us and Monson.", I said. "Let's camp here."

As soon as we set up the tent and dove in, the wind and rain picked up steam. The water was pouring off the visor of the rain fly. We made another great call.

That night, the forecast called for snow flurries and arctic cold. But at least no more rain.

In the morning, I climbed up out of our camp spot and took a brief look back at Wayne, who was almost underway. He was looking down, putting his gloves on. I briefly considered yelling, "Meet you at the top" down his way, but decided against it.

It was cold enough to warrant wearing my rain jacket and pants. Flurries were flying and there was a dusting of snow on the trees, yet the footing on the rocks was remarkably good.

"At least it isn't raining", I said to myself as I emerged from a granite field of boulders to arrive at the base of Chairback Cliff. The climb was vertical and I loved both the challenge and the layout it presented. When I got to the top, I waited for Wayne while taking in the view. I didn't bother to take my pack off. It was too early in the day for that.

After waiting for Wayne for a half hour, I knew something was wrong. I went through the normal checklist: slipped on rocks - leg damage, slipped on rocks - cranial damage or went the wrong way on the trail.

The only known was that I had to go look for him. I thought about leaving my pack, so I wouldn't have do climb the cliff with it again, but decided that was a bad idea. I had food and first aid stuff with me. To dig them out would take even more precious time.

I down-climbed and worked my way back to the campsite as quickly as I could. The mud on the trail only contained my boot print, meaning he had never made it this far. "If he was going the wrong way, he wouldn't do it for long", I thought. He'd see the sign for East Chairback Pond about a mile back from where we had camped and realize he was headed back from where we came."

I got all the way back to last night's campsite (about 2 miles from the cliff where I had turned back) and started up a ridge, when I saw him coming toward me. He had blown past the sign and gone all the way down to the logging road where we had rejoined the trail yesterday afternoon.

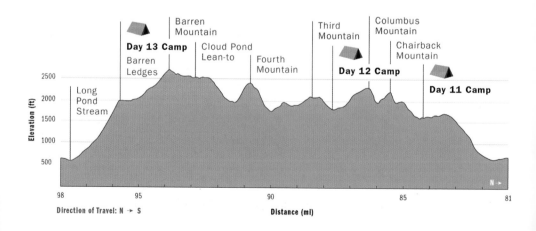

He was really pissed at himself, but I was more happy to see him in one piece.

"Shit happens.", I said.

And so at 11:00 a.m., the day began anew.

As we walked along, I said, "Call me crazy, but I'm actually looking forward to my second ascent of the cliff today."

"You're a machine.", he said.

That may be true at times, but even machines have their limitations. The two detours around rivers, Wayne's wrong turn, the powerful storm systems and now the cold were throwing sand in the gears.

The footing deteriorated in the afternoon and slowed our pace even more. Everything was wet, especially our feet, and the trail was covered in thin ice, which along with granite underneath made a dangerous combination.

The trail was nothing but puddles, roots, rocks and ice. I fell three times during the day, my right knee hitting granite each time.

It was time to consider other options. At this rate, we wouldn't be out of the woods until at least the day after we were due. I stood on the summit of Fourth Mountain knowing that it was time to cut the trip short. With considerable disappointment, I pulled the map out of my holster and took my bearings.

"Welcome to Fourth Mountain", I announced to Wayne upon his arrival.

Slumped shoulders and a few expletives mirrored my feelings on the subject.

"I'm thinking we should bail after Barren Mountain and do a road walk back to Monson.", I said. "We can come back and do the other 14 miles of trail in the spring."

Wayne immediately embraced the new plan. But we still had a lot of work to do to make it happen.

The wind was piercing through our wet clothes. We dropped down off the ridge and into a bog, where a series of logs, known appropriately as "bog bridges" would take us over the muck to the other side.

Unfortunately, there was a skim coat of ice on the logs. Halfway across the sea of mud, my left foot slipped off the bridge and sunk knee deep into the mud and icy water. My right knee wasn't having a good day at all. It slammed down onto the bridge, which I held tightly with both hands to keep me from falling in. Standing up on an icy bridge with 60 pounds on your back is some feat, I'll tell you. But I pulled it off like a tightrope walker nearing retirement.

When I got to the first stream, I plunged my leg in "boots and all" to get the mud off.

The climb of Barren Mountain warmed me right up again. Just after the side trail to Barren Ledges (amazing views, but winds that wouldn't let us stay long), we stopped to make our last camp. I told Wayne I would search for water if he set up the tent. The best I could find to work with was a giant puddle we had passed a quarter mile back. It was deep enough for me to use my water filter in and it yielded two quarts.

Back in the tent, I put dry clothes on, then turned on the radio. It would be sunny tomorrow. I briefly considered proposing that we walk the 14.5 miles into Monson via the trail, but decided that what I (and presumably we) needed was a full day of solid footing.

As it turned out, even though the plan was for less drama, we weren't out of the woods yet. The day started gloriously enough with a trip to Barren Ledges to watch the sun come up while drinking 20 oz. mugs of coffee. All we had to do was drop the 1,000 feet to Long Pond Stream, cross it, then take the logging road 12 miles into Monson.

When we arrived at Long Pond Stream, we were foiled yet again. At the AT crossing, someone had stretched a blue climber's rope from a birch tree on a tiny midstream island to the shore. Presumably at lower water, a series of rocks underneath combined with the security of the rope would allow safe passage.

On this day, the water was so high that it almost washed over the rope. So, for the third time on the trip, we began our long detour around a turbulent stream.

After several discussions about where we were and the best route out (and one unexpected plunge into a swamp that almost swallowed me up pack and all), we blasted through a tangle of deadwood that deposited us on the logging road to our salvation. After 95 miles of trail walking and almost 19 miles of bushwhacking, we had emerged from the Hundred Mile Wilderness.

It was a gorgeous Halloween Day and an enjoyable road walk into Monson. After all we had been through in recent days, it was a pleasure to simply let my mind move as freely as my feet. We ended up covering 17 miles to get back to the Wayne's car, arriving just as it got dark.

In the end, the Hundred Mile Wilderness had certainly given us our measure of adventure. Would I do it a fifth time? Absolutely.

Epilogue

Wayne and I returned to Monson the following spring with our friend Ed to do the 14.5-mile hike from Long Pond Stream to Monson. The temperatures hit the low 90s (there wasn't a snow flurry or rain cloud within sight). And we went swimming several times—on purpose.

SECTION 3

Caratunk, ME to Route 27, ME

TRIP STATS
October 12, 2009 - October 15, 2009
36.6 miles
North to South

The Kennebec River is most famous for the man who once used it as his means of traveling through Maine on his way toward Quebec. In the fall of 1775, Benedict Arnold left Cambridge, Massachusetts with 1,100 men. He led his troops north in boats via the Kennebec River, a decision that proved costly. Portaging the heavy boats through muddy bogs was grueling work. Several of the boats sprung leaks. Three hundred men turned back and 200 died on the way to Quebec. By the time the rag tag force reached Quebec in November, their attack was easily repelled.

While Benedict Arnold's March is often linked to the Kennebec, the place names on the thirty plus miles of Appalachian Trail between the Kennebec and Route 27 in the

Carrabassett Valley are permanent reminders of that event. East Carry Pond, Middle Carry Pond, West Carry Pond (places where they paddled or portaged boats), Arnold Point and Bigelow Mountain (named for one of Arnold's officers) are all places on the AT that were also visited by or seen by Arnold and his men more than 250 years ago.

Today, the Kennebec River is still an imposing obstacle, although for a different reason than Arnold's men faced. The river is still wide (at 70 feet or so, it's the widest unbridged crossing on the whole AT). And the water is fast. Even at low water, it wouldn't be wise to try to ford it. But today there also is dam upstream that can release large quantities of water with little warning.

For these reasons, the Maine Appalachian Trail Club sponsors a ferry service from late May to mid October. The craft used to ferry hikers across the river is actually a canoe, operated by an individual hired by the MATC to provide safe crossings.

As requested, we contacted the operator to ensure we could get a ride across the river, as we were closing in on the final days of the season.

On October 12, 2009, we parked the car at Route 27 (the southern terminus of the section) then waited for our shuttle ride to Caratunk. The foliage was stunning. It was just a few days past peak and the mountains were blanketed in reds and yellows. The Carrabassett Valley was as beautiful as I'd ever seen it. That was quite a claim, given the number of times I'd been there in the fall.

The shuttle man showed up right on time and dropped us off at the Caratunk

trailhead at 6:00. We had just enough light to get up the trail a few hundred yards and set up the dome. I was beyond exhausted and began the trip by sleeping for almost ten hours straight.

When I awoke, look out! I couldn't wait to get out on the trail. I had the coffee water on the stove before the sun had risen over the trees. You don't get many autumn days this prefect for hiking and I wanted to be in the woods enjoying every moment of it.

Wayne knew there was no stopping me. I was like the proverbial Irish Setter barking at the back door. We powered down our breakfasts, packed up, crossed Route 15 and walked down the embankment to meet the ferryman at the edge of the mighty Kennebec.

He was standing next to his well used aluminum canoe, leaning on a paddle when we arrived. His first comment was, "Man, you guys have got some old gear."

I laughed out loud. "It's not that old", I said. "It's just well loved."

"Whatever", he replied.

He paddled us over to the boulder laden far shore one at a time. On my way across, I tried to make small talk with him, but got one word answers in response. I flashed back to the ride to Baxter State Park when all I wanted was silence and the driver kept chit chatting.

"No more questions. Leave him alone.", I said to myself.

The canoe bumped the far shore. The ferryman had paddled this route so many times, he knew exactly where to slide the bow between the boulders. I stayed low, grabbing the gunwales to steady myself on the way out. I stood on a couple of flatish boulders and foisted my pack out of the canoe and onto a rock.

"Have a nice hike!", said the ferryman. He pushed off with his paddle and began his journey back toward the eastern shore.

I glanced over to Wayne and he nodded. A single gesture meaning "Yes, I'm ready to go" and "See you up the trail". I tightened my waist belt and to begin our own journey into beautiful Maine woods.

The ascent out of the Kennebec gorge was a gorgeous walk along Pierce Pond Brook. The trees glowed yellow and orange under the sun. Thick, green mosses blanketed the forest floor. And the brook offered endless entertainment. As we gained elevation, it revealed more waterfalls. There were mini side trails to several, and I often took the chance to step out from under the trees to grab a few moments in the sun.

On day two, we entered lake country. In a seven mile stretch, the AT passes all three of the "Carry Ponds" (East, Middle and West). The route here is reminiscent of the Hundred Mile Wilderness. It's a place of moss, beech trees, cedars, rocks, roots, mud and stellar lakefront views.

Late in the afternoon, we watched a front move in over West Carry Pond from Arnold Point. The lenticular clouds were forming in impressive fashion, but that wasn't a good sign for the coming days. Even as we sat on the shore, the wind shifted and the temperatures dropped.

"I have a feeling fall is coming to an end.", I said.

"Kind of our style to be here for it.", said Wayne.

I, too, had been thinking back to our Hundred Mile Wilderness trip.

On the third day, the sleet and snow started pelting the tent at 4:00 a.m. The funny

thing was that rather than having a sense of resignation about it, I felt the opposite. I had a feeling that walking through the frosted landscape was going to be really special.

I wasn't disappointed.

As the sun came up, the sleet and snow turned to fog and mist, which hung heavily over the mountains, lakes and woods all day. Walking through the gently frosted scene was ethereal. The thin dusting of snow over the grasses, moss, logs and ferns allowed their colors to still show through, yet winter's first statement was strong enough to leave its mark for the entire day.

When we turned up the north slope of Little Bigelow Mountain in the afternoon, we discovered that the snow had left a deeper impression at higher elevations. In fact, the combination of rain and snow on the trail had us downshifting to a one-mile-per-hour pace over the granite slabs and roots. If we had been trucks on the freeway, we would have been in the right lane with our emergency flashers on.

"No point in pushing it.", I thought. "To break an ankle here would be a real drag."

Looking around, I thought that it would be better to drop down off the ridge in an attempt to get out of the snow. There was a campsite down in Safford Notch that might do the trick. Yes, we'd have to lose our hard earned elevation to get there, but setting up the tent on damp flat ground was preferable to setting it up over a couple inches of snow on a slope.

I pitched the idea to Wayne on one of our rest stops.

"I'm up for it.", he said. "It's 3:00 now. I'd rather find a spot down there than be on the open summit looking for a spot at sundown."

We started looking for camp spots as soon as we started dropping down the Safford Notch trail. We were hoping to find a great site just below where the snow ended, but there weren't any.

We would have to go all the way to the floor of the notch, where the camp sites had been created (and the water flowed from a nearby spring).

It was worth the hike down. As we envisioned, there were indeed flat tent sites below the snow. As it turned out, that made the place popular with both campers and bears. There were signs posted advising campers to bear bag their food and hang it in trees. We decided to take our chances. I imagined that the bear was down in a warm spot far below us and didn't expect any yahoos would be coming through carrying shrimp Alfredo on their backs.

Our prudent approach paid off on day five when we topped Avery Peak and West Peak on Bigelow Mountain. I had climbed this mountain dozens of times to enjoy the view, but this experience was like none other. I emerged from tree line to climb into the world between autumn and winter.

Every step revealed a wider view of the incredible scene. The snow covered Bigelow Range stretched ahead of me, while the deep reds of autumn surrounded me on all sides. It was a day and an experience beyond any I could have imagined. And it was ours simply because we got out here to find it.

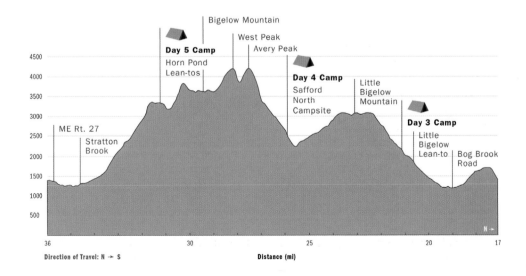

CHAPTER 22

360°
Euphoria

Successive days of incredible views keep our spirits high.

Nantahala, NC to Dick's Creek Gap, GA

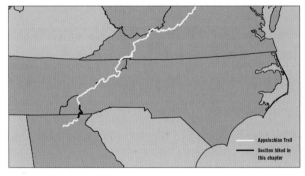

TRIP STATS
May 7, 2011 to May 14, 2011
75.2 miles
North to South

I have fought the urge to bite off more than I could chew my entire life. It began as soon as I learned how to eat solid foods. I remember being seated at the dinner table and having to remove pieces of chicken, steak or whatever from my mouth when people weren't looking and hide them in my napkin because they were too big for me to work with.

Over the years, this habit manifested in other ways. One of them was drinking. In my youth, there was no moderation. "If some beer was good, then more beer had to be better" became my mantra. This ridiculous notion/addiction got me into more trouble than I could ever admit until I stopped drinking altogether.

I seldom got into trouble in the mountains, however. Although there were many times that I pushed myself physically, there were only a few times I ever felt that I was in

harm's way. And those times were enough to teach me how to keep things in perspective. Some of us are not so lucky. For that I am blessed.

But, despite getting real about food, drink and outdoor exploits, there was one place I was chronically susceptible to over indulging. It was work.

Going into this next to the last trip on the Appalachian Odyssey, I still wasn't heading the advice I had offered myself so many times before. Almost every trip's journal entry started with some version of "it took an incredible effort just to get here". And even though on at least two trips my overworking was a precursor to illness, here I was yet again.

This time, Wayne was going to pick me up at the New Haven train station. We would drive to Georgia, park his car at an AT shuttler's house, have her give us a ride to the North Carolina trailhead and we would walk south toward her house.

The last five days going into the trip were a ridiculous whirlwind of writing binges wrapped around ten minute meal breaks, gear packing and almost no sleep. The night before I left, I slept for three hours, then got up to shower, drink coffee and get to the train.

I had promised Wayne that I would do the food shopping for the trip, which I hadn't gotten to. In addition, I needed to do some more work before I could set foot on the trail.

When I was de-training at New Haven, Wayne called to say he was running forty minutes late. I walked outside, leaned my pack against the station wall, then sat down beside it. I had a dull ache in the back of my neck and a barely functioning mind. I felt like dozing off, but didn't think this was the place or time.

It wasn't long before I heard the unmistakable exhaust system of the Waynemobile. I looked up to see his grin from behind the dash. Minutes after I settled into the car, I dozed off. When I woke up, I looked through the rear window to see the New York skyline disappearing behind us, then back to see the Meadowlands stretched out ahead.

I put my phone in the stand I had brought, set them on the dash and took out the keyboard I had brought to start crafting a work proposal as we sped down the highway. In retrospect, I believe this could be called the definition of insanity.

With only a brief stop in Harrisburg, PA for dinner, I kept typing, editing and reviewing from my dashboard work station. Finally, at 9:00 p.m., I pushed the "send" button signifying the true start to our next to the last adventure on the AT. I was free.

We made a Front Royal, Virginia hotel at 10:30 p.m. and wound down by watching a ballgame. My head was still going 65 miles per hour, even though my brain had pulled into a rest area an hour and a half ago.

We were up at 5:30 a.m. If we were going to meet our shuttle person at 5:00 p.m. in Georgia, every minute would count. The funniest part of the trip was our grocery shopping spree at the Bristol, Virginia Target store. I still can't believe what we pulled off in 15 minutes. We ran down aisles throwing oatmeal, soups, cold cuts, cheese, crackers and bread into the cart as we went. It was an incredibly orchestrated, efficient event.

Back on the road, we flew through a burger joint drive through in Franklin, Georgia, found a roadside spot to change into hiking clothes and arrived at our shuttle rendezvous spot fifteen minutes ahead of schedule.

The ride to the trailhead at Nantahala Outdoor Center was a beautiful trip through the mountains. It kept looking like it wanted to rain, but the clouds finally passed and it turned into a sunny late afternoon. The NOC was busy with kayakers, many of whom were strapping their kayaks on roof racks and calling it a day.

We couldn't call it a day until we got somewhere down the trail. We barely stopped at the trailhead AT sign, then began climbing up through the rhododendron and out of the gap. I found an informal side trail near the top of the ridge that led to a tent platform of all things. It was meant to be. In seven minutes, we were in the tent, listening to the roar of the Nantahala River below. Three minutes after that, another, louder sound joined it. That of Wayne's snoring. I could hardly believe he was first to go down for the count.

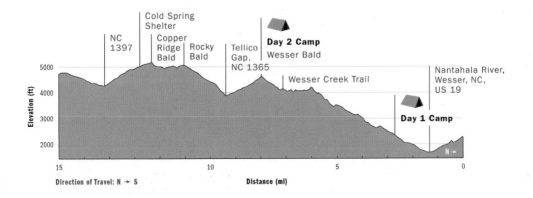

Everything about the first day out was spectacular. The temperatures were in the high 60s (excellent hiking temperatures), the spring flowers (including trillium and rhododendron) were in full bloom and the leaves were just a few days from bursting forth, lending beautiful coloration to the forest.

The hike out of the gap was epic. We spent all day climbing, which definitely helped me purge lingering thoughts of work. I was necessarily dealing only with the here and now, the hill that was immediately ahead of me. One of my ongoing concerns was my right hamstring. It was incredibly tight. If it popped, our trip would be over. I concentrated on pushing gently off my right foot until I could break my muscles in.

Our target for the day was the fire tower on Wesser Bald. When we were less than a mile away from the summit, we started meeting hikers coming down the trail warning us of a giant rattlesnake up ahead. Sure enough, when I turned up a short switchback, I saw the four foot snake just to the left of the trail and downslope from us. It was at least 3" in diameter and was looking perturbed. I had seen enough rattlers in Southern California to know when to give them an extra wide berth.

I put my hand out to the side as a warning to Wayne. He stood still as I climbed up and away from the snake.

Just then, a woman with a dog approached me coming down the hill. I stopped her to give her warning about the snake. "Hopefully, she'll leash her dog", I thought.

Nope.

Wayne was still standing still downslope when the woman decided to get a closer look at the snake. As she was looking, she lost her balance and fell directly into the path

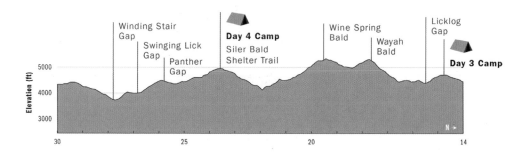

of the snake, landing only about 5 feet away. It was a miracle the snake didn't strike.

Wayne quickly helped the woman and dog escape and a crisis was averted. What a way to start a trip that would have been, helping her get off the mountain and to a hospital.

Minutes later, I climbed the 54 steps up the Wesser Bald Tower to one of the most scintillating views on the entire AT—an astounding 360° view of the southern Appalachians. We had appetizer and dinner hour there, watching the sun disappear over the mountain filled western horizon. It was a harbinger of days to come—incredible views from mountaintop fire towers.

Yes, it was great to be on the trail again.

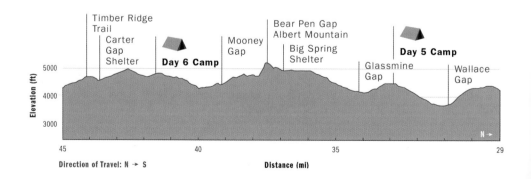

We began the next day the way we ended the preceding one, on top of the tower. I bolted up the stairs with coffee in hand at 5:45 to watch the sun come up over the mountains. Mother Nature was imploring me to come play in the mountains and I wasn't going to put up any fuss.

We broke camp at 8:30 and made our way down to Tellico Gap, where we found some interesting wooden retaining walls, a bag of food left hanging in a tree by a northbounder and the incessant sound of a weed whacker coming from someone's nearby yard.

One thing we saw more of on the trail than any other time in our AT escapades was fellow hikers. We counted more than 60 of them in the first two days we were out. This made sense, because it was May, the time most people leave Springer Mountain heading north with dreams of making Katahdin. Only around 25% of them would make it that far, but it was nice to know that at least this many people were willing to give it a try.

Lots of good things were happening for me on this trip. First off, my right leg rebounded. I didn't have to baby the hamstring anymore. More surprising was that I was hitting the end of the day with reserve energy. And bordering on miraculous was that I actually liked the ramen I ate for lunch.

The highlight of day three was the climb to the top of another tower, this one made of stone atop Wayah Bald. As we climbed to 5385', the temps had climbed into the low 80s, making the shade and breeze provided by the tower extra bonuses. The bugs had found me earlier in the day and they were hellacious. To stop was to be swarmed. The breeze was my savior.

Our lunch spot was near a spring on a Forest Service road down in the valley. Two older guys showed up on the scene. They had left Springer Mountain a few weeks before. It was their third attempt at the trail. Each time, they had gone back to the beginning.

"Say, what are you guys eating for lunch, so we know whether we should bonk you on the head and steal your food?", one asked.

"Ramen", I said.

"Shit.", he replied. "I guess you're safe then."

We spent the afternoon climbing to yet another great viewpoint, Siler Bald. We set up the tent in a shady spot and I dove in to get a break from the bugs. It was like a sauna in there, but it beat getting swarmed.

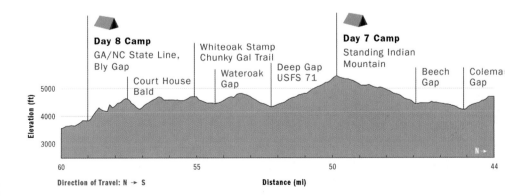

The next day was cloudy and warm. It got up to 80° again. Hydration was key. We stopped three times on the way to Panther Gap to tank up and drink as much as we could take in. By late afternoon, we passed a shelter on the way up a ridge. The trail guide indicated there were several springs ahead, so I kept climbing. The higher I got, the more I realized there would be no springs. I was down to 1 1/3 quarts of water. When Wayne arrived on the ridge top, he indicated he had 1 quart. Far from ideal, but we made it work.

An owl hooting directly above the tent woke me at 4:48 a.m. I turned on my headlamp and read about upcoming water sources in my trail guide. Glasmine Gap, one mile away, was the closest. When I got there at 8:45, I was completely dehydrated. I threw my pack to the ground, grabbed two water bottles and my filter and headed down the side trail to fill up. I drank a quart on the spot, then climbed back toward my pack, handing Wayne a full bottle when I got there.

One mile later, we came to another spring and filled up every vessel we had—seven quarts in all. We weren't going to be caught short again.

There was one more fire tower to climb, on the summit of Albert Mountain. When I arrived, I climbed up pack and all and waited for Wayne. It was another incredible view, but we wouldn't have it to ourselves for long. Two northbounders, then six weekend hikers joined us up there. It was getting a bit crowded, so we decided to give up our spots.

On the way down to Mooney Gap, I had a brainstorm. It was about ten degrees cooler in the rhododendron filled gaps then on the sunny summits. What if we ate lunch in the tent (to avoid bugs) down in the gap, waited a few hours, then climbed up to the ridge top to camp late in the day? That way, we wouldn't be baking in the tent.

"Brilliant."

Thus, from 1:15 to 3:45, we dined next to a stream in Mooney Gap, eating appetizers and hydrating. This became our new mode for the rest of the trip. It was inspired. One lunch even culminated in a trailside first—tuna melts served on bagels.

The afternoon we summited Standing Indian Mountain was intense. I got up there in time to see a gorgeous view from the ridge, but the weather was turning fast. I scouted

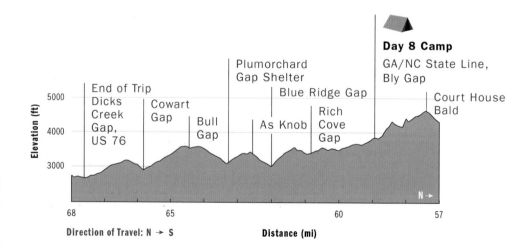

around for a camp spot and found a promising one. By the time Wayne arrived, the wind was blowing in a major storm. Within a half hour, a thunderstorm/squall was blasting through. We were glad to be protected by the rhododendron that surrounded us. If we had camped on the summit, the tent would have flattened over us.

I had been maintaining a three mile per hour pace for most of the trip, even on the climbs. It felt great to be this in shape again, still feeling strong at each day's end. Curiously, even though I was working hard, I wasn't sleeping well at all. The night of the squall on Standing Indian Mountain, I woke up at 2:30. And the last night on the trail, I was awake from 2:00 a.m. on. I listened to the radio for a while, which included the BBC special about the Yorkshire Ripper. In a completely unrelated, although similarly mournful development, the owls began hooting at 5:30 a.m.

We had less than nine miles to reach the end of the section, and I couldn't wait to get started. This, too, was new for me. Usually, I wanted to stay put for a while on the last morning. To savor every last moment I could squeeze out of the trip. I'm not sure what was propelling me toward the trail, but the force was undeniable.

By 8:15, I was on the path. Almost as soon as I started, I came to a tree with an old metal pipe embedded in it and a small American flag attached to it. There was also a wooden sign attached to it that said, NC/GA border.

I stopped and waited for Wayne. When he showed up a few moments later, we shook hands. There were twenty six years and thirteen states behind us. And one state left to go.

CHAPTER 23

Trail's End

28 years. 14 states. 2,181 miles. We could hardly believe the final hike was at hand.

Dicks Creek Gap, GA to Springer Mountain, GA

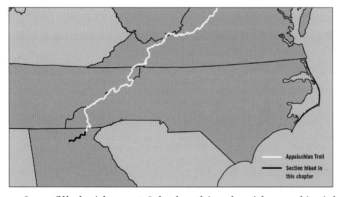

Appalachian Trail
Section hiked in this chapter

TRIP STATS
October 19, 2013
to October 29, 2013
66.8 AT miles (plus 8.8 to Amicalola State Park)
North to South

On the eve of the trip that would mark the end of our 28-year quest, I got four hours of sleep.

I was filled with angst. It had nothing do with grand insights about being on the AT for almost three decades or (this may surprise you) even staying up to finish work projects. It was something far more critical. I couldn't find my journal pouch.

Just before we started our Appalachian odyssey, I had been given a nylon travel pouch that turned out to be one of my favorite and useful items. It was the perfect size for carrying and protecting my favored spiral bound journal notebook and had a long zippered pocket that kept train tickets, credit cards and other things packed safely away. It even had a couple of pencil sleeves in it. When it was "journaling session" time (most often in the tent during morning coffee or evening appetizer time), I could reach for my trusty pouch and get started.

Now it was gone.

I looked everywhere. I ripped everything out of the car. I searched through all my gear (no small task). I drove to my office and looked through every drawer and box. I got up in the middle of the night, went up to the attic and searched through my gear again. Still no luck.

At 5:00 a.m., I gave up the search. I had to be on the 6:00 a.m. bus heading to Boston. My journal pouch would not be going on the final trip. I pulled a zip-seal bag out of a kitchen drawer, slid a new journal and two mechanical pencils in it and zipped it shut. I didn't want to carry my memories in a lousy plastic bag, but it was the best I could and would do.

"I hope whoever finds that journal pouch gets it back to me.", I thought. "It has my journal from the last trip in it." Even so, I wondered how that could happen. It didn't have any identifying materials in it, except possibly an Amtrak ticket stub from one of our trips in the early 90s that I used as a bookmark.

"If I ever do get it back, I need to zip a business card inside the pouch." I thought, as I slipped the plastic bag into the top pocket of my pack. I knew that every time I wrote on this trip would bring a fresh opportunity for me to play the "What the hell did I do with my journal pouch" game, which irked me even more.

"Ok. Enough morning news from the 'I lost my frigging journal pouch' channel", I said to myself. "It's time to change the station."

I certainly knew how to do that.

I put on my pack and walked out the front door. The final hike was underway.

Day one

Our train rolled into the Toccoa Georgia Amtrak station at 6:20 a.m. It had been a 22-plus hour ride from New York City (where Wayne joined me). I had been up for most of 48 hours, due to the search for my journal pouch and not being able to sleep more than 15 minutes at a time on the way down the east coast. (Somehow it wouldn't seem right to start any of these trips fully rested.)

It was still dark when we shouldered our heavy packs and walked into town to look for a breakfast joint. Not finding any open this Sunday morning, we headed back to the train station to eat our own food while we waited for our shuttle drivers to arrive. As our coffee mellowed in the French press travel mugs, the ladies from Hawassee, GA (the same women that had shuttled us to the Nantahala Outdoor Center on our last trip) drove up.

We arrived at Dick's Creek Gap around 9:20, grabbed a few photos, then crossed U.S. Route 76 to reconnect with the blessed path. The 2013 final tour was underway.

What a gorgeous day and time of year to be out! Bright sun, turning leaves (about 40% toward peak) and well designed trail. As is most often the case, our first few miles on the trail were a climb. In this case, we climbed 1,200 fee in the first 2.2 miles–a good steady workout, but not too crazy. There are certainly many steeper climbs on this trail.

I was incredibly happy to be here. At times like this, I knew I was destined to hike. Even after being largely sedentary for the past two months and climbing with a 70 lb. load on almost no sleep, I was in complete bliss.

We climbed steadily up through oaks and rhododendron, over Powell Mountain (3,850') and arrived at a side trail to a viewpoint. The sun had warmed the day enough that we sat in shirt sleeves, admiring extensive views of mountains rippling into the north and east, including Courthouse Bald, which we had climbed toward the end of our last hike. We broke out crackers and olive tapenade hummus for lunch. We decided that because we were so exhausted from getting here, we would keep the afternoon hike short. We would rest, eat some of the heavy food, then hit longer mileages the rest of the trip.

As I hiked along after lunch, I was serenaded by the jungle cries of pileated woodpeckers, flying slightly ahead of me, alighting on dead branches and inspecting

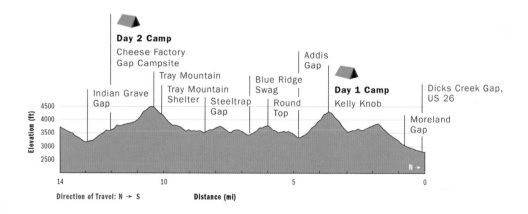

them for bugs. The woodpeckers have become my trail mates as of late. It seems like every time I had entered the woods, regardless of location and time of year, they had been there to greet me.

At 2:30, we found a gorgeous flat spot on top of Kelly Knob (4,276 and the highest peak between North Carolina and Tray Mountain).

Pasta Alfredo won the "heaviest meal in the pack" competition. It was topped only by my choice for dessert—hours and hours of sleep.

Day two

After sleeping a solid eight hours, I awoke at 4:19 to go out and look at the stars, then dove back into the sleeping bag for 3 more hours of shut eye.

It took a while for the sun to light up our ridge. We stayed in the tent and cooked dried eggs, Italian sausage and cheese burritos (the heaviest breakfast we had), brewed French press coffee and settled into the day – maybe a little too much. We didn't get underway until 10:00. It was time to start making mileage if we were going to finish on schedule.

We tanked up with two quarts of water each at Sassafras Gap and began a series of pleasant ups and downs along the ridge top and under the turning oaks. The splendid autumn day was making everyone happy, particularly the woodpeckers and gray squirrels.

The big climb of the day was Tray Mountain – 1,000' in about a mile. Again the southern trail was forgiving. The climb was steady and long, as opposed to so many New England approaches that are straight up. Nonetheless, it was work.

Sometimes on climbs, as was the case today, I began to hear a faint voice that wasn't there when I was younger. It says, "Why are you carrying 70 pounds up a mountain at your age? Thirty years ago, you were practically running up trails like this. Now you are barely making progress."

By now I knew that if little voice became the loudest one, I'd be miserable.

Yet, I couldn't simply deny the voice existed. To do that would be to deny myself an opportunity to acknowledge the kernel of truth in the message. It's better for me if I listen to that voice and find the positive message inside.

"It's true. This isn't 30 years ago. It's now. And now is pretty damned good. I'm still able to do this. And that is a blessing.", I said back to myself as I climbed up the hill.

Suddenly, the little, disparaging voice had no volume at all.

At 5.9 miles, I emerged onto the summit ridge and junctioned with the side trail to

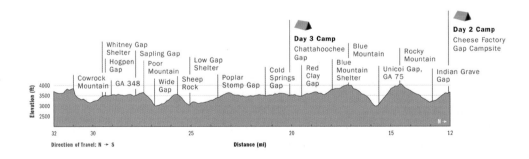

the Tray Mountain Shelter. I stopped just long enough to hear voices from the campsite, then climbed the last .3 to the rocky summit to stand at the highest point between me and Springer Mountain.

There were beautiful views to either side and I was bathed in bright sunshine. A blessing to be here indeed.

That night, I slept horribly. The muscle on my right leg that extended from my hip down toward my knee on was throbbing and I couldn't get it to stop. Rolling onto it and sleeping on that side seemed to help a little, but I was concerned about my ability to crank out a ten mile day on it.

Day three
We would need to get an early start to give me a chance to walk more slowly and still make the miles necessary to keep us on schedule. We decided to eat a bagel to save breakfast cooking and cleaning time. The hazelnut and chocolate spread I had found in the health food store a few weeks back was a huge hit.

We had a small "up and over" section to start the day, and my right leg protested from the start. Usually if my legs hurt, it is in isolated sections, say my calf muscles or my quads. It that's the case, I can usually adjust my gait for a while to work through the pain. This time, my whole leg was in pain, from the calf to the hip. It was going to take a lot to work through it.

Pushing off wasn't a problem. It was the landings. I compensated by leaning heavily on my right pole, then my left leg to take the pressure off.

No matter your age or physical condition, you can't really account for how spending your days climbing over mountains and hills will affect your muscles and joints. It's not an aerobic thing. It's the effect of roots and rocks.

Hiking the trail isn't like walking on a treadmill or running along a road. Your feet are constantly twisting and turning to accommodate the unpredictable tread–small stones that shift underneath you, boulders, roots and what have you.

There were two ways I could rehabilitate my leg right here and now. One was to rest, the other was to keep going.

I considered the ascent of Rocky Mountain as fine a chance as any to fine tune my relationship with my right leg, so I started up the hill. My right leg was initially an unwilling participant, but I thought that if I could get the blood flowing through, it would respond. About half way up the mountain, the concern about my leg was replaced by the incredibly addictive and completely un-purge-able melody from "Saved by Zero".

By the time I arrived at the 4097' summit, my leg was back! The stunning views certainly helped. The timing was good, because it was 11:00 and we had only covered a little over two miles. There was no way we were going to make our date with Springer Mountain and trail's end unless we picked up the pace.

I could hardly believe that the demon that took over my right leg muscle was completely exorcised, but it was. As an added bonus, the pain inflicted by the endless repetition of the "Saved by Zero" riff disappeared along with it.

We cruised down Rocky Mountain, crossed paved Unicoi Gap, where we found a briefly chatted with a northbounder from Michigan, scrambled up the bank across the street and cooked lunch. It felt like old times.

The trail obliged. The 1.5-mile climb up Blue Mountain featured a number of switchbacks (zig zags). I got stuck on the Schaeffer Beer jingle – the upbeat tempo and indication of my feeling stronger (at least stronger than Saved by Zero).

The mostly viewless summit didn't offer many reasons to linger. We scooted down through the turning oaks and beeches. There were still a lot of green leaves overhead, but splashes of yellow and rust were now mixed throughout. Gray squirrels were running all over the forest floor getting ready for winter. Cuttings of oak sprigs littered the trail, one sign of their relentless work.

At the nine mile mark, we hit Chattahoochee Gap. I was spent. We were close enough to our desired 10 mile per day pace and my leg was clearly on the rebound. We pledged to get an early start tomorrow.

As always, the squirrels were right. The temperatures dropped into the low 40s during the night.

Day four
We had a tremendous wake up call from nature's front desk. Just before dawn, a Barred Owl began serenading us with "Who cooks for? Who cooks for you?"

Fall arrived overnight. The wind turned to northwesterly – driving arctic air our way all day. We had to start making mileage today. Our profile map indicated that the terrain would help – the big ups and downs were subsiding.

Day five

We chose to finish off the bagels to speed us on our way again.

I selected my wardrobe for the day – shorts and gaiters. It was either that or shorts , long johns and gaiters. I didn't think the weather would be cold enough to warrant long underwear. (I detest wearing pants on the trail. They are so restrictive and make every knee bend a drag.)

We stepped into the brisk, overcast air and began climbing out of the gap.

Today was the crux day of the trip. In rock climbing, the crux move is the most important move on the climb. It's the point where you need to stretch to make a hand hold or toe hold that will enable you to move on. Sometimes it's a blind reach around a corner that makes upward mobility possible. You just need to trust your ability and judgment.

While we weren't facing anything quite as dramatic today, we were certainly aware that we needed to start hitting double digit mileage days or we would not make Springer Mountain on schedule.

This time, just when we needed it, the trail joined an old woods road for the next 3.8 miles. What a gorgeous stretch! The road wound around the shoulders of the range, making big "C" shaped curves as it traveled under the ridges and oaks. Periodically, the road would cross streams, some flowing, some not. At all of these crossings, the road was bolstered by particularly impressive stone walls that kept the road from eroding. I was reminded of some of the beautiful stonework under the Blue Ridge Parkway, where the trail offers views that people in cars passing above you can't see and probably don't ever imagine exist.

The leaf covered road was a really welcome sight. I reveled in the ability to make miles while lifting my feet one inch at a time, as opposed to climbing up and over roots and rocks. The sun was even making an attempt to join the celebration. The temps were in the mid 50s, but the wind made it feel colder.

We followed the road up over one final mountain shoulder and dropped into Low Gap Shelter for lunch. Six miles by noon. A big improvement over the past few days.

The shelter was tucked into a hollow. Bear bag cables dangled from surrounding trees, making it look like a giant puppeteer had been on the scene and left a big snarl. I didn't even want to put my pack in the shelter. Shelters are notoriously filled with mice, which I used to consider a mere nuisance. But now the risk of contracting the Hantavirus

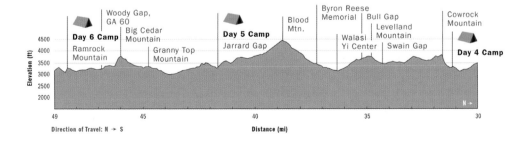

through contact with their droppings was an added concern. The outdoor picnic table was a safer choice.

The road section was over. We climbed 500' up through the blistering arctic wind, which also kept us moving. The 30 mph wind was turning the trailside leaves into gale force wind flags. If the leaves weren't falling off today, they would probably hold on for a few more weeks.

Up over the top of Sheep Rock, down 600' and up 700' over the next 2.5 miles. The wind was absolutely incessant – like hiking next to a freight train. Thankfully, at the top of Poor Mountain, we could take a sunny, nearly windless break for a few minutes.

We scampered down to Hogpen Gap, home of Georgia Route 348, where we also found three post collegiate section hikers who were cutting their hike short after covering the stretch from Springer Mountain to here. They were making cell phone calls and begging their friends to come save them, promising them hefty sums if they would give them a ride to the land of pizza and beer.

Across the paved road and back on the trail, we soon came to a side trail to a spring. Rather than take the side trip and have to carry more water up and over more hills, we decided to make another 1.4 miles to reach the next spring mentioned in the guide. That would give us a much needed 11.3 mile day. We drank one of my two remaining quarts before the climb.

Big mistake. First we blew right by the spring at the 1.4 mile mark- the side trail wasn't well marked. We soon realized we must have passed it and backtracked. We set up the tent, grabbed the water bottles and purifier, scrambled down the embankment in failing light and discovered a dry spring. Bummer.

We made due with the 1.5 quarts we had. It was enough to make chili and noodles and short cups of morning coffee, but it wasn't enough to sufficiently rehydrate after a day of hiking. Fortunately, we had a known source of water at Neel's Gap, 4 miles out.

From now to the end of the hike, water scarcity and how to deal with it would be a main theme.

Day six
The temps went down to the low 40s again last night. We only had short cups of coffee and granola bars for breakfast. Now the decision to eat bagels earlier in the trip reared its head. It would have been nicer to have a more substantial bagel and peanut butter breakfast to fight the chill. But, here on the trail, you need to live with your decisions, adapt and move on.

Minor ups and downs helped get me warm right off the bat. Then we descended to Neel's Gap, where there was a store! Working my way down through the oaks and beeches, visions of coffee, hot dogs, pizza – whatever was hot and ready to eat – danced through my head.

Well, the dream started out perfect enough. The store was an iconic stone building that housed restrooms and a backpacking/camping store that offered really expensive snack foods to thru hikers. I can't really blame them for charging what the market will bear, but when you are on foot and it's the only game in town, it stings a bit.

I bought two waters and two sports drinks and met Wayne out on the sunny deck. We spent 1.5 hours there talking to the numerous passers by, who were in general amazed

that these two old guys were still traipsing up and over mountains,

Now and then one of us would stand up and walk into the store for a supplemental feeding. One pair of section hikers, who were about our age and decided to try the hike north from Springer Mountain to Unicoi Gap, decided to terminate their hike here at Neel's Gap and called for a cab.

They told us there was no water for the next 15 miles, so we each filled up all of our bottles and then some – I filled an extra 20 oz. bottle, bringing my total to almost a gallon (10 pound's worth). I took the bait and weighed my pack on the scale the store had on the porch.

"Wow. 60 pounds. Actually not as bad as I thought.

Next we would climb 1300' in the next 2.4 miles to reach the summit of Blood Mountain, so named because of the legend that the fighting between the Cherokees and Creeks here was so fierce that the mountain ran red with blood.

One key indication that I was getting into trail shape is that I absolutely loved the climb. The trail ascended slowly and sanely from the gap in the first mile, making for a nice warm up. Then, we shot to the top. A wide rock slab heralded our arrival on the summit plateau. I dropped my pack and reveled in the sun and view.

It was a rock dancing scramble to the summit, the highest point on the Georgia AT. There was a large stone shelter with an even larger boulder pile next to it. We climbed up and sat in silence, enjoying the views of uninterrupted mountains before us and farm upon farm behind us. Quite a difference from the vibe of the Neel's Gap store! It was warm enough that I was able to briefly strip off my shirt and soak up the rays on "Blood Mountain Beach".

I took out the trail guide. It was 4:00. Our day of fits and starts had been fun and needed, especially the "relax and enjoy the views" part, but we had only covered 6.6 miles. We still had over 40 miles to cover to meet our ride on Sunday afternoon. Time for the masters to kick in the afterburners. At least it was mostly downhill from the highest peak to wherever we would be sleeping.

Another indication that I was getting into trail shape, but not quite there, was I felt really good until about 5:15, but then my footwork started getting sloppy in a hurry. After one or two episodes of my feet slipping off to the side, it was time to look for a camp spot.

We passed a trailside spring (thus, we did NOT have to carry all that water up and over Blood Mountain), drank a quart, then stopped at Jarrard Gap, featuring three great campsites. No more climbing. I was spent.

We spotted the tent as much out of the wind as possible and dove in, knowing we could fully rehydrate and cook whatever we wanted from what we had left in our food bags.

Both the day and I cooled down incredibly fast. The temps were plummeting and headed toward the low 30s. I threw on dry clothes and wrapped the down bag around me. Then I reached for my phone. It was time to check in.

In the early years of our adventure, the decision to carry a cell phone or not was easy. They didn't exist (at least in the way we have come to know them). As the years rolled by and the technology improved, I struggled with the idea of taking one on the trail. After all, one of the reasons we were out here was to get away from all the chatter.

Yet, there were sound reasons to carry a phone—the greatest being the ability to call out in the case of an emergency on the trail or receive information if something happened at home.

For this trip, we had arranged to have a childhood classmate that now lived in Atlanta to pick us up on Sunday afternoon, so we could catch our Monday night train out of Atlanta.

When I turned on my phone, I had received a text from my friend Joyce, saying that a family emergency had arisen and she couldn't get us on Sunday after all.

We pulled out the guidebook and maps and immediately adjusted our schedule, opting to stay one more night on the trail and walk into Amicalola State Park on Monday. Now nine mile days rather than eleven would be the norm.

Day seven

It's funny how adding the extra day to the trip immediately affected us. The first manifestation was hanging out in the tent for an extended breakfast. It took a while for the day to warm up and we weren't in as much of a hurry. Just knowing that we only needed to cover 9 miles per day for the rest of the trip was enough of an excuse to brew and extra cup of coffee and wait for the sun to do its thing.

When we left the gap at 10:00, it was still in the 40s. I was glad we saved the little climb til this morning, as that would warm us up. The trail was gorgeous – just a really fun walk through the late fall Georgia forest. The cold weather of the last few nights

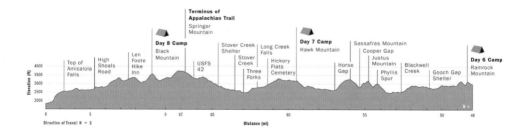

Preacher's Rock

would surely hasten the foliage to turn, but for now it was still mostly greens with splashes of yellow and rust.

With my muscles no longer barking at me, I was completely free to enjoy the hike, That, in turn, meant that I could easily dash off the 4.3 miles to the next landmark – a big, rocky slab on the side of Big Cedar Mountain (3737'), known as Preacher's Rock.

The view here was incredible. I put down my pack, curled up with my arms around my knees and drank in the lush green mountains that rippled ahead of me. Far beyond, in the flat land, I could pick out the white wisps of a paper mill. To the left, at the end of the rolling mountain range, was a lone rock faced peak. Two local guys (college kids) who had shown up and sat on the nearby rocks, told us that it was a training ground for Army Rangers. After making small talk for a while, one of them stood up to leave.

"Well, I guess it's time to go back to reality.", he said.

"This is reality.", I replied.

He paused a minute, looked back at me and exclaimed, "My god, you're right! You just blew my mind, man!"

After they started back down the trail, I could hear the guy I'd been talking to say, "I'm still thinking about what that dude said about reality." His friend responded, but by then they were too far down the trail to make out what he said.

We stayed on the slab in the now warm, nearly windless noonday sun. More lingering, but much needed for the soul.

Next up, a one mile plunge to Woody Gap, a knee knocking, "glad you have hiking poles" affair.

When we arrived, we de-packed at a picnic table in the sun and ran a few errands, namely throwing our trash in the garbage cans and calling Amtrak to change our departure city on Monday from Atlanta to Gainesville (closer to Amicalola State Park).

Just as we were getting ready to leave the Woody Gap parking lot, a guy drove in and dropped off two north bounders. He rolled down the window to ask if we were doing alright and also offered us water. We said yes to that.

Ron came over with a gallon jug and simultaneously poured Wayne a quart, while handing him a business card for his hiker shuttling enterprise. We asked him about availability on Monday to get us from Amicalola State Park to Gainesville. Unfortunately, he was booked.

Thankfully, he was up-to-date on the water situation ahead. He told us to tank up with jugged water at Cooper's Gap and stream water at Justice Creek.

As he departed, I shook his hand.

"Thank you, Ron. You're a godsend for everyone who hikes through."

We climbed up Ramrock Mountain and found a camp spot 50 feet from an overlook. Friday evening brought out the weekend hikers. One couple walked past our site on a side path. Soon thereafter, we smelled their campfire. They chose a good weekend to be out. I hoped the same for their campfire. The woods were incredibly dry.

Day eight

We were a little better at getting up and out for the day, It was another sun splashed one. We had been so spoiled on this trip. It was a lot easier hiking on a dry path with dry soles. Another bonus was that the temps stayed higher last night—in the upper 40s.

Lots of small up and downs were on the menu. We needed to do some nonstop work today. I guess you could call it our Crux Day II. An eleven mile day would set us up nicely to reach Springer Mountain tomorrow.

I started out in my fleece jacket and soon started overheating. Here is where my stubbornness kicks in. I've made my mind up to do some nonstop miles and don't even want the 2 minute interruption to strip off a layer and stuff it in my pack. I unzipped the pit zips and kept going until the 2.6 miles mark – Gooch Gap. There was a downed log in the clearing, so I made my clothing change and sat for the few minutes it took for Wayne to arrive.

Shortly after Gooch, the trail headed left and became less worn than the path we'd been traveling on for the past week. Yup, we were on a re-lo. There are at least three telltale signs of a re-lo, and this section had all three.

First, the trail was less worn. It would take a few seasons for it to be traveled enough to look like the "mother trail". Second, the ends of logs and stumps that were cut to create the trail hadn't aged much. Third, the 6-inch x 2-inch white blazes were new.

The real issue with re-los is when there are no signs on the trail or in shelters indicating that a change has been made. If you don't have an eagle eye for when the new trail ties back in with the old, you don't know how much was added to (or subtracted from) the description you have.

Basically, we didn't have a clue. We could have just completed a glorious section that added 3 miles, chopped one mile off or anywhere in between. The descriptions in our guidebook were such that we couldn't hone in. Our guidebook said "cross stream" five times in 1.5 miles. Which crossing were we making when the trail tied back into the original again?

The only way to recalibrate was to keep walking until we reached a known landmark.

In this case, we knew we were back on the original path when we began the steep ascent of Justus Mountain. The trail had descended into a dark, coniferous, beautiful valley, crossed a big stream on five big boulders, then started climbing out of the gap on sets of log stairs. Up and up we went – out of the dark enchanted hollow and into the bright sun of the ridges above. I began thinking that my sweat alone might raise the water table.

Just when I was about to crest the first shoulder of the mountain, I encountered two college aged hikers from Miami who were section hiking.

"We're driving back to Miami tomorrow", said the lead guy. "We're only averaging about 8 miles a day."

"So are we", I said. "We're finishing up. It's been 28 years."

"Cool. I want to be you, man.", he said.

We descended 500 feet to Cooper Gap (a truly known commodity, as it had a sign). It also had many jugs of water that had been left by Ron – awesome. We grabbed a quart and left the rest for others.

The whole afternoon was ups and downs, including a 500 foot climb of Sassafras Mountain. I was moving pretty slowly toward the top, but concentrated on my progress, not my speed. The next thing I knew, I was walking along the summit ridge using a completely different set of muscles than I was using only 5 minutes before.

Another sign I was getting in shape – no need to rest. The muscle changeover gives my legs enough rest.

On the way down, we stopped to make soup at a sunny trailside spot with limited views. We were 8.7 miles in and feeling good.

After lunch, two climbs to go – up and out of Horse Gap and up and out of Hightower Gap. I was really getting into the climb out of Horse Gap. I just settled into first gear and let the climb happen. The squirrels were running all about on the forest floor. After a while, I kind of stopped paying attention to them – at least the noise.

What I couldn't help notice was something big moving to my right. I stopped as eight huge wild turkeys slowly walked along the top of the small ridge to my right, walked right across the trail in front of me, then kept walking down the hill. Clearly they didn't feel threatened enough to either blast to the treetops to perch or do their ski jumper move, where they extend their wings and soar off the hilltops.

I was still reveling in the turkey sightings, when I heard a huge commotion to my right. Not 30 feet away, a mother bear came crashing down out of a big oak tree. She quasi fell the last 8 feet or so, made a huge crashing sound when she hit the leaves and branches below, then bolted down the mountain and across the trail just below Wayne.

Wow!

But the show was far from over. Her two cubs were still in the tree, and descended one by one, just as mama had. Except they whimpered toward that bottom leap to the ground. They also ran in the direction of mama bear and disappeared down the trail.

I could hardly believe our luck—both that we had seen the bear family and that mama bear hadn't decided to charge us instead of bolting down the mountain.

The buzz of the bear sightings certainly kept us on a high for the rest of the afternoon! Just before we reached Hightower Gap, there were two guys camped in separate tents to the right of the trail. I stopped long enough to warn them of bear activity and to suggest that they bear bag their food (suspend it from a tree branch) as an extra precaution.

Down at the gap, only 200 yards or so beyond them, was a woman standing on the dirt road with her arms akimbo. She asked us about the water situation. We told her it was pretty bleak between here are Justus Creek. She then asked us if there were many ups and downs between here and there.

I couldn't help chuckling. "Yes, there are a few.", I managed to say, thinking to myself, "you ARE hiking in the mountains you know", but stifling the response.

Then she asked us if there was water at Gooch Gap.

"Yes, there's a creek there."

"When were you there?"

"Eleven or so this morning. We stayed there about an hour."

"Well, that's pretty lame isn't it?"

I was speechless. Calling us out? Really? 8.9 miles plus a re-lo, which added confusion if nothing else to slow us down?

Wayne did better. "Well we are 56 years old", he said.

Awkward silence.

"Well, good luck.", I said, and we made our way up and out of Hightower Gap.

Half a mile up, we entered the clearing that marked the side trail to Hawk Mountain Shelter. A solo south bounder who had pitched his tent there, foretold of water below the shelter and a massive group of scouts camped in the clearing next to it.

We pitched the tent on the other side of the clearing, grabbed the water bottles and headed down.

My water filter was being a beast. There was so much sediment in it that it felt like we were trying to push concrete mix through a straw. I offered to filter four quarts for drinking, if Wayne would agree to boil the rest for cooking or coffee.

On the walk up, I was incredibly stiff. My muscles were cooling down and my feet were tingling with little aches and pains from the day. I was really looking forward to getting some solid ground pad time.

As I drifted off to sleep, it began to sink in that tomorrow would be Springer Mountain Day. That after 28 years of hiking this trail, I would be standing at its terminus.

Day nine

Today was the day a 28 year journey would come to an end.

I awoke and sat up in my ground pad/lounger, waiting for the sun to rise above the ridge and bring daylight to our camp.

At 7:00, it was still mostly dark when we heard the legions of scouts walking past our tent, heading north on the AT to end their weekend excursion. So good to see kids out in the mountains. Nature is such an underrated stimulant to the imagination.

Now the clearing was left to we two old guys and our neighbor, the north bounder, whose presence was periodically announced by a hacking cough. I fired up the coffee

and oatmeal water and pored over the map and guide.

We were 7.6 miles from Springer Mountain. I knew that the miles would fly by today. It's always that way toward the end of a trip – finally in trail shape and carrying a pack that was just about as light as it would get. As an added bonus, most of the first 4.5 miles would be gently rolling terrain.

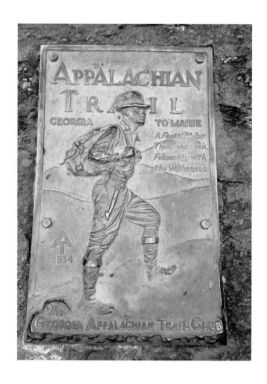

I ducked out of the tent to scope out the weather. It was overcast and chilly, but no threat of rain, true to the forecast. The fellow camper was gone. We didn't even hear him leave. We packed in a hurry and started up the trail.

Reflecting on this day, the thing I remember most is wearing a perpetual smile. I was in full information receiving mode – those aching muscles from earlier in the trip weren't a primary concern and I was free to simply enjoy my surroundings. The leaves underfoot had lost some of their vibrancy during the week. The kaleidoscope was still beautiful, yet muted. The leaves were still mostly green overhead, but the change was undoubtedly happening. More yellows and rusts were mixing in.

I felt fantastic. There was no bittersweet mixed in as there was on my last day on the Pacific Crest Trail 30 years before. Back then, I was getting off a trail that had been my daily home for 6 1/2 months. This time was different. Maybe it's because it hadn't yet sunk in that I was really finishing the trail. I wondered if it would take until next winter, when there would be no section to do next year.

We dropped down to a gorgeous place called Three Forks – where the convergence of three streams form the Noontootla River and a virgin stand of hemlocks towers above. Nearby USFS road 58 provides access to this beautiful river walk along an abandoned dirt road. There were lots of people out enjoying this autumn Sunday.

As we climbed out of the gap and left the weekend crowd behind, the trail took a couple of hairpin turns. I briefly wondered whether Wayne would make them all. In one place, it looked like the trail continued straight on the dirt road we were on. Only a downed tree across the path indicated it was the wrong way. (This is a frequent method trail stewards use to indicate that you shouldn't proceed, but sometimes it's easy to think that the tree is simply a blowdown from a storm.)

Meanwhile, I began the initial climb of Springer Mountain. Partway up, I met a northbound marine in full camo, asking about places to camp. He had a really sore foot, so I suggested he pass some time at Stover Creek Shelter to recoup. It wasn't long after we parted ways that I heard him talking to Wayne – who had obviously navigated the hairpins. Wayne caught up to me and asked me if it was ok to talk the rest of the way to

Springer or whether I wanted contemplation time. I said it was ok to talk. We did chat a bit, but it wasn't about our adventures on the trail. That would come later, I guessed.

As we ascended the mountain, I heard the jungle cry of a pileated woodpecker, followed by three very loud knocking sessions. I smiled, knowing that I was being chaperoned to the end of the trail by one of my favorite birds, the giant among woodpeckers. While I had seen wood shavings indicative of pileated visits earlier on the hike, I had only seen and heard smaller woodpeckers. Now one of the big boys was out, most likely looking for ants under the bark of a tree.

Compared to its terminus cohort, some 2,141 miles away, Springer Mountain is remarkably accessible. While you don't reach Katahdin without a concerted hiking effort, you can drive to within less than a mile of the top of Springer Mountain. In fact, the trail crosses through a large dirt trailhead parking lot .9 from the summit.

We briefly stopped (while still wearing packs) to look at the kiosks, brimming with info and maps. A few people were milling about, either just returning from or just setting off for the summit.

It was our turn. As we hiked up toward the top, I was thankful that it was another dry day. "It may not be sunny, but at least it's not drizzle or worse, pouring rain", I thought. We'd certainly been fortunate this trip.

A few tenths of a mile shy of the summit, we came to the junction with the Benton MacKaye trail. Named for the visionary who birthed the concept for the AT, it departed for its 300 mile trip through Georgia and North Carolina to arrive at the northern edge of the Smokies.

We decided not to stop, nor take the side trip to the first (or last) shelter on the AT. We could hear a gathering of people there and preferred to keep our completion ceremony short and private.

Hiking along, I climbed a small hill to find three women taking pictures at a trailside boulder. "You're almost there!", one said. Over the years, I've come to learn that this phrase can mean anything from being accurate to being several miles off, so I tended to think I was still a ways from the top.

Boy, was I wrong. I literally walked 50 yards into a clearing and there was the summit plaque. "Appalachian Trail – Georgia to Maine. A footpath for those who seek fellowship with the wilderness. — The Georgia Appalachian Trail Club." I was stunned. The ending stood in stark contrast to the 28 years it took to get here.

I took my pack off, flung my arms into the air, then walked over to give Wayne a hug. He asked me to put my hand on the plaque with him, then offered a toast.

Amazing. 28 years worth of memories flooded through me like a fast speed slide show. A devastatingly hot hike through the Shenandoahs in May, the hard earned granite summits of the Whites, the high mileage jaunt through Massachusetts and Connecticut, meeting Helen twice at her Port Clinton Hotel in Pennsylvania and so much more. Every trip had its own character. Every section its own charm. And now, at 2:35 on this October afternoon, it was complete.

We got chatting with a college student named Corey, who graciously offered to take our picture. After 20 minutes or so of discussion and general celebration, it was time to go. We still had an 8.7 mile hike ahead of us to reach the end – the visitor's center of Amicalola State Park.

The trail ahead

We still had some work to do, namely to get down to park headquarters and get a ride to the Gainesville Amtrak station between now and tomorrow night at 9:00 p.m. If we got in a few more miles today, we'd be in good shape. 1.5 miles down, we hit the junction for Black Gap Shelter. It was pretty busy for a Sunday night. I could smell the campfires long before we saw the tents or the trail to the shelter.

Opposite the shelter trail, there was a trail to a spring. We ditched our packs and walked way, way down to the spring below. "Damn that filter", I thought. "I need to replace that cartridge as soon as I get back. At least it's the last time we'll need it."

The walk back up, even without a pack, was a drag. It seemed to take forever. I half wanted to just find a flat spot and call it a day. We took out the trail guide. There was a flat ridge just over one mile away. We went for it.

Yes, it was flat, but there weren't any established camp spots there. We were loath to create a new one. We soldiered on. We crossed a dirt road 2.8 from Springer's summit in Nimblewill Gap. Someone had parked a black Chrysler there. Must have been some of the campers from Black Gap.

We tried to find a flat spot for the tent. The pickings were scarce. We noted how many sites we had seen from Springer Mountain north and how few between Springer and here.

We climbed a woods road and found a spot that looked passable on the right. When we got the tent set up, however, it was awful. Not flat enough.

One of the great things about the Pleasure Dome, is that you can move it intact to a different location. Wayne climbed the ridge across the street and I passed the tent up to him. We set it down in a better location. "That's it. Camp is established."

What a day! 6.0 to hike tomorrow and then to find a ride.

Day ten

The last day of a trip is a wild mishmash.

On the one hand, you are in trail shape. Your pack feels (and is) lighter. You have let go of the tether that ties you to the harried ways of the world.

On the other hand, the harried ways of the world await you at the end of the day's hike. There you must confront the real need to get from the trail to the train station—a challenge that held even more urgency today, for we didn't have a clue who would heed our call.

One predictable manifestation of "last-day-on-the-trail-itis" is that I want to hold onto the present for as long as possible.

I awoke before light, sat up in my ground pad/lounger and replayed the trip in my mind, starting with our arrival in Georgia nine days ago. These recaps bring me another round of joy and help etch trips in my mind, much like reviewing your notes after the professor has left the lecture hall.

Part of this exercise is noting the takeaways. For this trip, it wasn't hard. Lesson one: I'm not young enough to get up from behind a desk, get on a mountain trail and not feel it for several days. Lesson two: despite that, I absolutely still love life on the trail.

Wayne began stirring, so I fired up the coffee and oatmeal water. The food bags, once overstuffed, were now like empty holiday stockings. Oatmeal, coffee and a rogue package of ramen or two.

The conversation was about as sparse. We seemingly packed in seconds (on the last day, knowing exactly where everything is in the pack isn't nearly as important). Won't need to access the tent or smelly clothes for a while. The only things you need at the ready are your wind shell and your wallet.

We climbed up the first hill and found the perfect campsite. Oh well, water under the bridge. Last night's was just fine.

The next five miles would be a beautiful jaunt through the woods that was mostly downhill, but there would be two small climbs first. As I hiked along, I thought of a promise yet unkept.

One of my childhood friends, John, had ALS. My thoughts turned to him several times on this trip. John loves the outdoors and would love to have been doing what I was on this day. But the fact of the matter was that the mountain he was climbing was far greater than those I faced on the trail. Just thinking about that put a fine point on how lucky I was to be out here exploring.

Before I left Maine, John's wife, Linda asked me if I could hold up a sign that simply said, "Hope" in support of John.

On the summit of Frosty Mountain, the last significant summit of the trip, I held up my sign, had Wayne take a photo and posted it to my Facebook account. Promise kept. Thank you, John. I admire the way you face your climbs more than you know, my friend.

The trip was winding down — this truly epic, 28 year hike with half a lifetime full of memories that I would carry with me forever. As we walked down toward the state park, we started talking about next adventures. Not surprisingly, our options included doing the AT again, because no hike, even one taken on the same trail, is the same as the one before.

The only thing we knew with any certainty was that more life on the trail was - and would always be - in order.

The adventure continues.

Epilogue

When the first warm days of spring came to New England in 2014, I got an email from Wayne.

"How bout a hike?" he asked. "Maybe something in southern New England? There's no snow there."

I went up to the attic, grabbed my favorite 3-day pack and loaded it up for the trip. When I put it on, it didn't feel quite right. Something was poking me between the shoulder blades.

I took everything out of the pack and put it on again. "There it is again.", I thought. "What the heck is that?"

I inspected the pack more closely. Something had somehow gotten wedged between the pack's foam back and the inside of the pack. Even though the pack looked empty, something had found its way into the big pocket that held the foam pad inside.

I reached in and pulled the rogue item out. I couldn't believe it. It was my long lost journal pouch - the one that now has a business card zipped into it.

CHAPTER 24

Carrying the Load

"Are you kidding me? You're crazy!"

— hiker in Vermont (upon lifting my pack)

What I take with me

Every trip is different, yet one thing stays remarkably constant—my gear list. The only variables that change are the food (the length of the trip and season may influence choices), which sleeping bag I bring (I have several of them, covering ranges from -30°F to 40°F) and clothing (fall and winter hiking require more and heavier clothes).

Some hikers are fanatics about carrying the lightest load possible. They are known to drill holes in toothbrush handles and such. I am not one of them. My tastes tend toward eating well and being comfortable. Some of my gear choices may be a bit indulgent in that regard, but it's worked pretty well for thousands of miles and I'm happy with the results.

If I come back from a trip and have used everything in my pack at least once, I consider it a good measure of my preparedness. The only exceptions are my rain gear, the first aid kit, spare hiking pole parts and a packet or two of oatmeal. If I don't use them, it's fine by me.

16 All Season Performers

L.L. Bean® Cresta Hikers
Supportive, protective, provide a good grip and wear like iron.

Smartwool™ Socks and Polypro Liners
The liners help prevent chafing (blisters) and move moisture away from your feet.
The outer socks have a nice cushiony feel and dry fast. They also last and last and last.

Gaiters
These nylon sleeves are elasticized at top and bottom to snug down over your boot tops and keep dirt, pine needles, snow and other debris out. No need to stop to take pebbles out of your boots and your socks even stay clean!

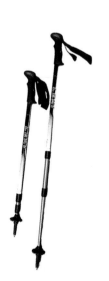

Leki® Poles
Made in Germany. I'd go all the way there to get a pair if I needed to. I hike all day with them. They save your knees on descents, provide two extra feet on stream crossings and extra stability on ascents. In between, they help me keep a good pace (at least for an old guy).

Polypro Long Johns (or Compression Shorts)

By now you may be asking, "Does this guy wear anything but polypropylene?" Well, one thing. Keep moving around the list and you'll find it. Polypropylene is the best active fabric invented do date. It wicks moisture and dries fast. There's an old saying, "cotton kills". It may seem overdramatic, but not by much. Cotton retains water and keeps moisture plastered against your skin. In cold weather, that could put you on the fast track to hypothermia. No thanks.

Unlined nylon shorts with pockets

Because nobody should see me walking around with Lycra® on and pockets come in handy for picking up granola bar wrappers and other litter people leave in their wake.

Polypro shirts

The moisture wicking marvels. I bring at least one long sleeve and a few short sleeved.

Stove

In the early years, we took the Svea (shown here). In 1995, we switched to Camping Gaz cylinders. As of this writing, we'll have to look for a new cylinder stove because they don't make Camping Gaz cylinders anymore.

16 All Season Performers

Guidebook holster

You can't underestimate the ability to check the guidebook or map (or take a picture with your phone) at a moment's notice. No more taking your pack off! Everything is within reach. I found his indispensable little gem in the 1990s and it's been with me ever since.

Gregory® Shasta Carbon fiber mountaineering pack

I'd wanted one of these packs for years, but they were too expensive. When I found when in a mountaineering shop's "going out of business" sale, I pounced. With carbon fiber stays (supports) instead of aluminum, these bad boys weigh about half as much as their counterparts. There's one place I could shave off some serious pack poundage!

Bean's Backpacker's Dome Tent

They make 'em lighter. They make 'em smaller. But the one we carry has been with us since 1995 and is still going strong. I wouldn't trade the extra space or the incredible reliability of what we've dubbed "The Pleasure Dome" for anything. More than 1,000 nights in the same tent in every season and weather condition imaginable speaks volumes. Sadly, they don't make this model anymore.

Bandanas

Gotta have 'em. Better than a visored hat (no failing to see overhead branches) and great for mopping up coffee or soup spills in the tent. They hardly weigh anything either.

French Press Travel Mug

I'll admit it. I'm a wicked coffee snob. I just can't drink freeze dried. The insulated mug doubles as my food bowl.

Sleeping Bag/Compression Stuff Sack

The bag I take depends on the season, but they are all filled with goose down. Synthetic bags weigh too much for my liking. The compression stuff sack cinches down to make the sleeping bag pack to about 1/3 its regularly stuffed size—more room for food!

ThermaLounger®

Another concession to luxury. Yes, a full nylon ground pad cover with aluminum back stays and straps is heavy. My rationale: when you're not hiking, you're resting. You might as well carry the most restful sleeping and lounging set up there is. If you've ever spent three days in a tent leaning on your elbow waiting for the rain to stop, you'll gladly carry a lounger.

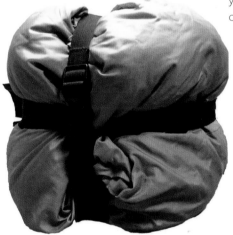

Water filter

The best defense against water borne illnesses and hands down, one of the most important pieces of gear we carry.

Glossary

Baxter State Park
In the 1930s, former Maine Governor Percival Baxter began purchasing plots of land, starting with Katahdin itself, with the idea of establishing a state park. In subsequent years, he kept buying adjacent parcels (27 more, totaling over 200,000 acres), which he turned over to the state of Maine to increase the size of the park. There were a few conditions attached. One of the most important ones was that the park would "remain forever wild".

Blaze
A trail marking system consisting of 2" x 6" rectangles, often painted on trees or rocks. The Appalachian Trail is marked by white blazes. Another color (usually blue) is used to mark side trails. Two blazes painted one atop the other (or with the top blaze offset to the left or right) indicate a turn, a trail junction or another tricky to navigate area ahead.

Bog Bridges
Bridges often constructed of planks or logs placed over perpendicular logs or rocks that allow hikers to stay on the trail without walking through puddles, streams or mud.

Bushwhacking
The act of hiking across land without the benefit of a trail.

Cirrus
Cirrus clouds (wispy formations that often look like fine paint brush strokes) form high in the sky, signaling the approach of a weather system. In my experience, rain generally appears within 48-hours of spotting cirrus clouds, so I plan my trail mileage and campsites accordingly.

Food Drop
A method of restocking with food on a long hike, whereby a box of food is mailed to a post office to be held in the hiker's name. This is particularly useful in rural locations, where getting hiking condusive foods is often difficult and time consuming.

Howard Johnson's
Founded in the 1920s in Quincy, Massachusetts as a pharmacy/soda fountain operation, "HoJo's" was one of the earliest and most successful chains in American history. By the mid 1970s, there were over 1,000 restaurants and 500 Howard Johnson motor lodges throughout the U.S. and Canada. By 2015, all the Howard Johnson's restaurants (including the one we ate breakfast in at Rockfish Gap) were defunct.

Hunt Trail
Blazed by Irving O. Hunt between 1904 and 1908, the Hunt Trail climbs to the summit of Katahdin (northern terminus of the AT) and is also the Appalachian Trail along its entire route.

Irving O. Hunt

Owner of a sporting camp who initially blazed a trail to the summit of Katahdin in the early 20th century. The trail would go on to bear his name and ultimately, become the final 5.4 mile stretch of the Appalachian Trail.

Katahdin

The northern terminus of the Appalachian Trail. The summit of Katahdin is 5,269'. The mountain's name comes from the Penobscot Indian term meaning "the greatest mountain". Among those who have visited Katahdin is Henry David Thoreau (1846). There is considerable debate as to whether the word "Mount" belongs in front of "Katahdin" as the mountain's name. Because the translated version then becomes, "Mount the greatest mountain", I am among those who prefer it simply be known as "Katahdin" and refer to it as such.

Killington Peak

The second highest peak in Vermont (4235') is a quick side trip from the Appalachian Trail.

Long Trail

The first long distance hiking trail conceived and built in America, the Long Trail, traverses the length of Vermont for 273 miles—from the Massachusetts border to Canada. The Long Trail was the inspiration for the Appalachian Trail.

Pacific Crest Trail

Established as a National Scenic Trail the same year as the Appalachian Trail (1971), the PCT runs from Mexico to Canada. Along the way, it passes through several National Parks and other federally protected lands. Highlights include the Mojave Desert, Mount Whitney (the highest peak in the continental U.S.) and the Cascade Range of Oregon and Washington.

Profile Map

A cutaway perspective of the trail that indicates general elevation loss and gain. Profile maps are helpful for getting a quick read for what the trail will be like on any given day.

Ramen

A Japanese noodle and broth soup that is popular hiking fare because it is lightweight, inexpensive and easy to pack. In general, the least expensive brands also pack lots of sodium. Although ramen is available in several flavors (beef, chicken, pork, etc.), my own theory is that there is only one flavor, and they just change the labels.

Shelter

The Appalachian Trail features hundreds of shelters along the way (also known regionally as lean-tos and waysides). These generally 3-sided open front shelters provide protection from wind and rain, as well as sleeping space on their raised wooden floors. Shelters are often located near water sources.

Switchback
A bend in the trail designed to both make climbing easier and minimize erosion. A switchbacked section of trail commonly traverses a section of a ridge, then "switches back" on itself to make the climb more gentle by using a zig zags technique.

Trailhead
The place where a section of trail begins. Commonly, a trailhead includes parking for at least a few cars.

Trayfoot fountain
When we hiked through Shenandoah National Park in 1991, there was a water fountain at the Trayfoot Overlook. When I visited the park again 1n 2014, the fountain was gone, along with all indications it
ever existed.

Wind Gap
A valley once occupied by a stream or river that was captured by another stream and diverted away.